Taking Off Teacher's Edition

Beginning English

Susan Hancock Fesler
Christy M. Newman

Teacher's Edition Writer: Gerry Strei

Taking Off: Beginning English Teacher's Edition, First Edition

Published by McGraw-Hill/Contemporary, a business unit of The McGraw-Hill Companies, Inc., 1221 Avenue of the Americas, New York, NY 10020.

 This book is printed on recycled, acid-free paper containing 10% postconsumer waste.

3 4 5 6 7 8 9 0 QPD/QPD 0 9 8 7 6 5 4

ISBN: 0-07-282065-9
Editorial director: Tina B. Carver
Senior managing editor: Erik Gundersen
Developmental editor: Mari Vargo
Director of North American marketing: Thomas P. Dare
Director of international marketing and sales: Kate Oakes
Production manager: Genevieve Kelley
Interior designer: Eileen Wagner
Copyeditor: Sophia Wisener

www.mhcontemporary.com

The McGraw-Hill Companies

Table of Contents

Introduction

The *Taking Off* Teacher's Edition provides support to teachers using the *Taking Off* Student Book. Each unit of the Teacher's Edition begins with a table listing the unit's lesson titles, the learning points covered within each lesson, and the corresponding Student Book page numbers. Below that, there are suggestions for how to use the unit-opening illustration to present new language from the unit. Additional suggestions for activities related to the unit openers are provided in the Color Transparencies package.

Learning points, new language, and teaching instructions are provided for each lesson. Seasoned teachers can use the instructions as a quick refresher, while newer teachers, or substitute teachers, can use the step-by-step instructions as a helpful guide for conducting the Student Book activities in the classroom. Listening scripts and Student Book answers are conveniently located within the teaching instructions for each individual activity. Dialogues appear in shaded grey boxes with torn-paper edges while all other listening scripts appear in shaded grey boxes with straight edges.

Chalkboards: Chalkboard illustrations provide examples of what the teacher may want to write or draw on the board in order to help clarify upcoming tasks for students.

Speech Bubbles: Speech bubbles provide examples of exchanges that the teacher can expect to have with students in order to model an activity.

Expansion Activities: Each unit contains four to six *Expansion Activities*, which are designed to reinforce or review specific learning points in new ways.

Additional Features of the Teacher's Edition:

- Two-page reproducible unit tests
- Answer keys for the Workbook and the tests
- A listening script for the tests
- A Student Book page reference in the top right corner of each page
- A Workbook page reference at the bottom of each page

Color Transparencies: A separate set of Color Transparencies (ISBN: 0-07-285951-2) is available as a teacher resource for *Taking Off*. This component includes color transparencies of the unit-opening scenes in the Student Book and a set of supplementary activities. For each transparency, teachers will find a unit-opening and unit wrap-up activity. The wrap-up task can be used as an informal oral assessment tool.

Many of the activities included with the Color Transparencies are accompanied by reproducible blackline masters. The transparencies and activity sheets are three-hole-punched so that they can be easily stored in a teacher resource binder.

Teaching strategies

Repetition: On almost every page of *Taking Off*, students have the opportunity to listen to and repeat new vocabulary and structures. They need this structured practice in a low-anxiety environment before they are asked to manipulate this language in reading, writing, listening, or speaking activities. Repetition allows them to learn the pronunciation of individual words, internalize word order, and better approximate the stress and intonation pattern of native speakers. Although the audio program provides for repetition, students may need more frequent repetition drills to reinforce pronunciation or word order. One strategy is to say the new word or phrase and have the class repeat chorally, then call on individual students. You can use the color transparencies of the unit-opening illustrations to introduce or review new language in this way.

When students are practicing conversational structures, you can lead them through a progression of activities. First, you read one role and the students respond chorally. Then, divide the class into two: one half reads one role chorally, and the other half responds chorally. Then model the conversation with a student, or have two students model the conversation for the class. Finally, students can practice with partners. In this way, they acquire confidence as they gradually become more independent in using the new language.

Modeling: Before students are asked to produce language in a new context, they need the opportunity to see it demonstrated and then to practice it in a structured setting. Whenever there is an activity that calls on students to personalize the language, the instructor should model how this is done. For example, on page 20 of the Student Book, students are asked to talk to a partner, completing the sentence "I have ______________ eyes." You should point to your eyes and say, "I have…" You can then pause, and prompt students to say the color of your eyes. Repeat the sentence, including the color of your eyes. After you have modeled the new language, more advanced students can provide additional examples of appropriate responses (e.g., "I have brown eyes."). Less proficient students can follow their examples.

Elicitation: Elicitation is an effective tool in making the classroom more learner-centered. When students contribute their ideas, they feel more secure about their abilities in the new language, and valued for what they already know. Asking questions and eliciting responses from the class will keep students more actively engaged in learning. More advanced students are often eager to respond, whereas the less proficient may be more reluctant. One way to level the playing field is to provide a sentence stem for the answer (e.g., "My name is ______"), and then have more advanced students model appropriate responses. Less proficient students can follow the pattern set by the students before them. Another strategy is to accept partial or one-word answers, and provide the rest of the sentence (e.g., "Tien," "Your name is Tien."). Allowing students to discuss the topic in small groups or pairs before you elicit responses from the whole class is also an effective strategy (see Modeling).

Error correction: When and how often to correct students is the subject of much debate. Research suggests that it is repeated exposure to accurate input rather than correction that helps a student internalize new language. Too much correction can cause a learner to feel insecure about his or her language ability and reluctant to take the risks necessary to becoming more fluent in a new language. When accuracy is the goal, as in the repetition of listening activities or completing a multiple-choice assessment, correction should be immediate and constructive. When fluency is the goal, as in the *Talk with a partner* activities, correction should be minimized, as it interrupts the conversational flow, and can make students more self-conscious. In many cases, students can self-correct if you provide a model of accurate language. For example, if a student says "Hello. I Carlos," you can respond, "Hi, Carlos. I'm Isabel." By emphasizing the correct form in your response, you can help students monitor their own speech. This technique is often referred to as "counsel correction." Another strategy is to pause before the error, gesturing for students to fill in the correct form.

Pair/group work: Students at a low beginning or literacy level are often reluctant to work in pairs or small groups, as they are insecure about their own language abilities and may be accustomed to a teacher-centered approach. However, pair and group work activities allow each student more opportunities to engage in conversation in English. To encourage student participation in these activities, walk around and listen to all of the pairs or small groups as they are working. Asking questions or helping with pronunciation makes students feel that the activity is purposeful and personally beneficial. Such monitoring also prepares students to speak in front of the whole group, and in authentic situations outside the classroom. To maximize interaction among the students, you can vary the seating arrangements or use strategies such as counting off that match students with different partners each time. Alternatively, you can engineer the groupings so that students complement each other, perhaps placing a more communicative student with one who has stronger literacy skills.

Using the audio program: Every unit in *Taking Off* includes substantive listening practice for students on realistic topics. This practice is important not only for assessment purposes, but also to help students become accustomed to listening to and comprehending voices other than that of the instructor. Such activities prepare students to navigate more successfully in the real world with other native speakers. Units are structured so that students first listen to vocabulary or conversational models as they associate the sound with the context, then they repeat the new language. When they have mastered the scripted conversation, they are then asked to personalize the new language in describing their own experiences.

Using realia: Adult students attend to and retain information when it is made relevant to their own needs and experience. Using real material such as authentic documents, maps, pictures, and objects not only helps students relate language learning to their own lives, it also appeals to a variety of learning styles. Each unit of *Taking Off* includes a form that helps students develop competence with authentic documents. Wherever possible, other realistic diagrams and visuals have been included in the units to help students place the language in real world contexts. Bringing in other authentic materials related to the unit topic can make concepts more tangible, and reinforce learning.

Pacing/time management: The student text is designed to provide 8-10 hours of instruction per 12-page unit. This permits an instructor to spend 45 minutes to an hour on each lesson of the unit. Although the language input is deliberately restricted in each lesson, the visuals provide opportunity for expansion and recycling of material. Learners benefit from continual recycling of skills and information. For example, in Unit 1, students will learn how to talk about things in a classroom. Pointing to objects in the classroom on page 2 and eliciting names for the objects reinforces this language. Specific ideas for how to extend the lesson can be found on the pages of the Teacher's Edition in *Expansion Activity* boxes.

How to work with reluctant learners: Sometimes adult students enter literacy and low beginning classes having had little experience in an educational setting. Others may have had negative experiences in school, or may feel that learning English at this stage in their lives is a burden rather than an opportunity. Such students may be reluctant at first to participate in class activities. Recognize that these students have a wealth of experience and knowledge on which to draw, and include activities that are relevant to their everyday lives. For example, in Unit 11, students learn to talk about jobs. Allow them to talk about the kind of work they do. Help them use the language provided in the unit to talk about their own jobs. In Unit 3, students begin to talk about families. Ask them to bring in photos of the people in their families. With every topic, be sensitive to the needs of your students. For example, those students whose families may have died or been left behind can either tell about their relatives or about the people they live with now.

Working with low beginners and literacy students in a multilevel setting: In most adult programs, low beginners and literacy students are placed in the same level. Low beginners are students who are literate in their first language, but are true beginners in English. Literacy students, on the other hand, usually do not have fundamental first-language literacy skills. This means that an instructor is often teaching two different skills sets, literacy and language. Using the *Taking Off* Workbook and the *Taking Off* Literacy Workbook to supplement the student book can help students practice skills at their level. However, an instructor can modify student book activities to provide additional skill practice for both groups of students.

When working with multilevel classes, pairing and grouping strategies can optimize learning for all students. For example, you may want to pair a low beginning student with a literacy student to reinforce alphabet recognition. On the other hand, putting students in small groups with others at the same level allows you to tailor activities to meet their individual needs. For example, in Unit 2, literacy students can practice letter formation, while low beginning students can take turns dictating letters of the alphabet to each other.

To the Teacher

Taking Off is a four-skills, standards-based program for low beginning students of English. Picture dictionary art pages teach life-skills vocabulary in a clear and visual way. The gradual pace of the course instills confidence in students as they establish a solid foundation in the basics of English.

Features

- **Four-skills foundation course** prepares students for Book 1 in a variety of popular series.
- **Activities correlated to CASAS, SCANS, EFF, and other key standards** prepare students to master a broad range of critical competencies.
- **Picture dictionary art pages** highlight life-skills vocabulary in engaging contexts.
- **Listening preparation activities** help students develop speaking, reading, and writing skills in a low-anxiety environment.
- **A *Numbers* page in each unit** helps students build numeracy skills for basic math work.
- ***In the Community* lessons** introduce students to critical civics topics.
- ***Grammar Spotlights*** present a small set of basic grammar points.
- **Literacy Workbook** provides reading and writing "on-ramp" activities for emerging readers and writers.

Components

- **Student Book** has twelve 12-page units with a wealth of individual, pair-, and group-work activities. In four special sections throughout the book, students and teachers will also find *Grammar Spotlight* and *Review* lessons for additional study and practice. Listening scripts are found at the back of the Student Book and in the Teacher's Edition.
- **Teacher's Edition with Tests** provides the following resources for each unit in the Student Book:
    - Step-by-step teaching instructions
    - Five to seven expansion activities
    - Two-page test
    - Listening scripts for all audio program materials
    - Answer keys for Student Book, Workbook, and test materials.
- **Color Transparencies** provide full-color acetates for unit-opening scenes in the Student Book.
- **Audiocassettes and Audio CDs for Student Book** contain recordings for all listening activities in the Student Book. Listening passages for each unit test are provided at the end of the audio section for that unit.
- **Workbook** includes supplementary practice for students who have basic reading and writing skills in their first language.
- **Literacy Workbook** provides reading and writing "on ramp" activities for emerging readers and writers. This component is designed for students who do *not* have foundational literacy skills in their first language. Like the Workbook, the Literacy Workbook offers supplementary activities for each unit in the Student Book.
- **Literacy Workbook Audiocassette and Audio CD** provide additional listening practice.

PROGRAM OVERVIEW

Guide to *Taking Off*

Consult the *Guide to Taking Off* on pages xvi-xix. This Guide offers teachers and program directors a visual tour of one Student Book unit.

Predictable lesson format

Most of the lessons in the Student Book are one page in length and contain three to five activities. This one-page lesson format allows teachers to "chunk" their instruction into short, manageable sections, allowing students to quickly complete lessons and feel a sense of accomplishment. The first activity in most lessons asks students to listen to and repeat new vocabulary and language. These listen and repeat activities help students prepare for speaking, reading, and writing skills in a low-anxiety environment. At the low beginning level, it is critical that students have a chance to listen to and repeat all new vocabulary and language before being asked to speak, read, or write.

Recurring cast of multicultural characters

Taking Off features an engaging cast of characters enrolled in a beginning English class. The authors developed the book around these characters to help students learn new language from familiar and engaging faces. Here is a profile of the characters in *Taking Off*:

Character	Nationality
Sandy Johnson (teacher)	American
Carlos Avila	Brazilian
Maria Cruz	Mexican
Leo Danov	Russian
Don Park	Korean
Tien Lam	Vietnamese
Grace Lee	Chinese
Paul Lemat	Haitian
Isabel Lopez	Colombian

Unit-opening illustrations

Each unit opens with a dynamic, full-page illustration, providing context for the key vocabulary items and language presented in the unit. This illustration sets the scene for the unit, activating students' background knowledge and encouraging them to share words they can say in English. Teachers can present the unit-opening illustrations on an overhead projector with the Color Transparencies.

CASAS, SCANS, EFF, and other standards

Program directors and teachers are often asked to benchmark student progress against national and/or state standards. With this in mind, *Taking Off* carefully integrates instructional elements from a wide range of standards including CASAS, SCANS, and EFF. Here is a brief overview of our approach to meeting these standards:

- **CASAS.** Many U.S. states tie funding for adult education programs to student performance on the Comprehensive Adult Student Assessment System (CASAS). The CASAS (www.casas.org) competencies identify more than 300 essential skills that adults need in order to succeed in the classroom, workplace, and community. Examples of these skills include: identifying or using appropriate non-verbal behavior in a variety of settings, responding appropriately to common personal information questions, and comparing price or quality to determine the best buys. *Taking Off* carefully integrates CASAS competencies that are appropriate for low beginning students.

- **SCANS.** Developed by the U.S. Department of Labor, SCANS is an acronym for the Secretary's Commission on Achieving Necessary Skills (www.wdr.doleta.gov/SCANS/). SCANS competencies are workplace skills that help people compete more effectively in today's global economy. The following are examples of SCANS competencies: works well with others, acquires and evaluates information, and teaches others new skills. A variety of SCANS competencies are threaded throughout the activities in each unit of *Taking Off.* The incorporation of these competencies recognizes both the intrinsic importance of teaching workplace skills and the fact that many adult students at the low beginning level are already working members of their communities.
- **EFF.** Equipped for the Future (EFF) is a set of standards for adult literacy and lifelong learning, developed by the National Institute for Literacy (www.nifl.gov). The organizing principle of EFF is that adults assume responsibilities in three major areas of life — as parents, citizens, and workers. These three areas of focus are called "role maps" in the EFF documentation. In the parent role map, for example, EFF addresses these and other responsibilities: participating in children's formal education and forming and maintaining supportive family relationships. Each *Taking Off* unit addresses one or more of the EFF role maps. The focus on the student as community citizen is particularly strong in Lesson 9 of each unit, which is devoted to *In the Community* activities.

Number of hours of instruction

The *Taking Off* program has been designed to accommodate the needs of adult classes with 96-216 hours of classroom instruction. Here are three recommended ways in which various components in the *Taking Off* program can be combined to meet student and teacher needs:

- **96-120 hours.** Teachers are encouraged to work through all of the Student Book materials, incorporating the *Grammar Spotlights* and *Review* lessons as time permits. The Color Transparencies can be used to introduce and/or review materials in each unit. Teachers should also look to the Teacher's Edition for teaching suggestions and testing materials as necessary.

  Time per unit: 8-10 hours.
- **120-168 hours.** In addition to working through all of the Student Book materials, teachers are encouraged to incorporate the Workbook and/or Literacy Workbook for supplementary practice.

  Time per unit: 10-14 hours.
- **168-216 hours.** Teachers and students working in an intensive instructional setting can take advantage of the wealth of expansion activities threaded through the Teacher's Edition to supplement their use of the Student Book and Workbook materials.

  Time per unit: 14-18 hours.

Assessment

Some teachers prefer to evaluate their students informally by monitoring their students' listening and speaking abilities during pair-work or group-work activities. These teachers may also maintain portfolios of student writing to show the progress students are making in writing skill development.

For teachers who need or want formal assessments of their students, the Teacher's Edition provides two-page, reproducible tests for each Student Book unit. Each test takes approximately 30 minutes to administer, and these tests are designed to assess vocabulary acquisition and listening comprehension skills. There are two listening activities on each test, and the recorded passages for these sections are found on the Student Book Audiocassettes and Audio CDs. Listening scripts for the tests appear in the Teacher's Edition.

SPECIAL FEATURES

Grammar Spotlights

Fundamental grammar points like the simple present tense of BE and HAVE are presented throughout the Student Book in two-page *Grammar Spotlight* lessons. These lessons appear at regular intervals throughout the book, but are not incorporated into the units themselves. In this way, teachers who address grammar in a direct way can call their students' attention to the *Grammar Spotlights* and to the corresponding grammar practice in the Workbook. Teachers who prefer not to present and practice grammar with their low beginning students can skip the *Grammar Spotlights*.

Numeracy skills for basic math

Learning basic math skills is critically important for success in school, on the job, and at home. As such, most national and state-level standards for adult education mandate instruction in basic math skills. With this in mind, Lesson 8 in each Student Book unit is dedicated to helping students develop numeracy skills they need for basic math work. In Unit 1, for example, students learn the numerals 1-10 and the English words for these numbers. Later in the book, students tackle activities like working with American money, reading Fahrenheit temperatures, and understanding numbers on a paycheck.

Civics and community involvement

Many institutions focus direct attention on the importance of civics instruction for English language learners. This type of instruction is often referred to as *EL/Civics*, and is designed to help students become active and informed community members. Lesson 9 in each Student Book unit explores a community-related topic. Labeled *In the Community*, these lessons have areas of focus like learning about garage sales, having a potluck dinner, using an ATM, and learning about health insurance.

Classes with literacy and low beginning students

A special *Taking Off* Literacy Workbook has been designed for literacy students enrolled in low beginning classes. Most low beginning students are true beginners in English who are literate in their first language. Literacy students, on the other hand, usually do not have fundamental first-language literacy skills. Literacy students often need specific instruction in letter formation and other fundamental reading, listening, and writing skills.

As teachers who have worked with mixed groups of literacy and low beginning students know, dealing simultaneously with the needs of each of these groups of learners is a great challenge. The Literacy Workbook offers a unique resource for teachers in such multi-level classes. Each Literacy Workbook unit provides essential support for key elements of the *Taking Off* Student Book. Working with or without a teacher's aide, literacy students can tackle basic reading, listening, and writing activities in the Literacy Workbook while their low beginning classmates tackle tasks at their ability level.

Scope and Sequence

Unit	Topics	Listening & Speaking Skills	Reading& Writing Skills
1 **Welcome to the classroom** *Page 2*	• Meeting new people • Alphabet • Greetings • Countries • Classroom language • Classroom objects • Emergency information form • Learning log	• Introduce yourself • Say the name of the country you come from • Listen and identify classroom objects • Say your telephone number, address, and email address • Ask for the spelling of words • Listen to and practice simple dialogs • Follow classroom directions	• Read and write alphabet letters • Interpret basic sight words • Write proper names, countries, and classroom words • Examine classroom commands/directions • Write and read personal information • Write new vocabulary in a learning log
2 **Where are you from?** *Page 14*	• Native language • Country of origin • Marriage • Physical appearance • Address • Identification form	• Collect information from classmates • Say the name of the country you come from • Say the language you speak • Recognize differences in marital status • Discuss hair and eye color	• Fill in information on a chart • Write personal information statements • Use writing to describe height • Identify vocabulary that describes physical appearance • Read and write words for select countries and languages
3 **This is my family.** *Page 26*	• Relatives • Name titles (Mr., Mrs., Ms.) • Family tree • Photo album • Ages • Census	• Ask questions about family • Discuss family members with classmates • Ask about someone's age • Listen to information about a census • Say name titles (Mr., Mrs., Ms.) • Recognize numbers 20-100	• Write family position words to complete a sentence • Read names using titles (Mr., Mrs., Ms.) • Make your own family tree • Examine classroom commands/directions • Read short sentences about a family • Complete a census form
Grammar Spotlight for Units 1-3 *Page 38*	• Pronouns (I, you, he, she, it, we, you, they) • Present tense of BE in long form (I am) and short form (I'm) • Present tense of BE with negatives (I'm not) • Present tense of HAVE (I have/she has)		
Review for Units 1-3 *Page 40*	• Matching activity: personal identification information • Listening activity: marital status • Community Challenge: find the address of the Registry/Department of Motor Vehicles		

Numeracy	Community Awareness	EFF	SCANS	CASAS
• Learn numbers 1-10 • Identify numbers used in context • Say and write telephone numbers with area code • Say and write addresses and e-mail addresses • Understand page references	• Complete an emergency information form • Identify your emergency contact person • Learn 911 for police and fire emergencies	• Communicate so that others understand • Develop and maintain relationships with others • Learn new skills • Respect others and value diversity	• Basic skills (reading, speaking, writing, listening, arithmetic) • Analyzes and communicates information • Knowing how to learn	**1**: 0.1.1, 0.1.4 **3**: 0.2.1, 0.1.6 **8**: 6.0.1 **9**: 0.2.2, 2.1.2
• Learn numbers 11-19 • Say and write numbers in an address • Say and write zip codes	• Complete a detailed identification form • Learn to write your name as follows: last name, first name, middle initial • Learn the components of an address	• Listen to and learn from others' experiences and ideas • Learn new skills • Respect others and value diversity • Communicate so that others understand	• Basic skills (reading, speaking, writing, listening, arithmetic) • Works with people of diverse backgrounds • Sociability	**1, 2, 3**: 0.1.2, 0.2.1, 2.7.2. **5**: 1.1.4 **8**: 6.0.1
• Learn numbers 20-100 • Say your age • Recognize number words • Write the number of family members in your household • Write the ages of family members	• Learn about the American census • Complete a census form for your family	• Find and use community resources and services • Develop a sense of self that reflects your history, values, beliefs and roles in the larger community • Recognize and understand your civic responsibilities	• Basic skills (reading, speaking, writing, listening, arithmetic) • Seeing things in the mind's eye	**2, 6**: 7.4.8 **8**: 6.0.2 **9**: 0.2.2 **GS**: 1.9.2

CASAS Standards: Numbers in bold indicate lesson numbers.
GS: Grammar Spotlight

Scope and Sequence

Unit	Topics	Listening & Speaking Skills	Reading& Writing Skills
4 **Welcome to our house** *Page 42*	• Rooms in a house • Items in a house • Types of houses • Household needs • Your dream house • Garage sales	• Listen to and recognize the rooms in a house • Discuss household items • Learn the names of different types of housing • Speak with a partner about household needs • Differentiate between numbers that sound alike (18 vs. 80)	• Write the names of the rooms in a house • Review a paragraph about a new apartment • Write and read about a dream house • Read a paragraph about garage sales
5 **I play soccer on Saturday.** *Page 54*	• Daily activities • Days of the week • Months and dates • Time • Movies • Appointments • Medical history form	• Discuss your daily activities • Say the days of the week • Say the months in a year • Talk about movie times • Use the telephone to make appointments • Listen to ordinal numbers	• Read the time on clocks and watches • Complete a calendar for the week • Recognize abbreviations for months • Write times on a calendar • Read information about study times • Write and read ordinal numbers • Complete a medical history form
6 **Let's go shopping.** *Page 66*	• Clothes • Colors • Clothing sizes • Money • Paying by check	• Listen to and identify articles of clothing • Ask for what you need in a store • Ask about clothing size • Say that clothing is too large or small • Say color words • Ask about favorite colors	• Read and write clothing words • Complete a chart about clothing sizes • Write sentences about your clothing size • Learn words for American coins and bills

Grammar Spotlight for Units 4-6 *Page 78*	• Singular and Plural Nouns Ending in *-ch, -sh, -s,* and *-x* • A/an (a house/an apartment) • Simple present tense of regular verbs
Review for Units 4-6 *Page 80*	• Matching activity: housing, clothing, and time information • Writing sentences about new furniture • Community Challenge: interpret a check-out page on an Internet shopping site

Numeracy	Community Awareness	EFF	SCANS	CASAS
• Differentiate between numbers with similar digits • Complete sentences using numbers • Understand page references	• Learn that garage sales are community activities • Recognize the different types of houses in a community	• Provide for physical needs • Get involved in the community and get others involved • Reflect on and reevaluate your opinions and ideas	• Basic skills (reading, speaking, writing, listening, arithmetic) • Responsibility • Knowing how to learn • Creative thinking	**1, 4**: 1.4.1 **7**: 7.1.1 **9**: 1.1.6, 1.3.1, 2.6.1 2.7.2
• Practice ordinal numbers • Recognize the days and dates on a calendar • Say the time a movie begins • Write your date of birth on a form	• Complete a health clinic information form • Learn about the following services: dental cleaning, car tune-up, and haircut • Keep community appointments on a calendar	• Recognize and understand your human and civic responsibilities • Manage time and resources	• Basic skills (reading, speaking, writing, listening, arithmetic) • Analyzes and communicates information • Uses time wisely	**1**: 0.2.4 **2, 3**: 2.3.2 **4**: 2.3.1 **6**: 2.1.8, 7.1.4 **7**: 7.1.4 **8**: 0.2.1, 6.0.1 **9**: 3.2.1
• Write a check • Recognize American coin and bill denominations • Match coins and bills to monetary values	• Shop at a department store • Buy clothes in a store • Recognize and use American money	• Participate in group processes and decision making • Figure out how economic systems work • Use technology and work tools	• Basic skills (reading, speaking, writing, listening, arithmetic) • Use technology to complete results • Problem solving	**1**: 0.1.3, 1.3.9 **3**: 8.1.2 **5**: 7.5.1 **6**: 1.1.9, 1.2.1 **7**: 1.2.2 **8**: 1.1.6, 6.0.2 **9**: 1.8.2

CASAS Standards: Numbers in bold indicate lesson numbers.

Scope and Sequence

Unit	Topics	Listening & Speaking Skills	Reading& Writing Skills
7 **I'm so hungry!** *Page 82*	• Grocery shopping • Food • Food groups • Containers for food • Meals • Potluck dinner	• Listen for the names of food items • Talk about a shopping list • Discuss breakfast, lunch, and dinner foods • Order in a restaurant • Ask and answer questions about foods you eat	• Make a shopping list • Read the names of food items • Complete a chart about location of foods in a supermarket • Read a paragraph about pot luck dinners
8 **How's the weather?** *Page 94*	• Weather • Seasons • Leisure activities • Temperature (Fahrenheit) • U.S. map	• Discuss different types of weather • Listen to and discuss leisure activities • Discuss activities you like to do in different seasons • Talk about temperature in a city	• Read and write about the seasons • Recognize weather-related vocabulary • Write sentences about weather • Interpret a weather map
9 **Where's the post office?** *Page 106*	• Neighborhood map • Places in the community • Banking • ATM (Automated Teller Machine)	• Talk about places you see in your neighborhood • Ask and answer questions about the location of neighborhood places • Ask your classmates what places they live near • Ask your partner where they do things	• Read a neighborhood map • Write sentences about the location of neighborhood places • Read about depositing money into a savings account • Read about how to use an ATM

Grammar Spotlight for Units 7-9 *Page 118*	• Present continuous (I am/I'm working) • Question words (where, how, what)
Review for Units 7-9 *Page 120*	• Matching activity: weather, seasons, and community-related information • Listening activity: weather, seasons, and leisure activities • Community Challenge: find addresses for community places (post office)

Numeracy	Community Awareness	EFF	SCANS	CASAS
• Write times of the day for meals • Use times of the day in sentences • Use container words to talk about food (a bunch of grapes)	• Explore a supermarket • Learn about a potluck dinner • Practice ordering food in a restaurant	• Provide for physical needs • Listen to and learn from others experiences and ideas • Get involved in community and get others involved	• Basic skills (reading, speaking, writing, listening, arithmetic) • Sociability • Understands how systems work • Analyzes and communicates information • Self-management	**1**: 7.1.2 **2**: 1.3.8 **3**: 1.3.7 **4**: 3.5.2 **5**: 8.2.1 **6**: 2.6.4 **7**: 3.5.9 **8**: 1.1.4 **9**: 2.7.2 **R**: 7.4.3
• Interpret a thermo-meter in degrees Fahrenheit • Write numbers using degrees Fahrenheit	• Read a weather map • Talk about the weather in your community • Discuss community-related leisure activities	• Find, interpret and analyze diverse sources of information • Listen to and learn from others' experiences and ideas • Reflect on and reevaluate your opinions and ideas	• Basic skills (reading, speaking, writing, listening, arithmetic) • Decision making • Reasoning • Seeing things in the mind's eye	**1**: 2.3.3, 5.7.3 **2**: 1.1.5 **6**: 0.2.4 **8**: 1.1.5 **9**: 1.1.3, 2.3.3 **R**: 7.4.2
• Read dates and money amounts on a bank deposit slip • Discuss a deposit slip • Complete a bank withdrawal • Use an ATM PIN number	• Interpret a neighborhood map • Recognize businesses in your community • Practice banking procedures	• Get involved in the community and get others involved • Find, interpret, and analyze diverse sources of information • Use technology and other work tools • Find and use community resources and services	• Basic skills (reading, speaking, writing, listening, arithmetic) • Seeing things in the mind's eyes • Understands how systems work • Uses technology to complete tasks • Acquires and evaluates information	**2**: 2.2.1, 2.2.5 **3**: 2.5.4 **7**: 0.2.4 **8**: 1.8.2 **9**: 1.8.1 **GS**: 2.1.1, 2.5.1, 2.5.5

CASAS Standards: Numbers in bold indicate lesson numbers.
R: Review
GS: Grammar Spotlight

Scope and Sequence

Unit	Topics	Listening & Speaking Skills	Reading& Writing Skills
10 You need to see a doctor. *Page 122*	• Health problems • Medicine • Healthy food • Exercise • Health insurance	• Listen and respond to dialogs about illness • Express physical pain • Make a doctor's appointment for your child • Discuss medicines and remedies • Listen to information about health insurance • Follow TPR (Total Physical Response) directions	• Recognize words for physical ailments • Chart health problems and remedies • Read about staying fit and healthy • Interpret a health insurance card
11 What's your job? *Page 134*	• Jobs • Workplaces • Driving • Want ads • Paycheck • Job application	• Talk about jobs • Say what job conditions you like (indoors, with people) • Say what work-related skills you can do (fix things) • Ask and answer questions with affirmative and negative responses	• Examine the tools different jobs require • Complete sentences about what you and others can do • Read want ads • Fill in a form about what your job was before • Complete sentences about paychecks • Practice with a job application
12 How do you get to class? *Page 146*	• Transportation • Directions to places in the community • Learner's permit • Road signs • Bus schedule	• Practice dialogs about methods of transportation • Differentiate among left, right, and straight ahead • Follow directions in the community • Listen to dialogs about time phrases • Ask when the next bus or train leaves	• Use a community map to give directions • Analyze a bus schedule • Complete sentences about a learner's permit • Read and respond to road signs

Grammar Spotlight for Units 10-12 *Page 158*	• Can/can't (I, you, he, she, it, we, they) • Prepositions of place(in, on, next to, between)
Review for Units 10-12 *Page 160*	• Matching activity: health, job, and transportation information • Listening activity: doctor's appointments • Community Challenge: interpret a bus schedule

Numeracy	Community Awareness	EFF	SCANS	CASAS
• Learn about health insurance co-payments • Say medicine dosages	• Complete health insurance forms • Understand a doctor's role in the community • Read a medicine label from a community pharmacy	• Provide for physical needs • Provide a nurturing home environment • Pursue personal self-improvement • Figure out how social service systems work	• Basic skills (reading, speaking, writing, listening, arithmetic) • Acquires and evaluates information • Problem solving • Self-management • Works within the system	**1, 2**: 3.1.1 **3**: 3.1.3 **4**: 3.3.1 **6, 7**: 3.5.9 **8**: 3.3.2 **9**: 3.2.3 **R**: 8.3.1
• Understand paycheck deductions • Learn about hourly wages • Review concept of depositing money in bank account	• Examine various jobs in the community • Recognize want ads as a community resource • Gain information about the job application process • Complete an employment application form	• Find and get a job • Meet new work challenges • Plan and renew career goals • Figure out how economic systems work • Balance and support work, career, and personal goals	• Basic skills (reading, speaking, writing, listening, arithmetic) • Use personnel resources • Understands how systems work • Reasoning • Self-esteem	**1**: 4.1.6 **2**: 4.1.8 **3**: 7.5.1 **5**: 4.4.2 **6**: 4.1.3 **7**: 4.1.2 **8**: 4.2.1 **R**: 4.1.3
• Read times related to public transportation • Practice time phrases • Write month, date, and year in numerical form (MM/DD/YY)	• Read schedule for community transportation • Review various forms of transportation (bus, train, subway) • Get around your community	• Identify and monitor problems, community needs, strengths and resources • Manage time and resources • Figure out how systems work	• Basic skills (reading, speaking, writing, listening, arithmetic) • Knowing how to learn • Self-management • Understands how systems work • Creative thinking	**1**: 2.2.3 **2, 3**: 2.2.1 **4**: 0.1.2 **5**: 2.2.4 **6**: 1.9.2, 2.5.7 **7**: 1.9.1, 2.2.2 **8**: 6.6.6 **9**: 2.2.4 **GS**: 2.6.3

CASAS Standards: Numbers in bold indicate lesson numbers.
R: Review
GS: Grammar Spotlight

Unit 1

Welcome to the Classroom

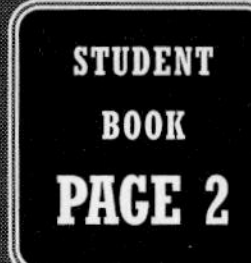

UNIT OVERVIEW

	LESSON:	LEARNING POINTS:	SB#
1.	**Welcome!**	Introducing yourself and greeting others	**p. 3**
2.	**The alphabet**	Understanding, saying, and writing the alphabet	**p. 4**
3.	**How do you spell that?**	Spelling your name	**p. 5**
4.	**What's in the classroom?**	Identifying things in the classroom	**p. 6**
5.	**Follow directions.**	Identifying and following classroom directions	**p. 7**
6.	**Open the book.**	Recognizing and saying classroom directions	**p. 8**
7.	**Point to the book.**	Recognizing and practicing direction words	**p. 9**
8.	**My phone number is 981-355-2305.**	Practicing numbers 0-10	**p. 10**
9.	**Emergency Information Form**	Writing and saying personal information	**p. 11**
10.	**Review**	Review Unit 1	**p. 12**

Suggestions for Unit Opener (Student Book page 2)

Brainstorm. Brainstorm with the students any language related to the classroom that they already know. Use your own classroom and the illustration to prompt students to say the words. Write the language on the board—for example, *chair*, *desk*, etc.

Model the language. Begin by reading the caption aloud—"Where are the students? What do you see?" Point to Sandy Johnson in the illustration and say, "teacher." Then point to other items in the illustration and name them. Use your own classroom to continue modeling the language. Write the words on the board.

Model the language again. This time have the class repeat the words after you. Then go around the room and have individual students repeat different words.

Point and say. Point to the words you've written on the board as you say them. Have the students repeat them after you.

Initiate pair work. Have the students work in pairs. Tell them to take turns pointing to items in the illustration and naming them. Demonstrate this by asking a student to point to someone or something and by saying the name yourself, then pointing to someone or something yourself and asking the same student to say the name. Go around the room and check students' work.

See Color Transparencies package for additional unit-opening activity. Many of these tasks include a reproducible blackline master.

1 Welcome!

STUDENT BOOK PAGE 3

LEARNING POINT
Introducing yourself and greeting others

NEW LANGUAGE

Hello.	I'm from _____.
My name is _____.	Nice to meet you (too).
Hi.	
I'm _____.	

A Listen.

Have the students listen with their books closed.

Paul: Hello. I'm Paul.

Isabel: Hi, Paul. I'm Isabel. Nice to meet you.

Paul: Nice to meet you too, Isabel.

Have the students listen again as they follow along with their books open. Ensure students' comprehension of the vocabulary and the situation by acting out the conversation with a student in front of the class.

Listen and say.

Have the class listen to and repeat each line of the conversation separately. Stop the tape or CD after each line or read aloud the separate lines with pauses.

B Talk with a partner.

Copy the open-ended conversation on the board. Pick a student to model the open-ended conversation with you in front of the class.

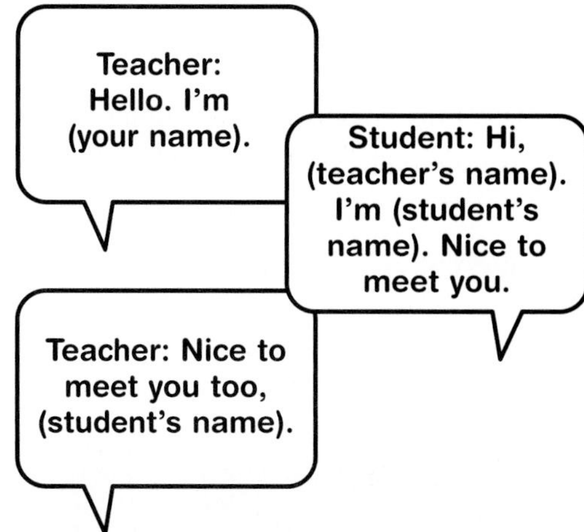

Teacher: Hello. I'm (your name).
Student: Hi, (teacher's name). I'm (student's name). Nice to meet you.
Teacher: Nice to meet you too, (student's name).

Have the students work in pairs to practice the conversation. Go around the room and check their work. Finally, call on different pairs to share their conversations with the class.

C Listen.

Repeat the procedure from the previous **Listen.**

Carlos: Hi. I'm Carlos. I'm from Brazil.

Tien: Hello. My name is Tien. I'm from Vietnam.

To help students understand the words *Brazil* and *Vietnam*, point out these countries on a map or globe. Alternatively, if you have students from these countries, ask them to point the countries out.

Listen and say.

Repeat the procedure from the previous **Listen and say.**

D Talk with a partner.

Repeat the procedure from the previous **Talk with a partner.**

1 Welcome!

STUDENT BOOK PAGE 3

E Read.

Have the students follow along in their books as you read aloud the contents of the name tag.

F Write your name.

Draw a name tag on the board and add your name.

Hello!
My name is
(your name)

Read your information aloud. Then have the students complete the activity. Go around the room and check their work.

Finally, call on individual students to read their name tags aloud.

EXPANSION ACTIVITY: Dialogue and Role Play

Have the students move around the room and introduce themselves to each other. Have them use the model dialogue in their books on page 3:

A: Hi. I'm _________. I'm from _________.

B: Hello. My name is _________. I'm from _________.

Go around the room and check the students' work.

2 The alphabet

STUDENT BOOK PAGE 4

LEARNING POINT
Understanding, saying, and writing the alphabet

NEW LANGUAGE

Brazil	Thailand
Colombia	USA
Japan	Venezuela
Mexico	Vietnam

A B C D E F G H I J K L M N O P Q R S T U V W X Y Z
a b c d e f g h i j k l m n o p q r s t u v w x y z

Listen.

Have the students listen with their books closed.

A B C D E F G H I J K L M N O P Q R S T U V W X Y Z

Have the students listen again as they follow along with their books open.

Listen and say.

Have the students listen to and repeat each letter separately. Stop the tape or CD after each letter or read aloud the separate letters with pauses.

Then call on individual students to listen and repeat after you.

Write.

On the board, write the alphabet with blanks under each letter.

Say "Copy" as you write the letters in the blanks.

Have the students copy the alphabet in their books. Go around the room and check their work.

Finally, call on different students to copy two to three letters of the alphabet on the board.

Write.

Repeat the procedure from the previous **Write.**

EXPANSION ACTIVITY: Write the letters.

Have the students write the letters of the alphabet on a separate piece of paper as you dictate them—first in sequence, then randomly. Be sure to write down your random sequence for later reference.

Have the students compare their work with a partner.

Write your random sequence of letters on the board so students can check their work.

Finally, go around the room and check students' work.

2 The alphabet

D Listen and say the letters.

Have the students listen with their books closed.

1. U-S-A

2. J-A-P-A-N

3. B-R-A-Z-I-L

4. M-E-X-I-C-O

5. V-I-E-T-N-A-M

6. T-H-A-I-L-A-N-D

7. C-O-L-O-M-B-I-A

8. V-E-N-E-Z-U-E-L-A

Have the students listen again as they follow along with their books open.

Have the students listen to and repeat each item separately. Stop the tape or CD after each item or read aloud the separate items with pauses.

Then call on individual students to listen and repeat after you.

To help students understand the names of the countries, point out the countries on a map or globe. Alternatively, if you have students from these countries, ask them to point the countries out.

E Listen and write.

Have the students listen with their books closed.

1. n-a-m-e

2. h-e-l-l-o

3. f-r-o-m

4. w-r-i-t-e

5. y-o-u

Write "1. _ _ _ _" on the board. Play or say the first item. Fill in the letters.

Have the students listen again and complete the activity. Stop the tape or CD, or pause after each item, so students have time to fill in the letters. Go around the room and check their work.

Have the students compare their answers with a partner. Then have them listen again as they check their work.

Finally, call on different students to read aloud the completed words as you write the answers on the board.

ANSWERS:

1. name

2. hello

3. from

4. write

5. you

3 How do you spell that?

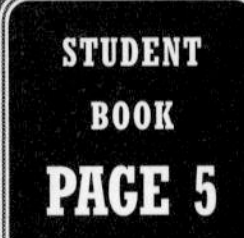

LEARNING POINT
Spelling your name

NEW LANGUAGE
first name
last name
What's your name?
How do you spell that?

Listen.

Have the students open their books and examine the illustrations.

Have the students listen with their books closed.

Maria: I'm Maria Cruz. What's your name?

Tien: My name's Tien Lam.

Maria: How do you spell that?

Tien: My first name is T-I-E-N. My last name is L-A-M.

Then have them open their books, look at the illustration, and listen again as they follow along.

Write your first and last names on the board and spell them aloud. Demonstrate the meaning of first and last. Point to your first name and say: "My first name is (your first name)." Then point to your last name and say: "My last name is (your last name)." Under your first name, write "first name." Under your last name, write "last name."

Listen and say.

Have the students listen to and repeat each line separately. Stop the tape or CD after each line or read aloud the separate lines with pauses.

Then call on individual students to listen and repeat after you.

B Talk with a partner.

Write the open-ended conversation on the board. Pick a student to model the open-ended conversation with you in front of the class.

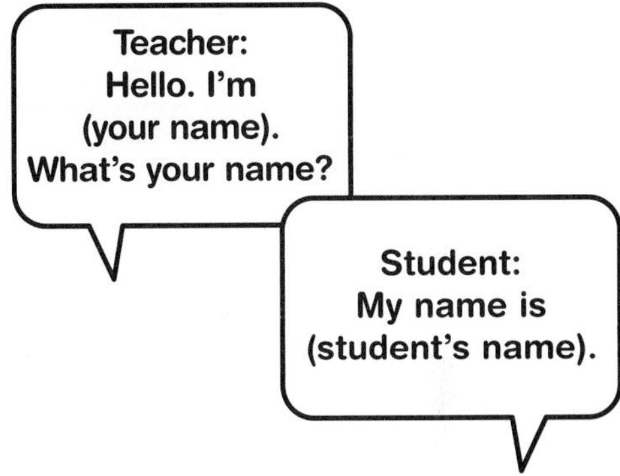

Teacher:
Hello. I'm
(your name).
What's your name?
Student:
My name is
(student's name).

Have the students work in pairs to practice the conversation. Go around the room and check their work.

Finally, call on different pairs to share their conversations with the class.

EXPANSION ACTIVITY:
Spell your name.

Use the dialogue in Activity A as a model and introduce yourself to a student. Model the dialogue with several students, then have the students walk around the room, introducing themselves to each other and asking each other to spell their names. Go around and join in the activity as you check their work.

Play *Alphabet Bingo*.

Explain to the students that bingo is a game, and that they are going to play it.

Copy the Bingo card on the board and fill it with random letters.

3 How do you spell that?

STUDENT BOOK PAGE 5

Say random letters of the alphabet. Each time you say a letter, ask the class whether or not the letter is on your card. As you say letters that are on your card, draw Xs over them. Once you've X-ed a complete diagonal, vertical, or horizontal row of letters, call out "Bingo!"

Have the students copy the Bingo card on paper and write any nine letters in the blanks. Check to make sure that students have not simply copied the letters you wrote on the board.

Read aloud random letters and when a student calls out "Bingo," check his or her work. Then have the winning student call the letters in the next round.

4 What's in the classroom?

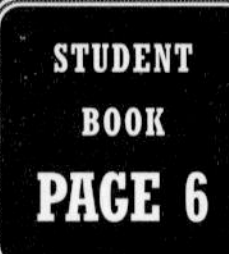

LEARNING POINT
Identifying things in the classroom

NEW LANGUAGE

backpack	door
board	notebook
book	paper
chair	pen
computer	student
desk	teacher

What's this?

EXPANSION ACTIVITY: Point and say.

Using the illustrations in the Student Book as a guide, point to people (teacher/student) and objects in your classroom as the class calls out the words.

Next, call on one student at a time, point to a person or object, and have the student say the word.

Finally, randomly point to different objects and prompt students to name them.

A Listen.

Have the students open their books and examine the illustrations.

Have the students listen with their books closed.

1. student
2. paper
3. desk
4. chair
5. pen
6. board
7. backpack
8. computer
9. teacher
10. notebook
11. door
12. book

Then have them open their books, look at the illustrations, and listen again as they follow along.

B Listen.

Have the students open their books and examine the illustration.

Have the students listen with their books closed.

Sandy: What's this?

Grace: A backpack?

Then have them open their books, look at the illustrations, and listen again as they follow along.

Listen and say.

Have the students listen to and repeat each line separately. Stop the tape or CD after each line or read aloud the separate lines with pauses.

Then call on individual students to listen and repeat after you.

C Talk with a partner.

Copy the open-ended conversation on the board. Pick a student to model the open-ended conversation with you in front of the class. Point to a chair and ask "What's this?"

4 What's in the classroom?

STUDENT BOOK PAGE 6

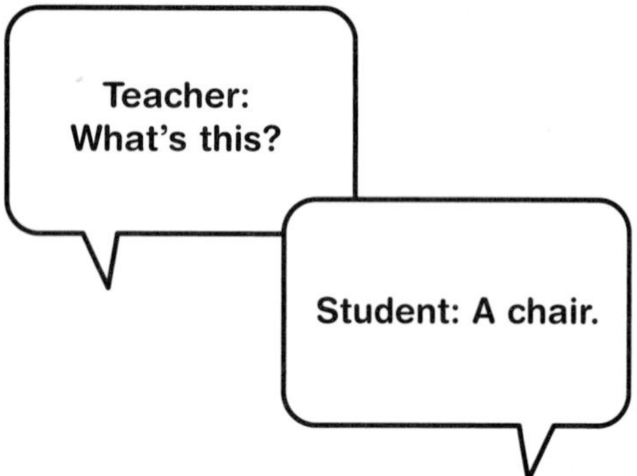
Teacher: What's this?
Student: A chair.

Have the students work in pairs to practice the conversation. Go around the room and check their work.

Finally, call on different pairs to share their conversations with the class.

5 Follow directions.

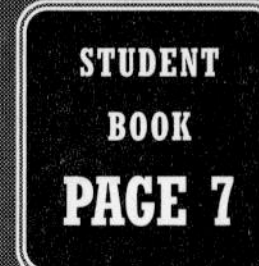

LEARNING POINT
Identifying and following classroom directions

NEW LANGUAGE
Check.
Circle.
Complete.
Match.

Read.

Copy the exercise on the board. Do not copy the circle, the check, the handwritten word *book*, or the handwritten letters *a* and *b*.

Have the students follow along as you read aloud the commands. Then read each command aloud again as you perform the action. For example, as you say: "Circle," draw a circle around the word *book*, and so on.

Circle.

Point out the example in the book. Write "c. pen" on the board and circle it as you say the word "Circle."

Teacher: Circle.

Refer the students to the item in their books and tell them to circle the appropriate word. Go around the room and check the students' work.

Have them compare their work with a partner.

Finally, call on a student to write the correct word on the board and circle it.

ANSWER: a. backpack

Check.

Point out the example in the book. Write "___ a. student" on the board and write a check on the line as you say the word "Check."

Refer the students to the item in their books and tell them to check the appropriate word. Go around the room and check the students' work.

Then have them compare their work with a partner.

Finally, call on a student to write the correct word on the board and check it.

ANSWER: d. desk

Complete.

Point out the example in the book and write it on the board, leaving the blank empty. Write the word "meet" in the blank. as you say the word "Complete."

Refer the students to the item in their books and tell them to complete the sentence. Go around the room and check the students' work.

Then have them compare their work with a partner.

Finally, call on a student to write the complete sentence on the board.

ANSWER: (student's name)

5 Follow directions.

STUDENT BOOK PAGE 7

Match.

Have the students examine the illustrations. Write the words and blanks in the first column on the board. Point to the first item and the door in the second column and write a "b" in the blank next to "door."

Have the students complete the activity. Go around the room and check their work.

Finally, write the answers on the board.

ANSWERS:

1. b

2. a

6 Open the book.

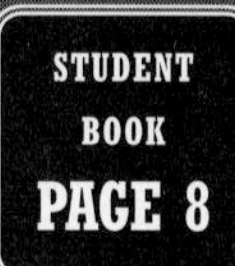

LEARNING POINT
Recognizing and saying classroom directions

NEW LANGUAGE

close	point to
go to	put away
open	take out

Listen.

Have the students open their books and examine the illustrations.

Have the students listen with their books closed.

1. Open. Open the book.

2. Close. Close the book.

3. Put away. Put away the book.

4. Go to. Go to the board.

5. Take out. Take out the pen.

6. Point to. Point to the computer.

Have them open their books, look at the illustrations, and listen again as they follow along.

Then have them listen a third time and watch you as you perform the actions.

Listen and say.

Have the students listen to and repeat each line separately. Stop the tape or CD after each line or read aloud the separate lines with pauses.

1. open

2. close

3. put away

4. go to

5. take out

6. point to

Then call on individual students to listen and repeat after you.

Listen and circle.

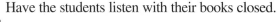

Have the students listen with their books closed.

1. Put away the paper.

2. Open the backpack.

3. Take out the book.

Point to the first item in the book.

Have the students listen to the first command. Circle the illustration on the left.

Then have the students listen again and complete the activity. Stop the tape or CD, or pause after each command, so students have time to circle the appropriate illustration.

Have the students compare their answers with a partner. Then have them listen again as they check their work.

Finally, for each item, ask the students whether they circled the first illustration or the second.

ANSWERS:

1. the illustration on the left

2. the illustration on the right

3. the illustration on the left

7 Point to the book.

STUDENT BOOK PAGE 9

LEARNING POINT
Recognizing and practicing direction words

NEW LANGUAGE

close	point to
go to	put away
open	take out

A Listen. Check √ what you hear.

Have the students listen with their books closed.

1. Open the door.

2. Go to the board.

3. Take out the pen.

4. Put away the notebook.

5. Open the door.

6. Put away the paper.

7. Point to the desk.

8. Take out the book.

Copy the first item on the board. Play or say the first command. Write a check next to "Open the door."

1. __ Close the door. √ Open the door.

Then have the students listen again and complete the exercise. Stop the tape or CD, or pause after each command, so students have time to check the appropriate column.

Have the students compare their answers with a partner. Have them listen again to check their work.

Finally, ask a student to copy the activity on the board and check (√) the answers.

ANSWERS:

1. Open the door.

2. Go to the board.

3. Take out the pen.

4. Put away the notebook.

5. Open the door.

6. Put away the paper.

7. Point to the desk.

8. Take out the book.

B Complete the sentences. Tell a partner.

Copy the first item on the board: "1. Open the __________." Point to the classroom door and then the blank as you prompt the class to answer, "door." Next write the word door in the blank.

Have the class members work individually to complete the sentences. Demonstrate that blanks may be filled with more than one correct answer by erasing the word door on the board and writing "notebook" in its place. Go around the room and check students' work.

7 Point to the book.

Pick a student to model the commands with you in front of the class.

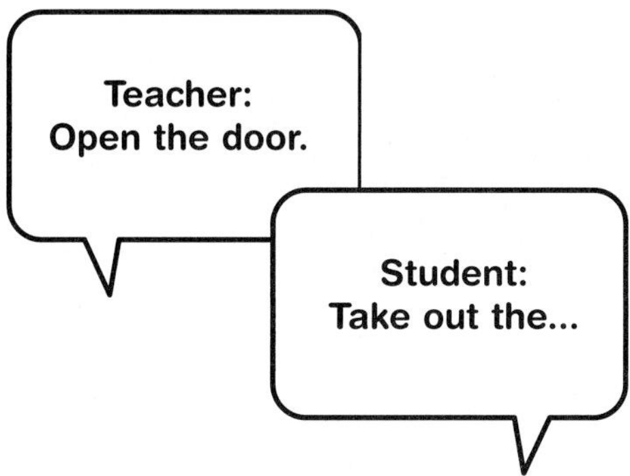

Teacher:
Open the door.
Student:
Take out the...

Have the students work in pairs to practice the commands. Go around the room and check their work.

SAMPLE ANSWERS:

1. Open the door/notebook/book.

2. Take out the pen/paper/notebook.

3. Close the door/notebook/book.

4. Go to the board/desk/teacher.

5. Put away the pen/notebook/paper.

6. Point to the board/notebook/desk.

C Play *Follow the Leader*.

Tell the students to complete the sentences in their books. Go around the room and check their work.

Tell your classmates.

Point out the illustration and explain that the student who is standing is the leader and that the others are following her. Tell the class that they will do the same thing as in the illustration.

Demonstrate the game. With a book in hand, be the leader and issue the first command, "Open the book," for the others to follow. Prompt the students to open their books.

Next put the students in groups of four to five. Explain that each group is to choose a leader who issues his or her commands for the others to follow.

Have the groups do the activity. Go around the room and check their work.

Every two or three minutes, stop the groups and have them choose a new leader.

SAMPLE ANSWERS:

1. Open the door/notebook/book.

2. Take out the pen/paper/notebook.

3. Close the door/notebook/book.

4. Go to the board/desk/teacher.

5. Put away the pen/notebook/paper.

6. Point to the board/notebook/desk.

8 My phone number is 981-355-2305.

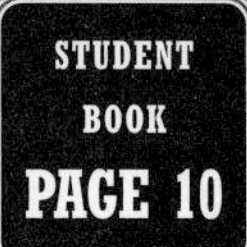

LEARNING POINT
Practicing numbers 0–10

NEW LANGUAGE
address
e-mail address
phone number
My ____ is ...

0	1	2	3	4	5	6	7	8	9	10
zero	one	two	three	four	five	six	seven	eight	nine	ten

A Listen.

Have the students open their books and examine the numbers.

Have the students listen with their books closed.

0, 1, 2, 3, 4, 5, 6, 7, 8, 9, 10

Then have them open their books, look at the numbers, and listen again as they follow along.

Listen and say.

Have the students listen to and repeat each number separately. Stop the tape or CD after each number or read aloud the separate numbers with pauses.

Then call on individual students to listen and repeat after you.

EXPANSION ACTIVITY: Show Me the Numbers

Prompt the class members to hold up the correct number of fingers as you say the numbers in order ("1, 2, 3, ...").

Next say numbers randomly and prompt the class to respond with the appropriate number of fingers.

Finally, call on individual students to hold up the correct number of fingers as you say random numbers.

B Write the number.

Copy the first item on the board.

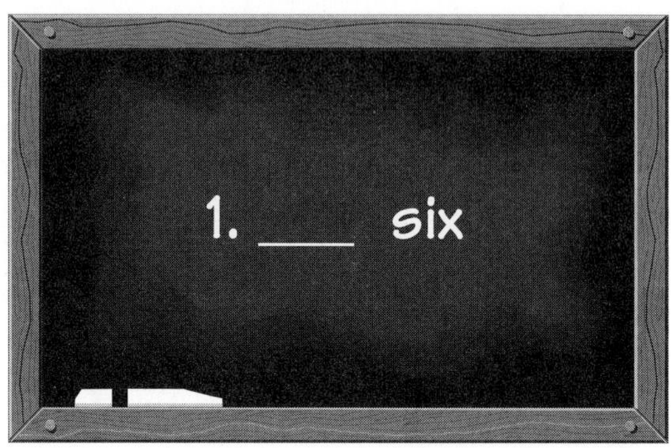

Then call a student to the board and say: "Write the number." Prompt the student to write the number *6* in the blank.

Have the students complete the activity and then compare their work with a partner. Go around the room and check their work.

Finally, write the items on the board. Then call on different students to fill in the blanks.

ANSWERS:

1. 6

2. 0

3. 5

4. 4

5. 10

6. 1

7. 7

8. 2

9. 8

10. 3

11. 9

8 My phone number is 981-355-2305.

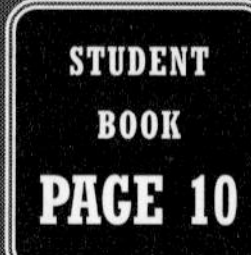

C Listen.

Have the students listen with their books closed.

Carlos: My phone number is 981-555-2305.

Leo: My address is 7 Paper Street.

Sandy: My e-mail address is wu046@hill.edu.

Have the students listen again as they follow along with their books open.

Listen and say.

Have the students listen to and repeat each line separately. Stop the tape or CD after each line or read aloud the separate lines with pauses.

Then call on individual students to listen and repeat after you.

Point out the learning note next to the conversation, which says "For: 2305 Say: two-three-oh-five or two-three-zero-five." Say the number both ways and have the students repeat after you.

D Write. Tell a partner.

Copy the incomplete sentences with the blanks on the board. Then read the sentences aloud as you fill in your own or fictitious information.

Teacher: My phone number is 981-555-5555.

Next have the students write in their own answers in their books. Go around the room and check their work.

Have the students work with a partner to take turns reading their answers aloud.

Finally, erase your answers from the board and have a student volunteer to fill in his or her information.

E Listen and circle.

Have the students listen with their books closed.

1. Six

2. Five

3. Ten

4. 5 Pen Avenue

5. 555-5050

6. 781-555-9876

Copy the first line on the board. Play or say the first item. Circle "six."

Then have the students listen again and complete the activity. Stop the tape or CD, or pause after each item, so students have time to circle the appropriate response.

Have the students compare their answers with a partner. Then have them listen again as they check their work.

Finally, call on individual students to write the items they circled on the board.

ANSWERS:

1. six

2. five

3. 10

4. 5 Pen Avenue

5. 555-5050

6. 781-555-9876

9 Emergency Information Form

STUDENT BOOK PAGE 11

LEARNING POINT
Writing and saying personal information

NEW LANGUAGE
Emergency Information Form

Read.

Have the students follow along in their books as you read aloud the information on the form. Introduce new language and explain what the form is for. Focus on the word *emergency*, making sure students understand what it means, providing and eliciting different examples of emergencies.

B Complete the form.

Copy the form on the board and fill in your own name and fictitious information.

Then read the contents of the form aloud for the class. Next have the students fill in their own information in their books.

Have the students work in pairs to share and compare the information on their forms. Go around the room and check their work.

Finally, erase the information you filled in the blanks on the board and then call on a student to fill in his or her own information. Have the student read aloud the information for the class.

C Talk to two students.

Copy the chart on the board.

Ask one or two students "What is your name?" "How do you spell that?" Then write their information on the board.

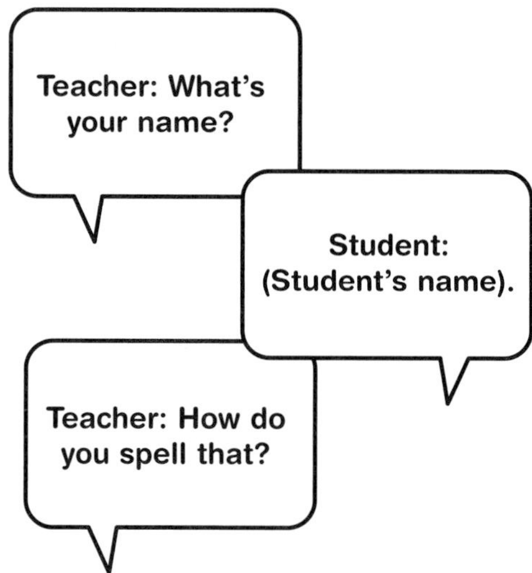

Teacher: What's your name?
Student: (Student's name).
Teacher: How do you spell that?

Have the students move around the room, talk to their classmates, and write their classmates' name on their charts. Go around and check their work.

Finally, have different students volunteer to copy the information they collected on the board. Have them spell the names and read them aloud.

10 Review

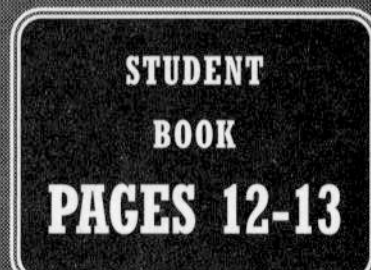

A Listen and write.

Have the students listen with their books closed.

Sandy: Hi. I'm Sandy. What's your name?

Don: My name is Don.

Sandy: Nice to meet you, Don.

Don: Nice to meet you too, Sandy.

Have the students open their books. Play or say first line and point out the example.

Have the students listen again and fill in the blanks with the words they hear. Stop the tape or CD, or pause after each line, so students have time to write. Go around the room and check their answers.

Have the students compare their answers with a partner. Then have them listen again as they check their work.

Finally, call on different students to read aloud the completed sentences as you write the answers on the board.

ANSWERS:

Hi

name

Nice

meet

B Listen and √ check the answer.

Have the students listen with their books closed.

1. What's your name?

2. Nice to meet you.

3. What's your name?

4. How do you spell that?

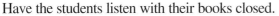

5. What's this?

6. What's your phone number?

Copy the first line on the board. Play or say the first item. Write a check mark next to "Don."

Then have the students listen again and complete the exercise. Stop the tape or CD, or pause after each sentence, so students have time to check the appropriate choices.

Have the students compare their answers with a partner. Have them listen again to check their work.

Finally, ask a student to copy the chart on the board and check (√) the answers.

ANSWERS:

1. Don.

2. Nice to meet you, too.

3. Isabel.

4. I-S-A-B-E-L

5. A chair.

6. 310-555-0123

10 Review

Listen and write.

Repeat the procedure from the previous **Listen and Write.**

Sandy: Hi. I'm Sandy. What's your name?

Grace: My name is Grace Lee.

Sandy: How do you spell that?

Grace: My first name is G-R-A-C-E.
My last name is L-E-E.

ANSWERS:

I'm

name

How

first

last

Write.

Point out the illustrations in the book and the sample answer. Have the students write the names of the different objects in the appropriate blanks.

Have them compare answers with a partner. Go around the room and check their work.

Finally, call on a student to write the answers on the board.

ANSWERS:

1. pen

2. book

3. desk

4. notebook

5. paper

E Learning Log

Write five words you remember.

Demonstrate to the class what a "learning log" is. Copy the directions—*Write five words you remember*—and the first column from the book on the board.

Then point to the word *remember* and say: "I remember…" as you tap your head with the forefinger of one hand and write additional words in the column with your other hand—*chair, book.*

Next point to the column and say: "This is a learning log. It has words I remember." Now copy the entire log on the board along with the headings and the sample words. Next prompt the class to think of an additional word for each column.

Tell the students to try to fill in the log without looking back in their books for words. Then have them compare answers with a partner.

Finally, call several students to the board and have them write one word in each column of the log. Check their work.

10 Review

STUDENT BOOK PAGES 12-13

SAMPLE ANSWERS:

Classroom	Numbers	Directions
desk	one	Circle.
chair	two	Open the book.
board	three	Close the door.
computer	four	Take out the pen.
door	five	Put away the paper.

√ Check what you can do.

Copy the checklist on the board and read the entries aloud as the students follow along. Explain the purpose of the checklist. Begin by demonstrating the meaning of the word *can*. For example, say: "I can say my phone number," then say your phone number. When you finish, put a check mark in the item No. 1 blank on the board.

Explain that for item number 5, the students are to add anything extra that they've learned to do. Prompt students to provide a possible answer and write it in the blank. If no one can come up with a possibility, provide one yourself—for example, "I can follow directions."

Tell the students to complete the checklist. Go around the room and check their work.

Finally, call on different students to read aloud the items they checked and what they filled in for item No. 5.

1. I can say my phone number. _____

2. I can say the alphabet. _____

3. I can read and complete a form. _____

4. I can write my name. _____

5. I can ____________________. _____

Looking Back

What do you see on page 2? Write three more words in your Learning Log.

Point out the final activity in the book. Explain the meaning of "Looking back." Tell the class that it means something similar to "Review."

Have the students look at the illustration on page 2 and add three words to their Learning Logs. Then have them compare their additions with a partner.

Finally, call on different students to read aloud the headings and the words they added.

See Color Transparencies package for unit wrap-up activity. This task can be used as an oral assessment tool. Many unit wrap-up activities include a reproducible blackline master.

Where are you from?

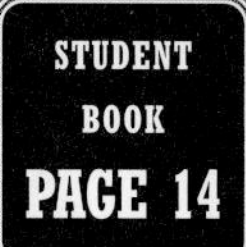

UNIT OVERVIEW

	LESSON:	LEARNING POINTS:	SB#
1.	**Where are you from?**	Saying where you're from	**p. 15**
2.	**What language do you speak?**	Saying what language you speak	**p. 16**
3.	**What language does he speak?**	Saying what language someone speaks	**p. 17**
4.	**Grace is married.**	Identifying marital status	**p. 18**
5.	**I am average height.**	Talking about height	**p. 19**
6.	**I have blue eyes.**	Talking about eye color and hair color	**p. 20**
7.	**He has brown hair.**	Identifying features	**p. 21**
8.	**What's your address?**	Practicing numbers 11-19 and saying your address	**p. 22**
9.	**Identification Form**	Writing down personal information	**p. 23**
10.	**Review**	Review Unit 2	**p. 24**

Suggestions for Unit Opener (Student Book page 14)

Brainstorm. Have students look at the unit-opening illustration. Ask them for words related to countries, languages, flags, and foods that they already know. Write the words on the board as students say them.

Model the language. Begin by reading the caption aloud—"Where are the students? What do you see?" Point to the people and items in the illustration and name them. Then point to other people and items in the illustration and name them. Write the words on the board.

Model the language again. This time have the class repeat the words after you. Then go around the room and have individual students repeat different words.

Point and say. Point to the words you've written on the board as you say them. Have the students repeat them after you.

Initiate pair work. Have the students work in pairs. Tell them to take turns pointing to the people, pets, and items in the illustration and naming them. Demonstrate this by asking a student to point to someone or something and by saying the name yourself, then pointing yourself and asking the same student to say the name. Go around the room and check students' work.

See Color Transparencies package for additional unit-opening activity. Many of these tasks include a reproducible blackline master.

1 Where are you from?

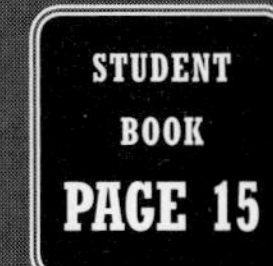

LEARNING POINT
Saying where you're from

NEW LANGUAGE
Brazil
China
Colombia
Korea
Mexico
Russia
Where are you from?
Where is _____ from?
He/She's from _____.

A Listen.

Have the students listen with their books closed.

Leo: I'm from Russia. Where are you from?

Don: I'm from Korea.

Have the students listen again as they follow along with their books open.

Listen and say.

Have the students listen to and repeat each line separately. Stop the tape or CD after each line or read aloud the separate lines with pauses.

Then call on individual students to listen and repeat after you.

B Talk with a partner.

Copy the open-ended conversation on the board. Pick a student to model the open-ended conversation with you in front of the class.

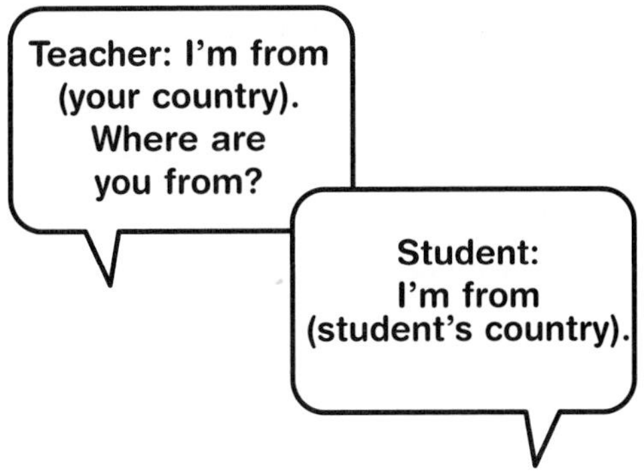

Teacher: I'm from (your country). Where are you from?
Student: I'm from (student's country).

Have the students work in pairs to practice the conversation. Go around the room and check their work.

Finally, call on a pair to share their conversation with the class.

C Listen.

Repeat the procedure from the previous **Listen.**

Grace: Where is Carlos from?

Maria: He's from Brazil.

Grace: Where is Isabel from?

Maria: She's from Colombia.

Point out these countries on a map or globe. Alternatively, if you have students from these countries, ask them to point them out.

Listen and say.

Repeat the procedure from the previous **Listen and say.**

WORKBOOK PAGE 11

1 Where are you from?

STUDENT BOOK PAGE 15

Talk with classmates.

Copy the open-ended conversation on the board. Pick a student to model the open-ended conversation with you in front of the class.

Teacher: Where is Grace from?
Student: She's from China.

Have the students work in pairs to take turns playing the roles of A and B. Tell them to use the words in the Word List. Go around the room and check their work.

Finally, call on different pairs to share their conversations with the class.

EXPANSION ACTIVITY: A Map Game

Use a large world map. Have a student volunteer to model the game with you in front of the class. Ask the student to point to his or her home country on the map. Then ask, "Where is (student's name) from?"

Have class members volunteer to answer by raising their hands. Pick a student to say the answer aloud.

Have different students come up to point to their home countries on the map. Ask for volunteers to answer the question "Where is (student's name) from?"

 WORKBOOK PAGE 11

2 What language do you speak?

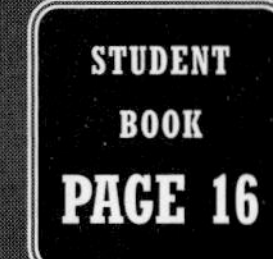
STUDENT
BOOK
PAGE 16

LEARNING POINT
Saying what language you speak

NEW LANGUAGE
Chinese
Portuguese
Spanish
I speak _____.
What language do you speak?

Listen.

Have the students open their books and examine the illustrations.

Have the students listen with their books closed.

Isabel: I speak Spanish. What language do you speak?

Carlos: I speak Portuguese.

Then have them open their books, look at the illustration, and listen again as they follow along.

Listen and say.

Have the students listen to and repeat each line of the conversation separately. Stop the tape or CD after each line or read aloud the separate lines with pauses.

Then call on individual students to listen and repeat after you.

Talk with a partner.

Copy the open-ended conversation on the board. Pick a student to model the open-ended conversation with you in front of the class.

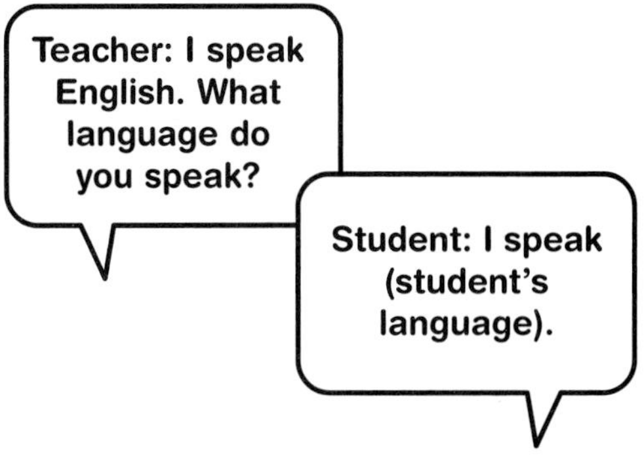
Teacher: I speak English. What language do you speak?
Student: I speak (student's language).

Have the students work in pairs to practice the conversation. Go around the room and check their work.

Finally, call on different pairs to share their conversations with the class.

Talk with three classmates. Complete the chart.

Copy the chart on the board.

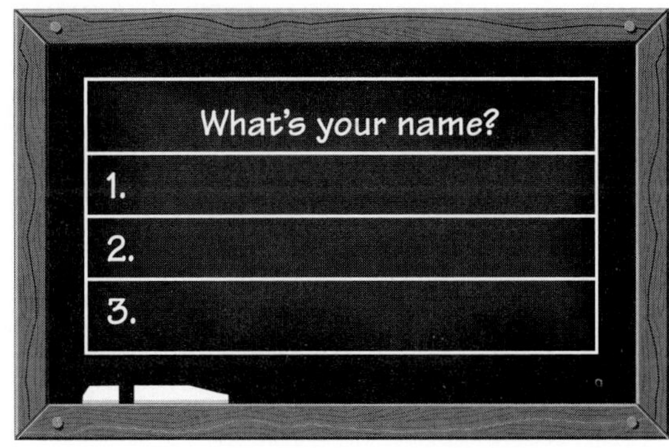
What's your name?
1.
2.
3.

Ask three students for their information and write it in the chart on the board.

Have the students move around the room, talk to their classmates and write their information in the chart.

Finally, erase the information in the columns on the board and have different students volunteer to fill in the information they collected. Have them read the information aloud.

WORKBOOK PAGE 12

2 What language do you speak?

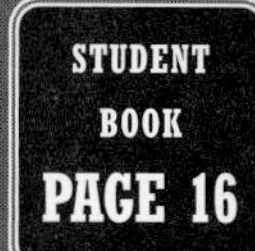

Write.

Copy the open-ended sentences on the board and add your own information. Then read your information aloud. Next have the students complete the activity. Go around the room and check the students' work.

Finally, call on individual students to read their information aloud. You can also have students write their sentences on the board as they read them aloud.

EXPANSION ACTIVITY: A Name Guessing Game

Note: This game is only appropriate for classes with students from various countries.

Write three open-ended sentences on the board.

Have the students copy the sentences on slips of paper and fill in their own information. Tell them to leave the third blank empty, but to write their names on the reverse side of the paper.

Fill out a slip of paper containing your own information to show students what to do. Go around the room and make sure everyone has done the job correctly.

Go around and collect the slips of paper. Demonstrate how to play the game by randomly picking up a slip of paper and reading aloud the two sentences. Read the third, incomplete sentence with a pause at the end to prompt the class to guess the student's name—"My name is . . ." Confirm the guess or guesses by turning over the paper and reading aloud the student's name.

Now call on different students to come to the front of the class and lead the game.

3 What language does he speak?

STUDENT BOOK PAGE 17

LEARNING POINT
Saying what language someone speaks

NEW LANGUAGE
Brazil
Korea
Korean
Mexico
Portuguese
Spanish
Vietnam
Vietnamese
_____ is from _____. What language does _____ speak?
_____ speaks _____.

 **Read. Complete the chart.**

Point out the chart and read aloud the names, the countries and the languages as the students follow along in their books.

Copy the last line on the board and fill it in with your information.

You: _____ _____

Have the students fill in the blanks with their own information. Go around and check their work.

 **Listen.**

Have the students listen with their books closed.

A: Carlos is from Brazil. What language does he speak?

B: He speaks Portuguese.

A: Tien is from Vietnam. What language does she speak?

B: She speaks Vietnamese.

Have the students listen again as they follow along with their books open.

Listen and say.

Have the students listen to and repeat each line separately. Stop the tape or CD after each line or read aloud the separate lines with pauses.

Then call on individual students to listen and repeat after you.

 **Talk with classmates about Carlos, Don, Tien, and Maria.**

Copy the open-ended sentences on the board.

Refer the students to Activity A and point out Carlos. Fill in the blanks with Carlos's information.

Pick a student to model the open-ended conversation with you in front of the class.

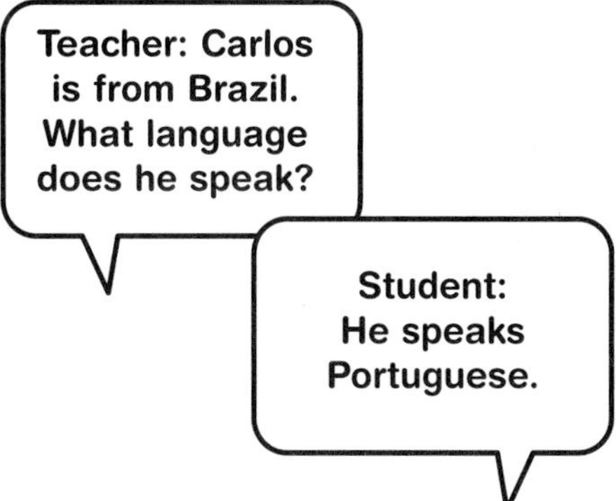
Teacher: Carlos is from Brazil. What language does he speak?
Student: He speaks Portuguese.

WORKBOOK PAGE 13

3 What language does he speak?

STUDENT BOOK PAGE 17

Have the students work in pairs to practice the conversation. Go around the room and check their work.

Finally, call on different pairs to share their conversations with the class.

 WORKBOOK PAGE 13

4 Grace is married.

LEARNING POINT
Identifying marital status

NEW LANGUAGE
divorced
married
single
widowed

Listen.

Have the students open their books and examine the illustrations.

Have the students listen with their books closed.

1. Married. She is married.

2. Single. They are single.

3. Divorced. Leo is divorced.

4. Widowed. Maria is widowed.

Then have them open their books, look at the illustrations, and listen again as they follow along.

If necessary, help students understand the new vocabulary by using gestures or words students already know. For example, if you are married and are wearing a wedding ring, say: "I'm married" as you point to your ring. For the word divorced, shake your head as you remove your ring.

Listen and say.

Have the students listen to and repeat each line of the conversation separately. Stop the tape or CD after each line or read aloud the separate lines with pauses.

married
single
divorced
widowed

Then call on individual students to listen and repeat after you.

Listen and circle.

Have the students listen with their books closed.

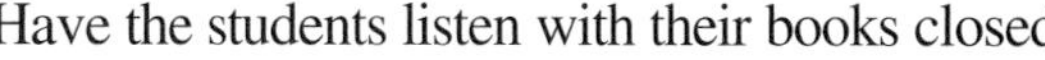

1. They are married.

2. He's widowed.

3. They are single.

Have the students open their books. Point out the first pair of illustrations in the book. Play or say the first item as you make a circling gesture around the illustration of the married couple.

Then have the students listen again and complete the activity. Stop the tape or CD, or pause after each sentence, so students have time to circle the appropriate illustration.

Have the students compare their answers with a partner. Then have them listen again as they check their work.

Finally, have a student come to the front of the class and point to the appropriate illustrations as you read the sentences aloud.

ANSWERS:

1. illustration on the left

2. illustration on the left

3. illustration on the left

5 I am average height.

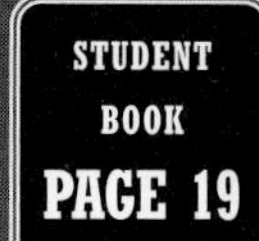
STUDENT
BOOK
PAGE 19

LEARNING POINT
Talking about height

NEW LANGUAGE
average height
short
tall

Listen.

Have the students open their books and examine the illustration.

Have the students listen with their books closed.

Paul: I'm average height.
Leo is tall.
Tien is short.
Don and Carlos are average height.

Then have them open their books, look at the illustration, and listen again as they follow along.

Listen and say.

Have the students listen to and repeat each line separately. Stop the tape or CD after each line or read aloud the separate lines with pauses.

average height
tall
short

Then call on individual students to listen and repeat after you.

Talk with a partner.

Copy the first open-ended sentence on the board. Pick a student to model the open-ended sentence with you in front of the class.

Teacher: Tien and Maria are...
Student: short.

Have the students work in pairs to complete the sentences. Go around the room and check their work.

Finally, call on a pair to share the answers with the class.

ANSWERS:

Tien and Maria are short.

Grace is tall.

Sandy is average height.

Write about three classmates.

Copy the first item on the board.

1. _____ is _____.

Then point out a student in the classroom and fill in the blanks with the appropriate information—the student's name and height—as you read the sentence aloud.

5 I am average height.

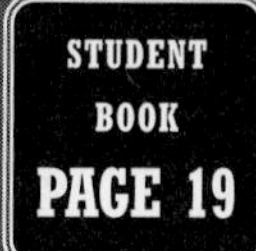

Have the students complete the activity. Have them stand up and move around as they fill in the blanks.

Next have the students read their answers with a partner.

Finally, call on different students to read their sentences aloud and to write them on the board.

6 I have blue eyes.

STUDENT BOOK PAGE 20

LEARNING POINT
Talking about eye color and hair color

NEW LANGUAGE

black	glasses
blond	green
blue	hair
brown	white
eyes	

_____ has _____ eyes/hair
_____ have _____ eyes/hair
_____ wear/wears glasses.
_____ don't wear glasses.

A Listen.

Have the students open their books and examine the illustrations.

Have the students listen with their books closed.

Leo has green eyes.

Isabel has blue eyes.

Leo and Isabel don't wear glasses.

Tien has brown eyes. She wears glasses.

Then have them open their books, look at the illustrations, and listen again as they follow along.

Listen and say.

Have the students listen to and repeat each sentence separately. Stop the tape or CD after each line or read aloud the separate lines with pauses.

Then call on individual students to listen and repeat after you.

B Talk to a partner.

Copy the open-ended sentences on the board. Pick a student to model the open-ended sentence with you in front of the class.

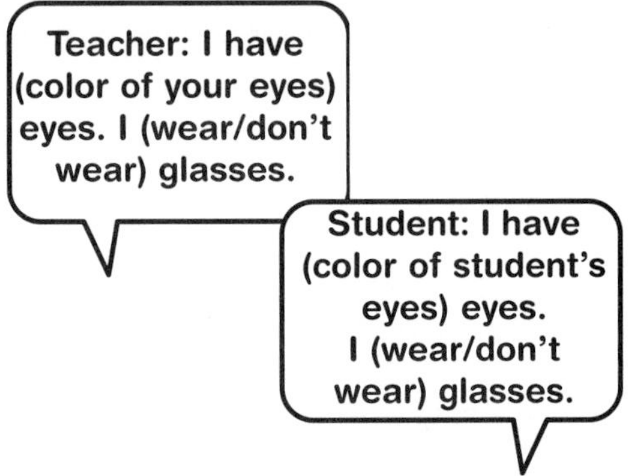

Teacher: I have (color of your eyes) eyes. I (wear/don't wear) glasses.
Student: I have (color of student's eyes) eyes. I (wear/don't wear) glasses.

Have the students work in pairs to practice the sentences. Go around the room and check their work.

Finally, call on a pair to share their sentences with the class.

C Listen.

Repeat the procedure from the previous **Listen.**

Sandy: I have red hair.
Paul and Tien have brown hair.
Leo has white hair.
Isabel has blond hair.

To help students understand the new vocabulary, point out different characters in the illustration and say: "(The character's name) has (color) hair."

6 I have blue eyes.

STUDENT BOOK PAGE 20

Listen and say.

Repeat the procedure from the previous **Listen and say.**

D Complete the sentence.

Write the open-ended sentence on the board and fill in your own information as you read the completed sentence aloud.

Have the students complete their own sentences.

Finally, call on different students to read their sentences aloud.

E Write about three classmates.

Write the first item from the book on the board. Then point out a student in the classroom and fill in the blanks with the appropriate information as you read the sentence aloud.

Have the students complete the activity. Have them stand up and move around as they fill in the blanks. Next have the students read their sentences with a partner.

Finally, call on different students to write their sentences on the board and read them aloud.

WORKBOOK PAGE 15

7 He has brown hair.

STUDENT BOOK PAGE 21

LEARNING POINT
Identifying features

NEW LANGUAGE
Language from Lessons 4, 5, and 6.

Match.

Review the meaning of Match with the students by pointing out the sample item in the book. Then have the class complete the activity.

Next have the students compare answers with a partner. Go around the room and check their work.

Finally, call on students to say the answers as you write them on the board.

ANSWERS:

1. d

2. b

3. a

4. c

Listen. Write the number.

Explain to students that they will hear a number followed by a question and answer. Have the students listen with their books closed.

1. He has brown hair and brown eyes. He's from Brazil.

2. He has white hair. He's divorced.

3. She is tall. She's Chinese.

4. She has red hair. She's from the USA.

5. She is widowed. She's from Mexico.

6. She has blue eyes. She speaks Spanish.

Copy the names and blanks on the board. Play or say the first item and write a "1" next to "Carlos."

Have the students listen again and complete the activity. Stop the tape or CD, or pause after each item, so students have time to write a response. Go around the room and check their answers.

Have the students compare their answers with a partner. Then have them listen as they check their work.

Finally, call on different students to read aloud the names and numbers as you write the answers on the board.

ANSWERS:

5 Maria

3 Grace

6 Isabel

4 Sandy

2 Leo

1 Carlos

8 What's your address?

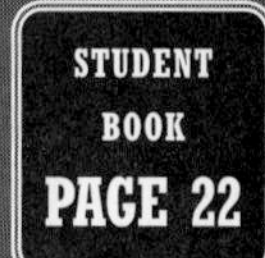

LEARNING POINT
Practicing numbers 11-19 and saying your address

NEW LANGUAGE
address
zip code

What's your _____?
My _____ is _____.

11	12	13	14	15
eleven	twelve	thirteen	fourteen	fifteen
16	17	18	19	
sixteen	seventeen	eighteen	nineteen	

Listen.

Have students listen with their books closed.

11, 12, 13, 14, 15, 16, 17, 18, 19

Have the students listen again as they follow along with their books open.

Listen and say.

Have the students listen to and repeat each number separately. Stop the tape or CD after each number or read aloud the separate numbers with pauses.

Then call on individual students to listen and repeat after you.

Write the numbers.

Write an example of this kind of activity on the board to demonstrate how to fill in missing numbers.

Demonstrate the procedure to the class as you fill in the missing numbers—2, 4, and 5.

Have the students do the activity and then compare their answers with a partner.

Finally, call on a student to write the complete sequence on the board.

ANSWERS:

11 12 13 14 15 16 17 18 19

C Write the number.

Copy the first item on the board.

Then call a student to the board and say: "Write the number."

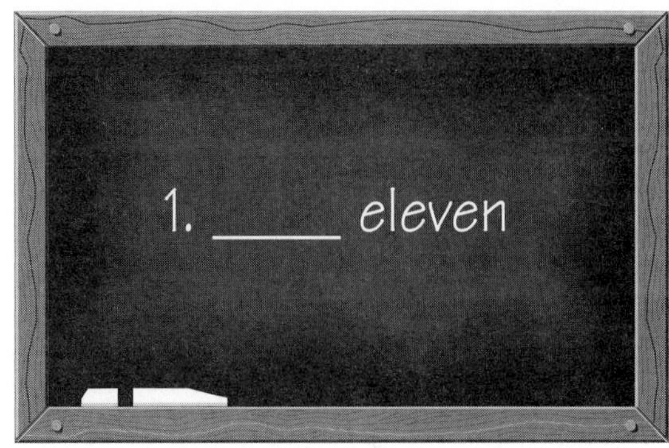

Prompt the student to write the number *11* in the blank.

What's your address?

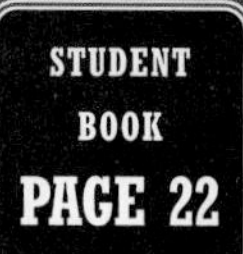

Have the students complete the activity and then compare their work with a partner. Go around the room and check their work.

Finally, copy the items on the board. Then call on different students to fill in the blanks and to say the numbers aloud as they do so.

ANSWERS:

1. 11

2. 16

3. 17

4. 13

5. 12

6. 18

7. 15

8. 14

Listen.

Have the students listen with their books closed.

Don: What's your address?

Paul: My address is 1714 Brown Street.

Don: What's your zip code?

Paul: My zip code is 01313.

Have the students listen again as they follow along with their books open.

Listen and say.

Repeat the procedure from the previous **Listen and say.**

Complete. Talk with a partner.

Copy the incomplete sentences on the board and fill in your own information as you read the completed sentences aloud.

Then have the students complete their own sentences.

Finally, call on different students to read their sentences aloud. Have several students write their sentences on the board and read them aloud.

EXPANSION ACTIVITY: Say and write the number.

Write the numbers 11–19 on the board. Randomly point to a number and prompt the class to say it. Continue with additional random numbers. Then call on individual students to say numbers that you point to.

Say random numbers from 11–19 and have the students write them down. Write the numbers on a piece of paper as you say them for later reference. Then call on a student to write the numbers on the board so the students can check their work.

9 Identification Form

STUDENT BOOK **PAGE 23**

LEARNING POINT
Writing down personal information

NEW LANGUAGE
identification form
marital status
MI = middle initial
state

Read.

Have the students follow along in their books as you read the information on the form aloud.

Teacher: Last name, Danov.

Explain that MI stands for "Middle Initial" and demonstrate by telling the class your second name and writing the initial for it on the board.

Demonstrate "type or print" by saying "type" as you mimic typing, and by saying "print" as you print your last name on the board.

Talk about forms used in the community. Refer the students back to page 11 in Unit 1 and compare that form to the one in this activity. For example, point out the different order of blanks for first and last names and tell the students that different forms have different orders. Also, show that on one form, the middle initial is required, but it's not required on the other form.

Complete the form.

Have the students complete the form with their own information. Then have them compare and share their work with a partner. Go around the room and check their work.

10 Review

STUDENT BOOK PAGES 24-25

Listen and write.

Have the students listen with their books closed.

Grace: I am tall.

Leo: I speak Russian.

Tien: I wear glasses.

Isabel: I have blond hair. I have blue eyes.

Copy the first sentence on the board. Play or say the first item. Write "tall" in the blank.

Then have the students listen again and complete the activity. Stop the tape or CD, or pause after each sentence, so students have time to fill in the blank.

Have the students compare their answers with a partner. Then have them listen again as they check their work.

Finally, call on individual students to read the completed sentences aloud.

ANSWERS:

tall

speak

glasses

blond; blue

Listen and √ check.

Have students listen with their books closed.

1. What language do you speak?

2. Who has red hair?

3. Where is Don from?

4. What's your zip code?

Copy the first line on the board. Play or say the first item. Write a check next to "I speak Vietnamese."

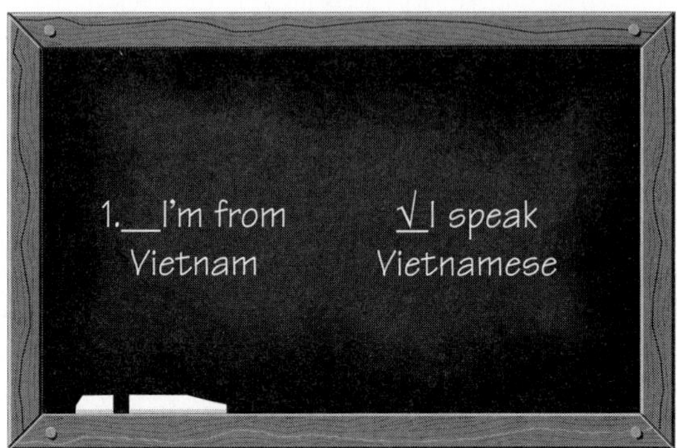
1.__I'm from Vietnam
√ I speak Vietnamese

Then have the students listen again and complete the activity. Stop the tape or CD, or pause after each question, so students have time to check the appropriate choices.

Have the students compare their answers with a partner. Have them listen again to check their work.

Finally, ask a student to copy the items on the board and check the answers.

ANSWERS:

1. I speak Vietnamese.

2. Sandy has red hair.

3. Korea.

4. 02090.

Play *Guess Who!*

Write about a classmate.

Read your sentences to the class. Say, "Guess who!"

10 Review

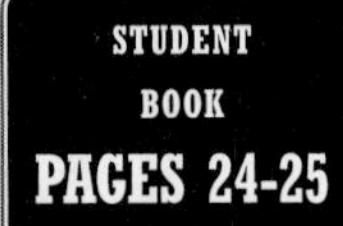

Tell the students they are going to play a game. Model the game for the class. Copy the sentences on the board and fill in the blanks to describe a student in the classroom.

Read the sentences aloud.

Then say, "Guess who!" and prompt the class to answer.

Have students fill in the blanks on their own, then take turns reading their sentences to the class and saying, "Guess who!"

Write. Complete the sentences.

Tell the students to carefully examine the illustrations. Go over the first item to help them get started. Then have them complete the activity.

Have the students compare answers with a partner. Go around and check their work.

Write the incomplete sentences and blanks on the board. Call on different students to write the answers in the blanks for you to check.

ANSWERS:

1. green

2. red

3. brown

4. blue

5. wears

Learning Log

Write five words you remember.

Review the purpose of a learning log. Tell the students to try to fill in the log without looking back in their books for words. Then have them compare answers with a partner.

Finally, copy the Learning Log on the board. Call several students to the board and have them write one word in each column of the log. Check their work.

SAMPLE ANSWERS:

Countries	Colors	Numbers
Brazil	black	twelve
China	blue	thirteen
Korea	brown	fourteen
Russia	green	eighteen
Vietnam	white	nineteen

√ Check what you can do.

Tell the students to complete the checklist. Go around the room and check their work.

Finally, call on different students to read aloud the items they checked and what they filled in for item No. 5.

1. I can say my hair and eye color. ____

2. I can ask people where they are from. ____

3. I can write my country's name. ____

4. I can say my country and language. ____

5. I can ____________________. ____

10 Review

STUDENT BOOK PAGES 24-25

EXPANSION ACTIVITY:
What can you do?

Have students volunteer to act out items they checked in *Check what you can do.* Tell each volunteer to read aloud the checked item and then perform the action in front of the class. For example, for item No. 3—I can write my country's name—have a student write his or her country's name on the board.

Looking Back

What do you see on page 14? Write three more words in your Learning Log.

Have the students look at the illustration on page 14 and add three words to their Learning Logs. Then have them compare their additions with a partner.

Finally, call on different students to read aloud the headings and the words they added.

See Color Transparencies package for unit wrap-up activity. This task can be used as an oral assessment tool. Many unit wrap-up activities include a reproducible blackline master.

This is my family.

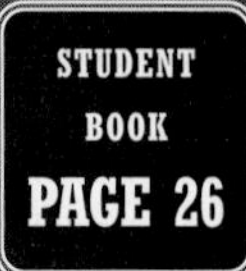

UNIT OVERVIEW

	LESSON:	LEARNING POINTS:	SB#
1.	**Sandy Johnson's family**	Saying the names of family members	**p. 27**
2.	**My relatives**	Identifying family members	**p. 28**
3.	**Who is Arthur?**	Asking and answering questions about family members	**p. 29**
4.	**Do you have children?**	Asking and answering questions about family members	**p. 30**
5.	**Mr., Mrs., and Ms.**	Recognizing and writing titles	**p. 31**
6.	**Carlos's relatives**	Identifying family members by name	**p. 32**
7.	**She is young.**	Understanding and writing personal descriptions	**p. 33**
8.	**How old are you?**	Practicing numbers 20-100 and saying your age	**p. 34**
9.	**Completing a census form**	Understanding and filling out a census form	**p. 35**
10.	**Review**	Review Unit 3	**p. 36**

Suggestions for Unit Opener (Student Book page 26)

Brainstorm. Have students look at the unit-opening illustration. Ask them for words related to family and family members that they already know. Write the words on the board as students say them.

Model the language. Begin by reading the caption aloud—"Who do you see on this page?" Point to the people and items in the illustration and name them. Use yourself and your students to continue modeling the language. Write the words on the board.

Model the language again. This time have the class repeat the words after you. Then go around the room and have individual students repeat different words.

Point and say. Point to the words you've written on the board as you say them. Have the students repeat them after you.

Initiate pair work. Have the students work in pairs. Tell them to take turns pointing to people and items in the illustration and naming them. Demonstrate this by asking a student to point to someone or something and by saying the name yourself, then pointing yourself and asking the same student to say the name. Go around the room and check students' work.

See Color Transparencies package for additional unit-opening activity. Many of these tasks include a reproducible blackline master.

1 Sandy Johnson's family

STUDENT BOOK PAGE 27

LEARNING POINT
Saying the names of family members

NEW LANGUAGE

brother	husband
daughter	mother
family	son
father	

What's your _____'s name?
His/Her name is _____.
And your _____'s name?

A Listen.

Have the students open their books and examine the illustrations.

Have the students listen with their books closed.

1. Mother. This is Sandy's mother.

2. Father. This is Sandy's father.

3. Brother. This is Sandy's brother.

4. Husband. This is Sandy's husband.

5. Daughter. This is Sandy's daughter.

6. Sons. These are Sandy's sons.

Then have them open their books, look at the illustrations, and listen again as they follow along.

Listen and say.

Have the students listen to and repeat each line separately. Stop the tape or CD after each line or read aloud the separate lines with pauses.

1. mother

2. father

3. brother

4. husband

5. daughter

6. sons

Then call on individual students to listen and repeat after you.

B Listen.

Have the students listen with their books closed.

Julia: What's your father's name?

Sandy: His name is Arthur. And your father's name?

Julia: His name is Mark.

Have the students listen again as they follow along with their books open.

Listen and say.

Repeat the procedure from the previous **Listen and say.**

C Talk with a partner.

Copy the open-ended conversation on the board. Pick a student to model the open-ended conversation with you in front of the class.

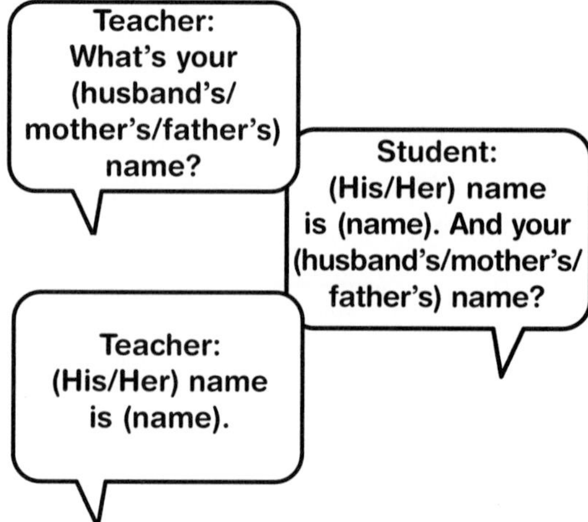

Teacher: What's your (husband's/ mother's/father's) name?
Student: (His/Her) name is (name). And your (husband's/mother's/ father's) name?
Teacher: (His/Her) name is (name).

1 Sandy Johnson's family

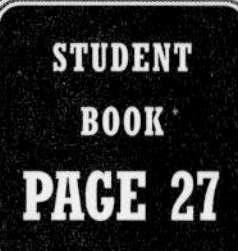

Have the students work in pairs to practice the conversation. Tell them to use the words in Activity A and the Word List. Go around the room and check their work.

Finally, call on different pairs to share their conversations with the class.

2 My relatives

STUDENT BOOK PAGE 28

LEARNING POINT
Identifying family members

NEW LANGUAGE
niece sister-in-law

Listen.

Have the students open their books and examine the illustrations. Have the students listen with their books closed.

Sandy: This is my father, Arthur.
This is my mother, Ann.
This is my brother, John.
This is my sister-in-law, Tomiko.
This is my husband, Will.
This is my niece, Mary.
These are my sons, Justin and Andy.
This is my daughter, Alexandra.

Have the students open their books. Point out the illustration of Sandy's family tree. To help the class understand how a tree works, draw your own simple family tree on the board and point out yourself in relation to your family members.

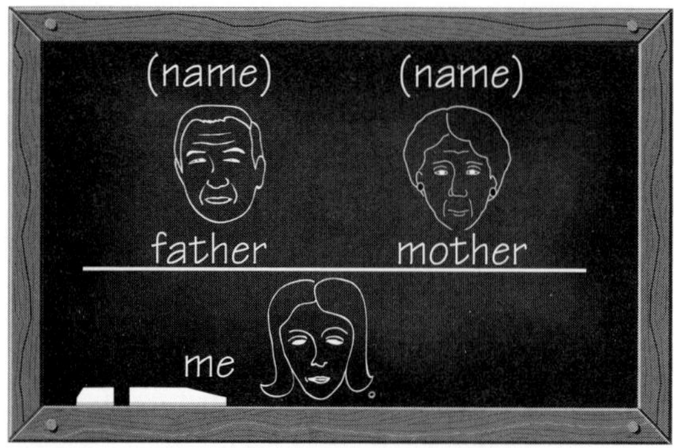

Then have the class listen again as they follow along with their books open.

Listen and say.

Have the students listen to and repeat each word separately. Stop the tape or CD after each line or read aloud the separate lines with pauses.

father
mother
brother
sister-in-law
husband
niece
sons
daughter

Then call on individual students to listen and repeat after you.

Listen and write.

Have the students listen with their books closed.

1. Justin is Sandy's son.
2. Alexandra is Sandy's daughter.
3. John is Sandy's brother.
4. Will is Sandy's husband.
5. Arthur is Sandy's father.
6. Ann is Sandy's mother.
7. Tomiko is Sandy's sister-in-law.
8. Mary is Sandy's niece.

Have the students open their books. Play or say the first item and point out the example.

 WORKBOOK PAGE 20

2 My relatives

STUDENT BOOK PAGE 28

Have the students listen again and complete the exercise. Stop the tape or CD, or pause after each sentence, so students have time to write a response. Go around the room and check their answers.

Have the students compare their answers with a partner. Then have them listen again as they check their work.

Finally, call on different students to write the completed sentences on the board.

ANSWERS:

1. son

2. daughter

3. brother

4. husband

5. father

6. mother

7. sister-in-law

8. niece

EXPANSION ACTIVITY:
Make your own family tree.

Have the students draw their own family trees. Explain that they can use Sandy's tree as a model, but that they might have a different arrangement of blanks. To make sure they understand, draw a modified version on the board to represent your own family tree or a fictitious one.

Go around the room and check the students' work. Have different students volunteer to draw their family trees on the board.

Tell the students to keep their family trees because they can use them in an Expansion Activity in Unit 3, Lesson 6.

WORKBOOK PAGE 20

3 Who is Arthur?

STUDENT BOOK PAGE 29

LEARNING POINT
Asking and answering questions about family members

NEW LANGUAGE
Who is/are _____?
_____ is/are _____.

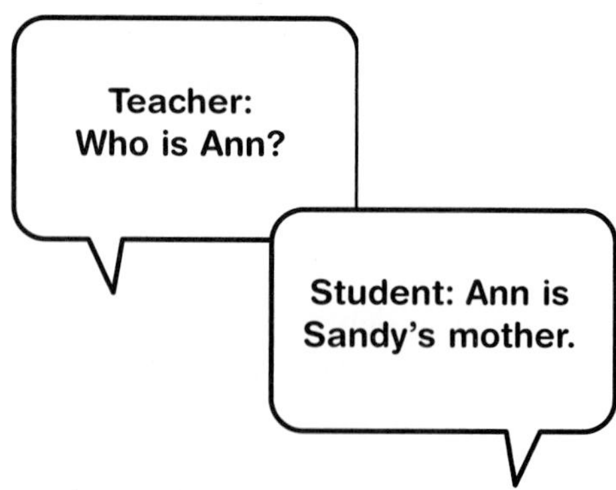
Teacher:
Who is Ann?
Student: Ann is
Sandy's mother.

Listen.

Have the students open their books and examine the illustration.

Have the students listen with their books closed.

Isabel: Who is Arthur?

Don: Arthur is Sandy's father.

Then have them open their books, look at the illustrations, and listen again as they follow along.

Listen and say.

Have the students listen to and repeat each line of the conversation separately. Stop the tape or CD after each line or read aloud the separate lines with pauses.

Then call on individual students to listen and repeat after you.

Talk with a partner. Look at the pictures on page 28.

Copy the open-ended conversation on the board. Pick a student to model the open-ended conversation with you in front of the class.

Have the students work in pairs to practice the conversation. Go around the room and check their work.

Finally, call on different pairs to share their conversations with the class.

Work with classmates. Read and circle.

Point out the first item. Ask "Who is Will?" and prompt the class to answer, "Sandy's husband."

Have the students work in small groups to do the activity. Have them take turns asking the questions and circling the answers.

Call on different groups to say the answers aloud as you write them on the board.

ANSWERS:

1. b **4.** b

2. b **5.** a

3. a **6.** b

4 Do you have children?

STUDENT BOOK PAGE 30

LEARNING POINT
Asking and answering questions about family members

NEW LANGUAGE
children
Do you have _____?
Yes, I have _____.
No, I don't.

Teacher: Do you have children?
Student: Yes, I have (number of children)./ No, I don't.

A Listen.

Have the students listen with their books closed.

Paul: Do you have children?

Leo: Yes, I have three daughters.

Tien: No, I don't.

Have the students listen again as they follow along with their books open.

Listen and say.

Have the students listen to and repeat each line of the conversation separately. Stop the tape or CD after each line or read aloud the separate lines with pauses.

Then call on individual students to listen and repeat after you.

B Talk with a partner.

Copy the open-ended conversation on the board. Pick a student to model the open-ended conversation with you in front of the class.

Have the students work in pairs to practice the conversation. Go around the room and check their work.

Finally, call on different pairs to share their conversations with the class.

C Listen.

Repeat the procedure from the previous **Listen.**

Tien: Do you have two brothers?

Carlos: Yes, I do.

Tien: Please sign here.

Carlos: Do you have a daughter?

Tien: No, I don't.

Listen and say.

Repeat the procedure from the previous **Listen and Say.**

Do you have children?

STUDENT BOOK PAGE 30

D Ask classmates. Complete the chart.

Copy the chart on the board.

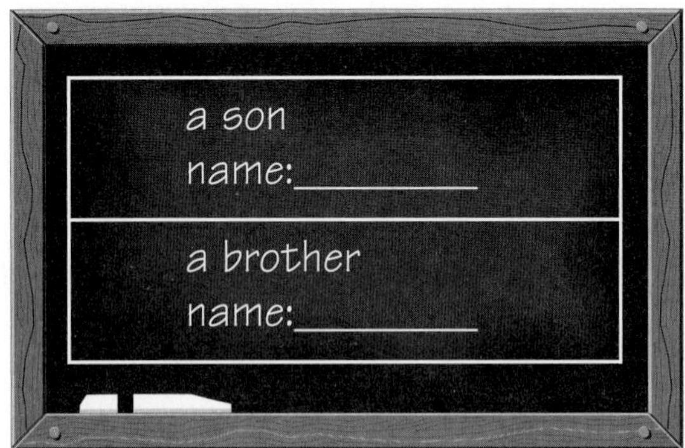

Ask students "Do you have _____?" until a student answers "Yes." Write that student's name in the appropriate space on the chart.

Explain to the class that they will use the chart to interview their classmates. Tell them to move around the room and ask their classmates "Do you have _____?" Remind them to write down their classmates' names if they answer "yes." Go around the room and check their work.

Finally, have different students copy their completed charts on the board.

EXPANSION ACTIVITY: Talk about your chart.

Point out one of the completed charts from Activity D on the board. Model a sentence or two describing the chart. Write the sentences on the board.

Teacher: (Student's name) has a son.

Then have the students work in pairs to make sentences about people on their charts. Go around the room and check their work.

5 Mr., Mrs., and Ms.

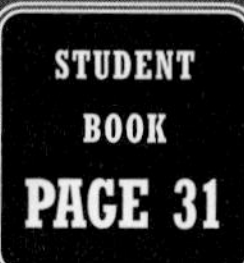

LEARNING POINT
Recognizing and writing titles

NEW LANGUAGE
Mr.
Mrs.
Ms.

Listen.

Have the students open their books and examine the illustrations.

Have the students listen with their books closed.

1. Mr. and Mrs. Hancock

2. Mr. Hancock and Ms. Tanaka

3. Ms. Lopez

Then have them open their books, look at the illustrations, and listen again as they read along.

Explain how the titles are used. Use yourself as an example; say: "I am (your title and name)."

Teacher:
I am
(your title
and name).

Next point to a student and say the student's appropriate title and name.

Listen and say.

Have the students listen to and repeat each line separately. Stop the tape or CD after each line or read aloud the separate lines with pauses.

Then call on individual students to listen and repeat after you.

Work with a partner. Write *Mr.*, *Ms.*, or *Mrs.*

Have the students examine the illustrations. Go over the sample answer with the class.

Have the students do the exercise. Go around the room and check their work.

Then write the exercise items and blanks on the board. Call on a student to fill in the blanks with the correct titles.

ANSWERS:

1. Mrs.

2. Mr.

3. Ms.

4. Mr.

6 Carlos's relatives

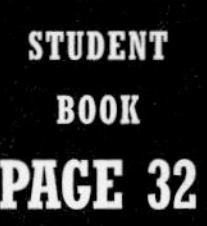

LEARNING POINT
Identifying family members by name

NEW LANGUAGE

aunt	relatives
grandfather	sister
grandmother	uncle

Write. Complete Carlos's family tree.

Have the students examine Carlos's family tree. Point out the blanks that are already filled in and relate them to the illustrations.

Teacher: Vera is Carlos's grandmother.

Have the students complete Carlos's family tree. Go around the room and check their work.

Have two students volunteer to copy Carlos's family tree on the board—the names and the blanks without the illustrations. Tell them to leave the blanks empty.

Point to each blank as you call on different students to say the answers. Have the two volunteers write the answers in the blanks.

ANSWERS:

Magda: mother

Rudolfo: father

Alfredo: brother

Write about your family.

Copy the first item on the board and fill in the blank with your own father's name.

Read the sentence aloud.

Have the students complete the activity. Go around the room and check the students' work.

Finally, have different students volunteer to write their sentences on the board.

**EXPANSION ACTIVITY:
Name the Relative**

Point out the family tree in Activity A. Hold up the book or use a transparency as you point to Rudolfo and say: "I am Rudolfo." Then point to Ricardo and prompt the class to finish your next sentence, "Ricardo is my … (brother)." Continue by pointing to other family members on the tree and by following the same routine.

Teacher: I am Rudolfo. Ricardo is my brother.

Make sure not to include relationships which the students haven't had yet—for example, brother-in-law.

If the students drew their own family trees for the Expansion Activity in Unit 3, Lesson 2, have them work in pairs to name their own relatives. If not, have them work in pairs with the family trees on pages 28 and 32 of the Student Book.

7 She is young.

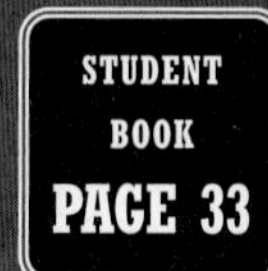

LEARNING POINT
Understanding and writing personal descriptions

NEW LANGUAGE
granddaughter
middle-aged
old
parents
young

A Listen and read.

Have the students open their books, examine the illustrations, and read the sentences.

Have the students listen with their books closed.

This is Don's family.

1. Don's grandfather is old.

2. His parents are middle-aged.

3. His aunt is middle-aged, too.

4. Sumin is his sister. She is young.

Then have them open their books, look at the illustrations, and listen again as they follow along.

B Complete the sentences about Leo's family.

Point out the first illustration and the sample answer as you read aloud the corresponding sentence. Then tell the students to look at each illustration and write the appropriate words in the blanks.

Go around the room and check the students' work.

Have the students compare their answers with a partner. Tell the pairs to take turns reading aloud the completed sentences.

Finally, call on two students to write the sentences on the board.

ANSWERS:

1. old

2. young

3. middle-aged

WORKBOOK PAGE 24

8 How old are you?

STUDENT BOOK PAGE 34

LEARNING POINT
Practicing numbers 20-100 and saying your age

NEW LANGUAGE

20	21	22	23	24
twenty	twenty-one	twenty-two	twenty-three	twenty-four

25	26	27	28
twenty-five	twenty-six	twenty-seven	twenty-eight

29	30	40	50	60	70
twenty-nine	thirty	forty	fifty	sixty	seventy

80	90	100
eighty	ninety	a hundred / one hundred

How old are you?
I'm _____ years old.

Listen.

Have the students listen with their books closed.

20, 21, 22, 23, 24, 25, 26, 27, 28, 29,
30, 40, 50, 60, 70, 80, 90, 100

Have the students listen again as they follow along with their books open.

Listen and say.

Have the students listen to and repeat each number separately. Stop the tape or CD after each number or read aloud the separate numbers with pauses.

Then call on individual students to listen and repeat after you.

Write the numbers.

Copy the first item on the board.

Then call a student to the board and say, "Write the number." Prompt the student to write the number *28* in the blank.

Have the students complete the activity and then compare their work with a partner. Go around the room and check their work.

Write the items on the board. Then call on different students to fill in the blanks.

ANSWERS:

1. 28
2. 30
3. 90
4. 60
5. 50
6. 40
7. 80
8. 70
9. 100
10. 41

 WORKBOOK PAGE 25

C Listen.

Repeat the procedure from the previous **Listen.**

Grace: How old are you, Sumin?

Sumin: I'm ten years old.

Listen and say.

Repeat the procedure from the previous **Listen and Say.**

D Talk with a partner.

Copy the open-ended conversation on the board. Pick a student to model the open-ended conversation with you in front of the class.

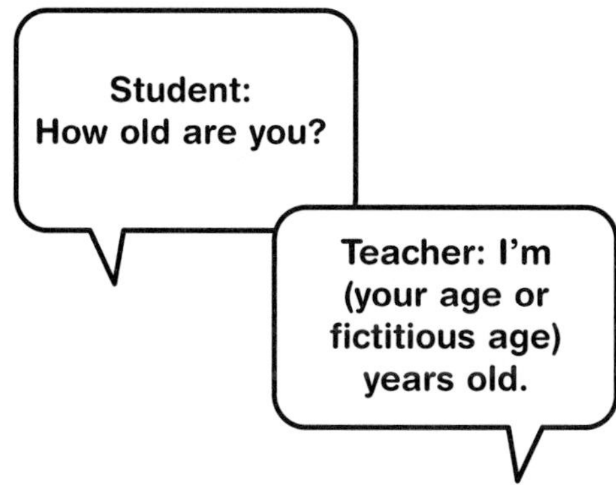

Student: How old are you?
Teacher: I'm (your age or fictitious age) years old.

Have the students work in pairs to practice the conversation. Go around the room and check their work.

Finally, call on different pairs to share their conversations with the class.

EXPANSION ACTIVITY: Say and write the number.

Write the numbers 20-100 on the board ("20, 21, 22,...30, 40, 50,..."). Randomly point to a number and prompt the class to say it. Continue with additional random numbers. Then call on individual students to say numbers that you point to.

Say random numbers from 20-100 and have the students write them down. Write the numbers on a piece of paper as you say them for later reference. Then call on a student to write the numbers on the board so the other students can check their work.

9 Completing a census form

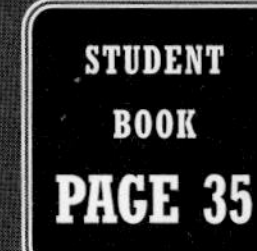
STUDENT BOOK PAGE 35

LEARNING POINT
Understanding and filling out a census form

NEW LANGUAGE
census form
count
List all the people at your address.

Listen and read.

Have the students open their books, examine the form, and read the sentences.

Have the students listen with their books closed.

This is a census form. The census is a count of all the people in a country. Families in the U.S. complete a census.

Have the students open their books. Point out the census form. Explain what a census is. Explain the word "count" by counting the students with your index finger.

Then have the students listen again as they follow along. Answer any questions students may have about the new language.

Complete the form.

Explain the meaning of "List all the people at your address."

Then have the students fill out the form. For students who live alone, have them use fictitious names and ages or relatives' names and ages. Go around the room and check the students' work.

Finally, have different students copy their completed forms on the board.

10 Review

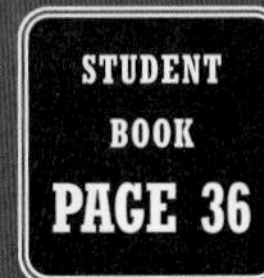

A Listen and write.

Have the students listen with their books closed.

1. My name is Ms. Redman.

2. I live at 60 Brown Road.

3. I am married.

4. My husband's name is Bill.

5. We have five children.

6. My sister has five children, too.

Have the students open their books. Play or say the first item and point out the example.

Have the students listen again and complete the exercise. Stop the tape or CD, or pause after each sentence, so students have time to fill in the blank. Go around the room and check their work.

Have the students compare their answers with a partner. Then have them listen again as they check their work.

Finally, call on different students to read the completed sentences aloud as you write the answers on the board.

ANSWERS:

1. Ms.

2. 60

3. married

4. name

5. children

6. sister

B Listen and √ check.

Have the students listen with their books closed.

1. How old are you?

2. Do you have children?

3. Is she married?

4. Who is Andy?

5. Who is Ann?

Copy the first item on the board. Play or say the first sentence. Write a check mark next to 35.

Then have the students listen again and complete the exercise. Stop the tape or CD, or pause after each question, so students have time to check the appropriate choice.

Have the students compare their answers with a partner. Have them listen again to check their work.

Finally, ask a student to write the items on the board and check √ the answers.

ANSWERS:

1. 35

2. Yes, I have two sons.

3. Yes, she is.

4. Sandy's son.

5. Sandy's mother

6. 12

7. 14

8. 50

C Listen and circle.

Have the students listen with their books closed.

1. eighty

2. sixty

3. nineteen

4. twenty-five

5. seventeen

6. twelve

7. fourteen

8. fifty

Copy the first item on the board. Play or say the first number. Circle "80."

Then have the students listen again and complete the activity. Stop the tape or CD, or pause after each item, so students have time to circle the appropriate choice.

Have the students compare their answers with a partner. Then have them listen again as they check their work.

Finally, call on individual students to write the items they circled on the board.

ANSWERS:

1. 80

2. 60

3. 19

4. 25

5. 17

D Write *Mr.*, *Ms.*, or *Mrs.*

Review titles as abbreviations and their use with the students. Then point out the example and review the use of Ms.

Next have the students do the activity. Have them compare answers with a partner.

Finally, call on a student to write the answers on the board.

ANSWERS:

1. Ms; Mrs.

2. Mr.

3. Ms.

4. Mr.

E Complete the chart. Write about your family.

Copy the chart on the board and fill in your own information as you explain the procedure to the class.

Your Family	Name	Married, Single, Divorced, Widowed
Mother		
Father		

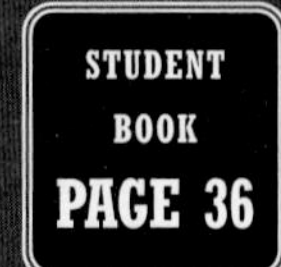

Have the students complete their own charts. Go around the room and check their work.

Finally, have different students copy their completed charts on the board.

Learning Log

Write five words you remember.

Review the purpose of a learning log.

Tell the students to try to fill in the log without looking back in their books for words. Then have them compare answers with a partner.

Finally, call several students to the board and have them write one word in each column of the log. Check their work.

SAMPLE ANSWERS:

Relatives	Ages	Numbers
mother	young	twenty-five
father	middle-aged	thirty-four
brother	old	fifty
sister		sixty-six
grandmother		ninety

√ Check what you can do.

Tell the students to complete the checklist. Go around the room and check their work.

Finally, call on different students to read aloud the items they checked and what they filled in for item No. 5.

1. I can talk about my family. _____

2. I can use Mrs., Ms., and Mr. _____

3. I can read a family tree. _____

4. I can say and write numbers from 1-100. _____

5. I can ____________________. _____

Looking Back

Who are the people on page 26? Write three more words in your Learning Log.

Have the students look at the illustration on page 26 and add three words to their Learning Logs. Then have them compare their additions with a partner.

Finally, call on different students to read aloud the headings and the words they added.

See Color Transparencies package for unit wrap-up activity. This task can be used as an oral assessment tool. Many unit wrap-up activities include a reproducible blackline master.

1-3 Grammar Spotlight for Units 1-3

STUDENT BOOK PAGES 38-39

A Pronouns

Singular	Plural
I	we
you	you
he	they
she	
it	

Point out the chart of pronouns and have the students repeat the word *pronoun*, the headings, and the actual pronouns after you.

Next point to yourself and say: "I." Then point to and look at a student and say: "you." Point to a male student and say: "he," to a female student and say: "she," to a book and say: "it." Then make a circling gesture with your index finger, pointing at yourself and the class members around the room as you say: "we." Next point to two or three students and say: "you."

Finally, hold up your book and point to the illustration of Sandy's family on page 28 and say: "they."

Circle the pronouns.

Point out the sample answer in the book. Tell the students to circle only the pronouns in the sentences.

Have the students compare answers with a partner.

Finally, call on students to read the sentences and the pronouns.

ANSWERS:

1. I

2. We

3. He

4. She

Present Tense of *BE*

Point out the chart and have the students repeat the contents after you. Then call on individual students to repeat one or more of the forms. Explain that the contractions—'m, 's, and 're—are alternate versions of the full forms.

I **am**	I'**m**
He **is**	He'**s**
She **is**	She'**s**
It **is**	It'**s**
We **are**	We'**re**
You **are**	You'**re**
They **are**	They'**re**

Write *am, is,* or *are.*

Point out the example and relate it to the chart.

Have the students complete the activity.

Have the students compare answers with a partner. Then call on a pair of students to write the completed sentences on the board and read them aloud.

ANSWERS:

1. is

2. are

3. are

4. is

5. are

6. am

Write *'m*, *'s*, or *'re*.

Go over the example with the students. Then have them fill in the blanks with the appropriate contracted form. Remind them to write about themselves in the last item. Go around and check their work.

Have the students compare answers with a partner. Then call on a student to write the answers on the board. Ask other students to read their final sentences aloud.

ANSWERS:

1. 'm

2. 're

3. 're

4. 's

5. 're

6. 'm from (country).

EXPANSION ACTIVITY: Say the other form.

Have the students look at the chart in Activity B. Say each of the full forms from the left side of the chart and prompt the class to say the contractions on the right. For example, say, "He is" and prompt the class to say "He's." Then reverse the process—say the contracted forms and have the class say the full ones.

Next call on individual students.

Finally, have the students close their books and repeat the process.

C *BE* with Negatives

Model the forms for the students. You can help them understand the meanings by shaking your head and moving your index finger back and forth to indicate negation as you say sentences with "I'm not," "He's not," etc.

I'm not	He's not	We're not
	She's not It's not	You're not They're not

Point out the chart and have the students repeat the forms after you. Then have individual students repeat different forms.

Make up sentences using the forms and have the class and individual students repeat them after you.

Teacher: I'm not married/single/divorced/widowed.

1-3 Grammar Spotlight for Units 1-3

STUDENT BOOK PAGES 38-39

Write negative sentences.

Copy the first item on the board and show the relationship between the two sentences by pointing to the word "married" and shaking your head as you write "She's not" in the blank. Remind the students that the completed sentences will help them fill in the blanks. Have them complete the activity.

Have the students compare their work with a partner. Then call on a pair of students to write the completed sentences on the board and read them aloud.

Finally, call on different students to share their final sentences with the class.

ANSWERS:

1. She's not

2. We're not

3. They're not

4. I'm not (student's marital status).

D Present Tense of *HAVE*

Point out the grammar chart and have the students follow along as you read aloud the contents. Then use the chart to make up complete sentences. Use realia and/or gestures to help students understand the meaning. For example, hold your book to your chest as you say: "I have a book."

I **have**	We **have**
You **have**	You **have**
He **has**	They **have**
She **has**	
It **has**	

Write *have* or *has*. Then write a sentence about you.

Read the directions aloud as the students follow along in their books. Next go over the sample answer with the class. Relate the word "have" to the phrase "They have" in the chart.

Have the students complete the activity and then compare answers with a partner. Go around and check their work.

Finally, call on a student to write the answers on the board.

ANSWERS:

1. have

2. has

3. have

4. has

5. I have (personal information about eye and/or hair color).

Grammar Spotlight for Units 1-3

STUDENT BOOK PAGES 38-39

EXPANSION ACTIVITY: Say who has what.

Tell the students to make up five sentences with "has" and "have." Provide some examples—write them on the board and say them aloud.
For example:

Pointing to your hair I have (color of your hair) hair.

Pointing to two students (The students' names) have books.

Pointing to a student (The student's name) has brown eyes.

Have the students write their sentences down on a separate piece of paper.

Call on different class members to stand up and read their sentences aloud. You can also have them write their sentences on the board.

WORKBOOK PAGES 28–29

1-3 Review for Units 1-3

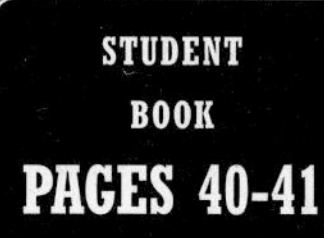

Match.

Point out the example and read the question and answer aloud. Explain that students will match questions and answers. Then have the students complete the exercise. Go around the room and check their work.

ANSWERS:

1. f **5.** a

2. b **6.** c

3. e **7.** d

4. g

B Listen and √ check.

Have the students listen with their books closed.

1. Mary is young. She has brown hair.
She is single.

2. Peter is old. He has white hair.
He is single.

3. Anna is young. She has black hair.
She is married.

Have the students open their books. Play or say the first item as you indicate a check mark in the blank next to "a" in your book.

Have the students listen again and complete the activity. Stop the tape or CD, or pause after each item, so students have time to check the appropriate response.

Have the students compare their answers with a partner. Have them listen again to check their work.

Finally, ask a student to write the items on the board and check the answers.

ANSWERS:

1. a.

2. b.

3. b.

Circle the words.

Hold up your book and demonstrate how to do the activity by pointing out the sample answer. Then have the students circle the words. Have them compare their answers with a partner.

ANSWERS:

~~AVERAGE~~, ~~BACKPACK~~, ~~DAUGHTER~~, ~~EIGHTEEN~~,
~~FORTY-SIX~~, ~~OPEN~~, ~~PARENT~~, ~~THREE~~, ~~ZERO~~, ~~ZIP~~

B	X	D	A	U	G	H	T	E	R
A	Y	I	P	K	6	I	L	I	I
C	P	E	A	V	E	R	A	G	E
K	T	D	L	B	D	W	L	H	R
P	A	R	E	N	T	O	D	T	F
A	H	V	B	N	T	H	R	E	E
C	W	Z	I	P	I	I	Q	E	S
K	D	E	W	M	O	P	E	N	L
P	C	R	X	W	O	D	A	U	O
U	F	O	R	T	Y	-	S	I	X

D Community Challenge

Work with a partner. Where do you get a driver's license?

Have the students work with a partner. Make telephone directories available so that the pairs can look up the information. Go around the room and check their work.

Have a pair of students write the information on the board. Call on two students to read the information aloud.

Unit 4 Welcome to our house

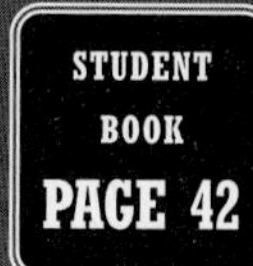

UNIT OVERVIEW

	LESSON:	LEARNING POINTS:	SB#
1.	**He's in the kitchen.**	Identifying rooms and asking and saying where people are	**p. 43**
2.	**Is there a lamp in the bedroom?**	Asking and answering questions about furnishings in rooms	**p. 44**
3.	**There's a shower in the bathroom.**	Identifying places and things in a house	**p. 45**
4.	**Where do you live?**	Talking about where you live	**p. 46**
5.	**I need a refrigerator.**	Talking about the furniture you need	**p. 47**
6.	**Where do you study?**	Identifying the rooms where you do specific things	**p. 48**
7.	**My dream house**	Describing houses	**p. 49**
8.	**18 or 80?**	Differentiating between pairs of numbers	**p. 50**
9.	**A garage sale**	Talking about things you need and how how much they cost	**p. 51**
10.	**Review**	Review Unit 4	**p. 52**

Suggestions for Unit Opener (Student Book page 42)

Brainstorm. Have students look at the unit-opening illustration. Ask them for words related to rooms and furniture that they already know. Use your own classroom and the illustration to prompt students to say the words. Write the words on the board as students say them.

Model the language. Begin by reading the caption aloud—"Where is everyone?" Point to the people and rooms in the illustration and name them. Use your own classroom to continue modeling the language. Write the words on the board.

Model the language again. This time have the class repeat the words after you. Then go around the room and have individual students repeat different words.

Point and say. Point to the words you've written on the board as you say them. Have the students repeat them after you.

Initiate pair work. Have the students work in pairs. Tell them to take turns pointing to the different people, rooms, and items in the illustration and naming them. Demonstrate this by asking a student to point to someone or something and by saying the name yourself, then pointing yourself and asking the same student to say the name. Go around the room and check students' work.

See Color Transparencies package for additional unit-opening activity. Many of these tasks include a reproducible blackline master.

1 He's in the kitchen.

STUDENT BOOK PAGE 43

LEARNING POINT
Identifying rooms and asking and saying where people are

NEW LANGUAGE

bathroom	kitchen
bedroom	living room
dining room	yard

Where is _____?
_____ is in the _____.

Listen.

Have the students open their books and examine the illustrations.

Have the students listen with their books closed.

1. Kitchen. This is the kitchen.

2. Living room. This is the living room.

3. Bedroom. This is the bedroom.

4. Dining room. This is the dining room.

5. Bathroom. This is the bathroom.

6. Yard. This is the yard.

Then have them open their books, look at the illustrations, and listen again as they follow along.

Listen and say.

Have the students listen to and repeat each word separately. Stop the tape or CD after each word or read aloud the separate words with pauses.

1. kitchen

2. living room

3. bedroom

4. dining room

5. bathroom

6. yard

Then call on individual students to listen and repeat after you.

Listen.

Have the students listen with their books closed.

Will: Where is Justin?

Sandy: He's in the dining room.

Will: Where is Arthur?

Sandy: He's in the yard.

Have the students listen again as they follow along with their books open.

Listen and say.

Repeat the procedure from the previous **Listen and say.**

Talk with a partner. Look at page 42.

Copy the open-ended conversation on the board. Pick a student to model the open-ended conversation with you in front of the class. Point to Andy in the bathroom in the illustration on page 42.

1 He's in the kitchen.

STUDENT BOOK PAGE 43

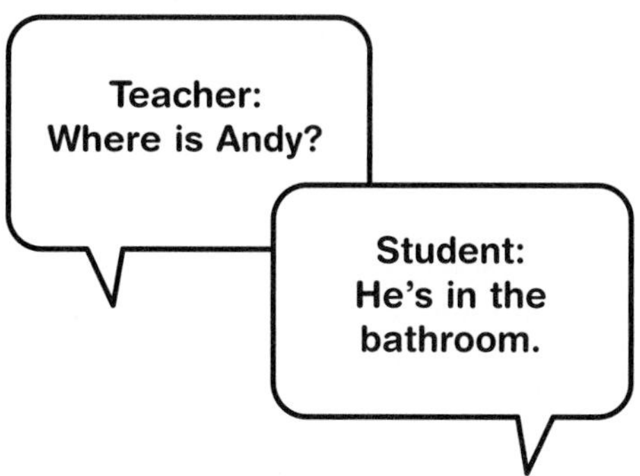
Teacher:
Where is Andy?
Student:
He's in the bathroom.

Have the students work in pairs to practice the conversation. Tell them to use the illustration on page 42 and the words in the Word List. Go around the room and check their work.

Finally, call on different pairs to share their conversations with the class.

WORKBOOK PAGE 31

2 Is there a lamp in the bedroom?

STUDENT BOOK PAGE 44

LEARNING POINT
Asking and answering questions about furnishings in rooms

NEW LANGUAGE

bed	lamp
CD player	rug
dresser	sofa
fireplace	table

Is there a _____ in the _____?
Yes, there is. / No, there isn't.

Listen.

Have the students open their books and examine the illustrations.

Have the students listen with their books closed.

1. Table. Is there a table in the dining room?
2. Sofa. Is there a sofa in the living room?
3. Bed. Is there a bed in the bedroom?
4. Lamp. Is there a lamp in the bedroom?
5. CD player. Is there a CD player in the living room?
6. Fireplace. Is there a fireplace in the living room?
7. Dresser. Is there a dresser in the bedroom?
8. Rug. Is there a rug in the bedroom?

Then have them open their books, look at the illustrations, and listen again as they follow along.

Listen and say.

Have the students listen to and repeat each word separately. Stop the tape or CD after each word or read aloud the separate words with pauses.

1. table
2. sofa
3. bed
4. lamp
5. CD player
6. fireplace
7. dresser
8. rug

Then call on individual students to listen and repeat after you.

Listen.

Repeat the procedure from the previous **Listen.**

Carlos: Is there a fireplace in the living room?

Man: Yes, there is.

Carlos: Is there a lamp in the bedroom?

Man: No, there isn't.

Listen and say.

Repeat the procedure from the previous **Listen and say.**

2 Is there a lamp in the bedroom?

STUDENT BOOK PAGE 44

Talk with a partner.

Have the students look at the illustration in Activity B. Write the open-ended conversation on the board. Pick a student to model the open-ended conversation with you in front of the class.

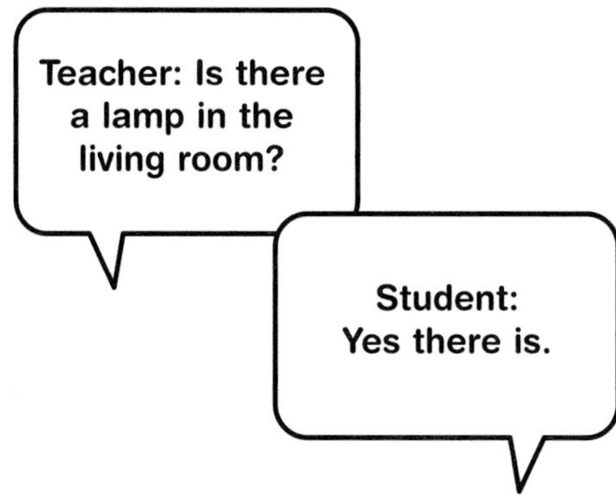

Teacher: Is there a lamp in the living room?
Student: Yes there is.

Have the students work in pairs to practice the conversation. Tell them to use the illustration in Activity B and the words in the Word List. Go around the room and check their work.

Finally, call on a pair to share their conversation with the class.

EXPANSION ACTIVITY: Things in the Classroom

Have the students work in small groups. Tell them to brainstorm and make a list of all the objects they've learned about that they might find in a room. To help them get started, prompt them to come up with a possible first object for their lists and write it on the board—for example, "chair." Tell them to try not to use their books at first.

Next call members from different groups to the board to write down the names of the objects.

Have the students work in pairs to take turns playing the roles of A and B from activity C. Tell them to use the list on the board to ask each other—"Is there a _____ in the classroom?" To help them get started, model a sample exchange with a student in front of the class.

Finally, call different students to the front of the room to play the role of A with the entire class.

3 There's a shower in the bathroom.

STUDENT BOOK PAGE 45

LEARNING POINT
Identifying places and things in a house

NEW LANGUAGE

barbecue	shower
closet	sink
hall	stove
microwave oven	tub
refrigerator	window

There's a _____ in the _____.
There are two _____ in the _____.

A Listen.

Have the students open their books and examine the illustrations.

Have the students listen with their books closed.

1. Shower. This is a shower.
2. Hall. This is a hall.
3. Sink. This is a sink.
4. Stove. This is a stove.
5. Window. This is a window.
6. Microwave oven. This is a microwave oven.
7. Closet. This is a closet.
8. Refrigerator. This is a refrigerator.
9. Tub. This is a tub.
10. Barbecue. This is a barbecue.

Then have them open their books, look at the illustrations, and listen again as they follow along.

Listen and say.

Have the class listen to and repeat each word separately. Stop the tape or CD after each word or read aloud the separate words with pauses.

1. shower
2. hall
3. sink
4. stove
5. window
6. microwave oven
7. closet
8. refrigerator
9. tub
10. barbecue

Then call on individual students to listen and repeat after you.

B Listen and circle.

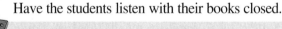

Have the students listen with their books closed.

1. There's a tub in the bathroom.
2. There's a barbecue in the yard.
3. There's a sink in the kitchen.
4. There's a closet in the bedroom.
5. There's a window in the dining room.
6. There's a refrigerator in the kitchen.

Copy the first item on the board. Play or say the first sentence. Circle "tub."

Then have the students listen again and complete the exercise. Stop the tape or CD,

3 There's a shower in the bathroom.

or pause after each sentence, so students have time to circle the appropriate choice.

Have the students compare their answers with a partner. Then have them listen again as they check their work.

Finally, call on individual students to read aloud the items they circled.

ANSWERS:

1. tub

2. barbecue

3. sink

4. closet

5. window

6. refrigerator

Complete.

Write the first sentence on the board. Point to the list of words in the exercise and fill in the blank with "kitchen."

Read the sentence aloud.

Teacher:
There's a sink in the kitchen.

Have the students complete the activity.

Have the students compare answers in small groups. Tell them to take turns reading aloud the completed sentences. Go around and check their work.

Finally, call on two students to write the completed sentences on the board.

ANSWERS:

1. kitchen

2. bathroom

3. yard

4. living room

4 Where do you live?

STUDENT BOOK PAGE 46

LEARNING POINT
Talking about where you live

NEW LANGUAGE
apartment
house
rented room

Where do you live?
I live in a/an _____.

Listen.

Have the students open their books and examine the illustrations.

Have the students listen with their books closed.

1. I live in a house.

2. I live in a rented room.

3. I live in an apartment.

Then have them open their books, look at the illustrations, and listen again as they follow along.

Listen and say.

Have the students listen to and repeat each line separately. Stop the tape or CD after each line or read aloud the separate lines with pauses.

Then call on individual students to listen and repeat after you.

Talk with classmates.

Copy the open-ended conversation on the board. Pick a student to model the open-ended conversation with you in front of the class.

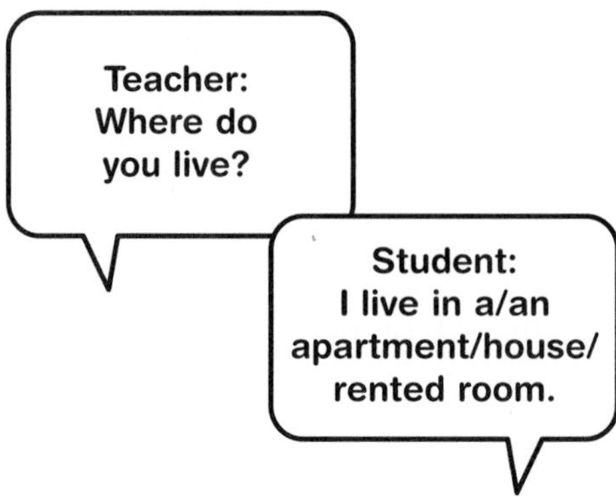

Teacher: Where do you live?
Student: I live in a/an apartment/house/ rented room.

Have the students move around the classroom to practice the conversation with different classmates. Go around and check their work.

Finally, call on different pairs to share their conversations with the class.

Write. Work with a partner.

Have the students look at the illustrations and the list of words. Demonstrate the procedure by pointing out the sample answer and the corresponding illustration.

Then have the students work with a partner to fill in the blanks with the appropriate words from the list.

Finally, call on a student to write the answers on the board.

ANSWERS:

1. a house
2. an apartment
3. an apartment
4. a rented room
5. a house
6. a rented room

WORKBOOK PAGE 33

5 I need a refrigerator.

STUDENT BOOK PAGE 47

LEARNING POINT
Talking about the furniture you need

NEW LANGUAGE
furniture
garage

What do you need?
I need _____.
Do you need a _____?
No, I don't./Yes, I do.
Thanks.

A Listen and read.

Have the students open their books, examine the illustrations, and read the paragraph. Have the students listen with their books closed.

Carlos is happy with his new apartment. There is a bed and a dresser. There are five chairs. But Carlos needs a table. He needs other furniture, too. Paul has furniture for Carlos. The furniture is in his garage.

Have the students listen again as they follow along with their books open.

Help the students understand the meaning of the verb "need" and the noun "furniture" by using gestures or words they already know.

Now have the students relate the paragraph to the illustrations. Point out the illustration of Carlos and read the first five sentences aloud. Then point out the illustration of Paul and read the last two sentences aloud.

B Listen.

Have the students listen with their books closed.

Paul: What do you need?

Carlos: I need a table.

Paul: Do you need a refrigerator?

Carlos: No, I don't. Thanks.

Have the students listen again as they follow along with their books open.

Listen and say.

Have the students listen to and repeat each line separately. Stop the tape or CD after each line or read aloud the separate lines with pauses.

Then call on individual students to listen and repeat after you.

C Talk with a partner.

Copy the open-ended conversation on the board. Pick a student to model the open-ended conversation with you in front of the class. Tell the student to pretend he is Carlos and to play the role of B.

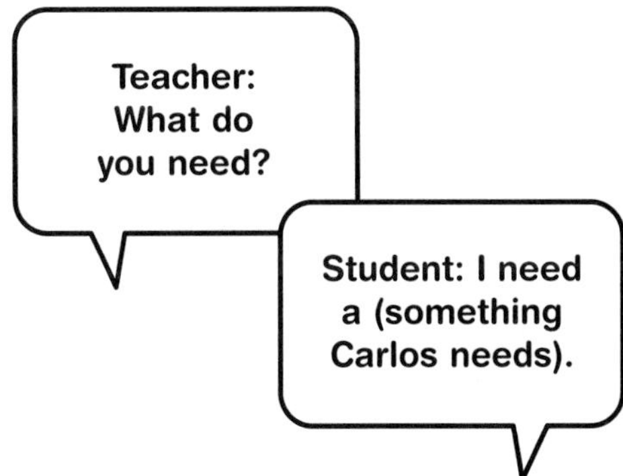

Teacher: What do you need?
Student: I need a (something Carlos needs).

5 I need a refrigerator.

STUDENT BOOK PAGE 47

Have the students work in pairs to practice the conversation. Tell them to use the illustrations and the words in the Word List. Go around the room and check their work.

Finally, call on different pairs to share their conversations with the class.

EXPANSION ACTIVITY: Describe and draw.

Describe and draw a room in your house or apartment. For example, draw a rectangle on the board and say, "This is my kitchen. There is a sink. There is a refrigerator. There is a window." Draw these items as you say them.

Have students work in pairs to describe rooms in their own houses or apartments. Tell them to draw their partners' rooms.

6 Where do you study?

STUDENT BOOK PAGE 48

LEARNING POINT
Identifying the rooms where you do specific things

NEW LANGUAGE
cook
eat
shower
sleep
study

Where do you _____?

Listen and circle.

Have the students listen with their books closed.

1. There's a stove in the kitchen.

2. There's a sofa in the living room.

3. There's a barbecue in the yard.

4. There's a table in the dining room.

Play or say the first item. Point to the illustration of a kitchen and mime drawing a circle around it.

Then have the students listen again and complete the activity. Stop the tape or CD, or pause after each sentence, so students have time to circle the appropriate illustration.

Have the students compare their answers with a partner. Then have them listen again as they check their work.

Finally, call on different students to say which illustrations they circled.

ANSWERS:

1. illustration on the left

2. illustration on the right

3. illustration on the right

4. illustration on the right

√ Check.

Point out the illustrations as you read the questions aloud.

Point out the sample checked answers on the chart as you ask and answer the question—"Where do you study?" "In the living room. In the bedroom."

Teacher: Where do you study? In the living room. In the bedroom.

Tell the students to answer the questions on the chart by checking the appropriate columns. Expect answers to vary. Go around the room and check the students' work.

SAMPLE ANSWERS:

1. living room, kitchen, bedroom

2. kitchen

3. bathroom

4. bedroom, living room

5. kitchen, living room

7 My dream house

STUDENT BOOK PAGE 49

LEARNING POINT
Describing houses

NEW LANGUAGE
also
dream house
at the beach
in the city/country /suburbs

Listen.

Have the students open their books and examine the illustrations.

Have the students listen with their books closed.

1. In the city. Leo's dream house is in the city.

2. In the country. Isabel's dream house is in the country.

3. At the beach. Paul's dream house is at the beach.

5. In the suburbs. Don's dream house is in the suburbs.

Then have them open their books, look at the illustrations, and listen again as they follow along.

To help students understand the new vocabulary, point to specific parts of each illustration as you say the new words. For example, say: "beach/at the beach" as you point to the beach in the illustration.

Listen and say.

Have the students listen to and repeat each phrase separately. Stop the tape or CD after each phrase or read aloud the separate phrases with pauses.

1. in the city

2. in the country

3. at the beach

4. in the suburbs

Then call on individual students to listen and repeat after you.

Listen and read.

Have the students listen with their books closed.

Leo's dream house

My dream house is in the city. There is a kitchen, a dining room, and a living room. My dream house also has five bedrooms for my family. There are three bathrooms. I love my dream house.

Have the students listen again as they follow along with their books open.

Write. Complete the sentences.

Copy the first item on the board and fill the blank with your own information. Then read the sentence aloud.

My dream house

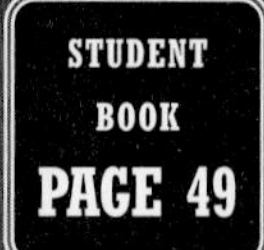

Next have the students complete the sentences in their books. Tell them to use Leo's paragraph as a guide. Go around the room and check their work.

Finally, call on individual students to write their completed sentences on the board.

SAMPLE ANSWERS:

1. in the country

2. a kitchen, a dining room, and a living room

3. a big bathroom

4. two bedrooms

5. I love my dream house.

D Read your sentences to your classmates.

Read the sentence you wrote on the board aloud.

Teacher: My dream house is...

Have the students form small groups. Tell the group members to take turns reading their sentences aloud. Go around the room and check their work.

EXPANSION ACTIVITY: Describe and draw.

Have a student read the paragraph about Leo's dream house aloud as you draw a floor plan on the board based on the pertinent sentences.

Next have the students draw floor plans for their own houses.

Finally, call on different students to come to the board and read aloud their dream house statements and draw their floor plans on the board.

8 18 or 80?

STUDENT BOOK PAGE 50

LEARNING POINT
Differentiating between pairs of numbers

NEW LANGUAGE
numbers

A Listen.

Have the students listen with their books closed.

1. twelve	twenty
2. thirteen	thirty
3. fourteen	forty
4. fifteen	fifty
5. sixteen	sixty
6. seventeen	seventy
7. eighteen	eighty
8. nineteen	ninety

Have the students listen again as they follow along with their books open.

Listen and say.

Have the students listen to and repeat each pair of numbers separately. Stop the tape or CD after each pair or read aloud the separate pairs with pauses.

Then call on individual students to listen and repeat after you.

B Listen and circle.

Have the students listen with their books closed.

1. sixteen	**5.** thirteen
2. nineteen	**6.** seventy
3. forty	**7.** twelve
4. eighteen	**8.** fifty

Copy the first item on the board. Play or say the first number. Circle "16."

Then have the students listen again and complete the exercise. Stop the tape or CD, or pause after each number, so students have time to circle the appropriate choice.

Have the students compare their answers with a partner. Then have them listen again as they check their work.

Finally, call on individual students to read aloud the items they circled.

ANSWERS:

1. 16	**5.** 13
2. 19	**6.** 70
3. 40	**7.** 12
4. 18	**8.** 50

8 18 or 80?

STUDENT
BOOK
PAGE 50

C Listen and write.

Have the students listen with their books closed.

1. My address is 50 Beach Street.
2. The house is 70 years old.
3. The rented room is at 20 Hall Road.
4. There are 13 apartments.
5. There are 19 windows.
6. I have 12 tables.
7. We need 40 chairs in the dining room.
8. He has 14 pens.
9. The house has 18 rooms.
10. There are 17 lamps in the garage.

Copy the first item on the board. Play or say the first sentence. Tell the students to listen for numbers. Write "50" in the blank.

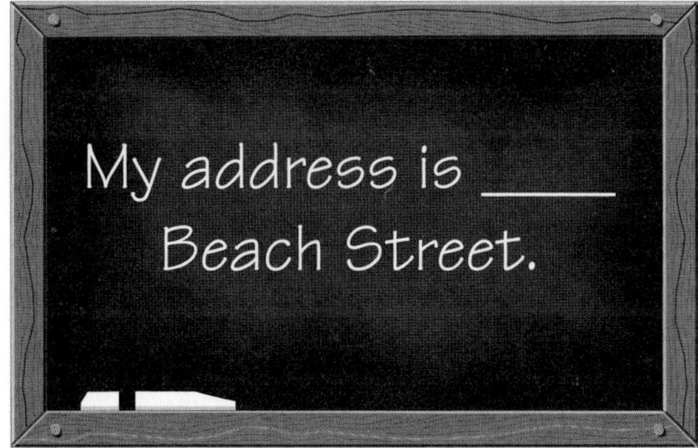
My address is _____
Beach Street.

Then have the students listen again and complete the exercise. Stop the tape or CD, or pause after each sentence, so students have time to write.

Have the students compare their answers with a partner. Then have them listen again as they check their work.

Finally, call on individual students to write the complete sentences on the board.

ANSWERS:

1. 50	**6.** 12
2. 70	**7.** 40
3. 20	**8.** 14
4. 13	**9.** 18
5. 19	**10.** 17

EXPANSION ACTIVITY: Write the numbers.

Dictate random numbers from this lesson and have the students write them down on a separate piece of paper. For a list of numbers, see the listening script for Activity A. Be sure to write down your random list of numbers for later reference. Have the students compare their work with a partner.

Say the numbers again as the pairs check their work.

Finally, call on a pair to write the numbers on the board.

9 A garage sale

LEARNING POINT

Talking about things you need and how much they cost

NEW LANGUAGE

backpack	garage sale
bike	good
CD	new
fan	pan
for sale	toaster
fun	

What do you need?
I need a _____.
I have a _____ for sale.

A Listen and read.

Have the students open their books, examine the illustration, and read the paragraph.

Have the students listen with their books closed.

Garage Sales

Americans love garage sales. There are books and furniture for sale. The books and furniture are good. But they are not new. Garage sales are fun.

Then have them open their books, look at the illustrations, and listen again as they follow along.

Point out the garage and the different things for sale as you explain what a garage sale is.

Answer any questions the students have about the new vocabulary.

B Listen and match.

Have the students listen with their books closed.

Sandy's students are at the garage sale. What do they need?

1. Isabel needs a lamp.

2. Carlos needs a backpack.

3. Don needs some CDs.

4. Maria needs a bike.

At the top of the board write "1. Isabel." Further down, on the right, write "b. lamp." Play or say the first item and draw a line from "1. Isabel" to "b. lamp" on the board.

Have the students listen again and complete the activity. Stop the tape or CD, or pause after each sentence, so students have time to write a response.

Have the students compare their answers with a partner. Then have them listen again as they check their work.

Finally, call on different students to say their answers aloud.

 WORKBOOK PAGE 37

A garage sale

ANSWERS:

1. b

2. d

3. c

4. a

Listen.

Have the students listen with their books closed.

Seller: What do you need?

Maria: I need a bike.

Seller: Good! I have a bike for sale.

Have the students listen again as they follow along with their books open.

Listen and say.

Have the class listen to and repeat each line of the conversation separately. Stop the tape or CD after each line or read aloud the separate lines with pauses.

Then call on individual students to listen and repeat after you.

Talk with a partner.

Copy the open-ended conversation on the board. Pick a student to model the open-ended conversation with you in front of the class.

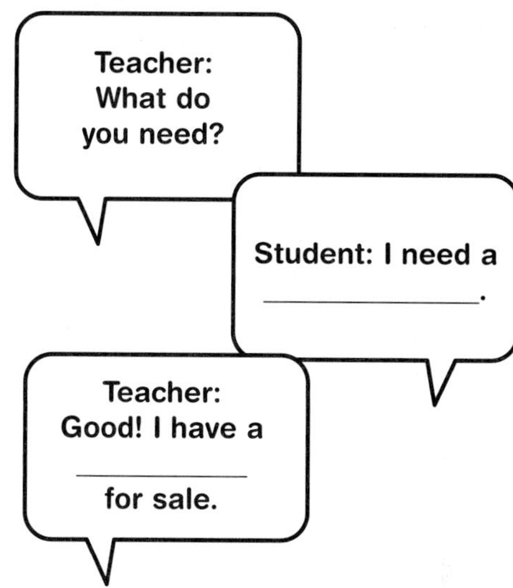

Teacher: What do you need?
Student: I need a ______.
Teacher: Good! I have a ______ for sale.

Have the students work in pairs to practice the conversation. Tell them to use the words in the Word List. Go around the room and check their work.

Finally, call on different pairs to share their conversations with the class.

10 Review

STUDENT BOOK
PAGES 52-53

Listen and circle.

Have the students listen with their books closed.

1. There is a sink in the bathroom.

2. There are books in the bedroom.

3. Paul lives in the suburbs.

4. Tomiko is 30.

Copy the first item on the board. Play or say the first item. Circle "bathroom."

Have the students listen again and complete the activity. Stop the tape or CD, or pause after each sentence, so students have time to circle the appropriate response.

Have the students compare their answers with a partner. Then have them listen again as they check their work.

Finally, call on individual students to read aloud the items they circled.

ANSWERS:

1. bathroom

2. bedroom

3. suburbs

4. 30

Listen and √ check.

Have the students listen with their books closed.

1. Where is Maria?

2. Is there a lamp in the living room?

3. What do you need?

4. Do you need a dresser?

Copy the first item on the board. Play or say the first item. Write a check mark next to "In the dining room."

Then have the students listen again and complete the activity. Stop the tape or CD, or pause after each question, so students have time to check the appropriate response.

Have the students compare their answers with a partner. Then have them listen again as they check their work.

Finally, ask a student to write the items on the board and check √ the answers.

ANSWERS:

1. In the dining room.

2. Yes, there is.

3. I need a pen.

4. Yes, I do. Thanks.

Complete the chart. Work with classmates.

Copy the chart on the board.

Room	Furniture and Things in the Room
1. bathroom	shower, tub
2. living room	
3. kitchen	

10 Review

STUDENT BOOK
PAGES 52-53

Ask students to think of other things that are in a bathroom. Write the words in the first row of the right column as students say them.

Then tell the students to write the names of furniture and things in the appropriate columns. Go around the room and check their work.

Next ask a student to copy the chart on the board.

Finally call on different students and have them write their answers in the columns for you to check.

SAMPLE ANSWERS:

1. bathroom: shower, tub, sink, rug

2. living room: sofa, table, lamp, fireplace

3. kitchen: sink, stove, refrigerator, microwave oven

Complete.

Tell the students to use the illustration and the words in the box to fill in the blanks. Go over the sample answer with the class. Then have the students fill in the blanks. Go around the room and check their work. Have the students compare their work with a partner.

Finally, copy the sentences on the board and call on students to fill in the missing information.

ANSWERS:

kitchen

stove

chairs

table

Learning Log

Write five words you remember.

Review the purpose of a learning log.

Tell the students to try to fill in the log without looking back in their books for words. Then have them compare answers with a partner.

Finally, copy the Learning Log on the board. Call several pairs to the board and have them write one word in each column of the log. Check their work.

SAMPLE ANSWERS:

Verbs	Furniture	Rooms
eat	chair	bedroom
cook	lamp	dining room
study	rug	living room
shower	sofa	kitchen
sleep	dresser	bathroom

√ Check what you can do.

Tell the students to complete the checklist. Go around the room and check their work.

Finally, call on different students to read aloud the items they checked and what they filled in for item No. 5.

1. I can name rooms and furniture. ____

2. I can say what I have and what I need. ____

3. I can write about my dream house. ____

4. I can say and understand numbers. ____

5. I can ____________________. ____

10 Review

STUDENT BOOK
PAGES 52-53

Looking Back

What do you see on page 42? Write three more words in your Learning Log.

Have the students look at the illustration on page 42 and add three words to their Learning Logs. Then have them compare their additions with a partner.

Finally, call on different students to read aloud the headings and the words they added.

> See Color Transparencies package for unit wrap-up activity. This task can be used as an oral assessment tool. Many unit wrap-up activities include a reproducible blackline master.

Unit 5 I play soccer on Saturday.

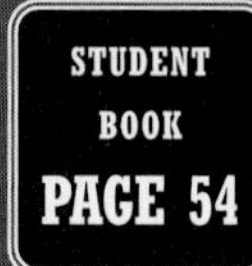

UNIT OVERVIEW

	LESSON:	LEARNING POINTS:	SB#
1.	**What do you do every day?**	Saying what you do every day	**p. 55**
2.	**Days of the week**	Recognizing, saying, and writing the days of the week	**p. 56**
3.	**Months**	Recognizing, saying, and writing months	**p. 57**
4.	**What time is it?**	Asking and saying what time it is	**p. 58**
5.	**It's 5:45.**	Saying what you do at different times of the day	**p. 59**
6.	**Making an appointment**	Making an appointment	**p. 60**
7.	**How often do you study?**	Saying how often you do something	**p. 61**
8.	**Ordinal numbers**	Recognizing and using ordinal numbers	**p. 62**
9.	**Completing a form**	Writing down personal information	**p. 63**
10.	**Review**	Review Unit 5	**p. 64**

Suggestions for Unit Opener (Student Book page 54)

Brainstorm. Have students look at the unit-opening illustration. Ask them for words related to daily activities that they already know. Write the words on the board as students say them.

Model the language. Begin by reading the caption aloud—"Where are the people?" Point to the items and activities in the illustration and name them. Use your own classroom to continue modeling the language. Write the words on the board.

Model the language again. This time have the class repeat the words after you. Then go around the room and have individual students repeat different words.

Point and say. Point to the words you've written on the board as you say them. Have the students repeat them after you.

Initiate pair work. Have the students work in pairs. Tell them to take turns pointing to the different people, rooms, and items in the illustration and naming them. Demonstrate this by asking a student to point to someone or something and by saying the name yourself, then pointing yourself and asking the same student to say the name. Go around the room and check students' work.

See Color Transparencies package for additional unit-opening activity. Many of these tasks include a reproducible blackline master.

1 What do you do every day?

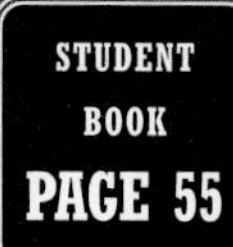

LEARNING POINT
Saying what you do every day

NEW LANGUAGE

brush my teeth	talk on the phone
eat breakfast	watch TV
play basketball	work on my computer
read the newspaper	

What do you do every day?
I _____.

Listen.

Have the students listen with their books closed.

Leo: I read the newspaper.

Paul: I work on my computer.

Justin: I brush my teeth.

Andy: I play basketball.

Carlos: I watch TV.

Maria: I eat breakfast.

Sandy: I talk on the phone.

Have the students listen again as they follow along with their books open.

Listen and say.

Have the students listen to and repeat each line separately. Stop the tape or CD after each line or read aloud the separate lines with pauses.

Then call on individual students to listen and repeat after you.

Listen and circle.

Have the students listen with their books closed.

Sandy: What do you do every day, Leo?

Leo: I read the newspaper.

Sandy: What do you do every day, Paul?

Paul: I brush my teeth.

Sandy: What do you do every day, Carlos?

Carlos: I watch TV.

Sandy: What do you do every day, Maria?

Maria: I eat breakfast.

Play or say the first item. Tell the students they will hear a conversation and that they should look for the illustration that matches what each person does every day. Point out the example.

Then have the students listen again and complete the activity. Stop the tape or CD, or pause after each conversation, so students have time to circle the appropriate illustration.

Have the students compare their answers with a partner. Then have them listen again as they check their work.

Finally, call on individual students to point to the items they circled.

ANSWERS:

1. illustration on the left

2. illustration on the left

3. illustration on the right

4. illustration on the right

1 What do you do every day?

STUDENT
BOOK
PAGE 55

C Listen.

Repeat the procedure from the previous **Listen.**

Sandy: What do you do every day?

Leo: I read the newspaper.

Listen and say.

Repeat the procedure from the previous **Listen and say.**

D Talk with a partner.

Copy the open-ended conversation on the board. Pick a student to model the open-ended conversation with you in front of the class.

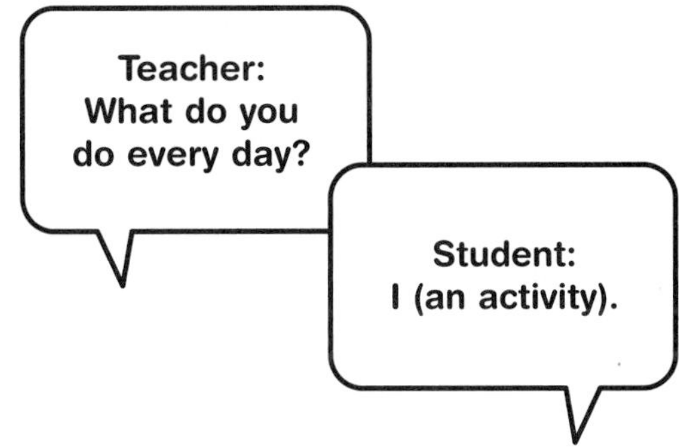
Teacher:
What do you
do every day?
Student:
I (an activity).

Have the students work in pairs to practice the conversation. Tell them to use the words in the Word List.

Go around the room and check their work. Finally, call on a pair to share their conversation with the class.

2 Days of the week

LEARNING POINT
Recognizing, saying, and writing the days of the week

NEW LANGUAGE
Sunday
Monday
Tuesday
Wednesday
Thursday
Friday
Saturday

A Listen.

Have the students listen with their books closed.

Sunday

Monday

Tuesday

Wednesday

Thursday

Friday

Saturday

Have them open their books, look at the calendar, and then listen again as they follow along.

Listen and say.

Have the class listen to and repeat each day of the week separately. Stop the tape or CD after each word or read aloud the separate words with pauses.

Then call on individual students to listen and repeat after you.

B Listen and circle.

Have the students listen with their books closed.

1. My sisters study on Monday.

2. My brothers cook dinner on Thursday.

3. I go to garage sales on Sunday.

4. Paul and Leo play basketball on Saturday.

Copy the first sentence on the board. Play or say the first item. Tell the students to listen for a day of the week. Circle "Monday."

Then have the students listen again and complete the activity. Stop the tape or CD, or pause after each sentence, so students have time to circle the appropriate response.

Have the students compare their answers with a partner. Then have them listen again as they check their work.

Finally, call on individual students to read aloud the items they circled.

ANSWERS:

1. Monday

2. Thursday

3. Sunday

4. Saturday

WORKBOOK PAGE 41

2 Days of the week

STUDENT BOOK PAGE 56

EXPANSION ACTIVITY: Circle what you hear.

Write the following numbered pairs on the board and have the students copy them on a separate piece of paper:

1. Sunday Monday
2. Tuesday Thursday
3. Wednesday Tuesday
4. Friday Thursday
5. Saturday Sunday

Tell the students to circle the day of the week they hear as you read aloud the following days: Sunday, Thursday, Wednesday, Friday, Saturday.

Have a student circle the answers on the board.

Repeat the activity with new pairs of words.

Listen and write.

Have the students listen with their books closed.

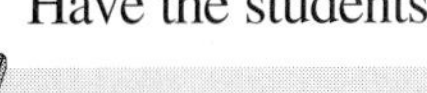

1. I play soccer on Thursday.

2. We go to my mother's house on Friday.

3. My nieces go to garage sales on Saturday.

4. I go to class on Monday.

5. I cook dinner on Tuesday.

6. Grace and I study on Wednesday.

Copy the first sentence on the board. Play or say the first item. Tell the students tao listen for a day of the week. Write "Thursday" in the blank.

Then have the students listen again and complete the activity. Stop the tape or CD, or pause after each sentence, so students have time to write a response.

Have the students compare their answers with a partner. Then have them listen again as they check their work.

Finally, call on different students to read the completed sentences aloud as you write the answers on the board.

ANSWERS:

1. Thursday

2. Friday

3. Saturday

4. Monday

5. Tuesday

6. Wednesday

3 Months

STUDENT BOOK PAGE 57

LEARNING POINT
Recognizing, saying, and writing months

NEW LANGUAGE

January	July
February	August
March	September
April	October
May	November
June	December

When is your birthday?
It's in _____.

A Listen.

Have the students open their books and examine the calendar. Have the students listen with their books closed.

January

February

March

April

May

June

July

August

September

October

November

December

Then have them open their books, look at the calendar, and listen again as they follow along.

Listen and say.

Have the students listen to and repeat each month separately. Stop the tape or CD after each month or read aloud the separate months with pauses.

Then call on individual students to listen and repeat after you.

B Listen.

Have the students listen with their books closed.

Don: When is your birthday?

Isabel: It's in October.

Explain the meaning of birthday. Draw a birthday cake on the board and write the day and month of your birthday next to it. Point to the date and say: "My birthday."

Have the students listen again as they follow along with their books open.

Listen and say.

Repeat the procedure from the previous **Listen and say.**

C Talk with three classmates.

Copy the open-ended conversation on the board. Pick a student to model the open-ended conversation with you in front of the class.

3 Months

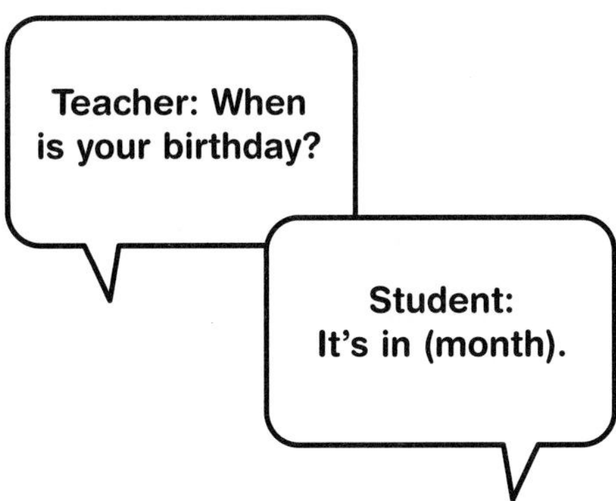

Teacher: When is your birthday?
Student: It's in (month).

Have the students talk to three classmates. Go around the room and check their work.

Finally, call on different pairs to share their conversations with the class.

D Write.

Have the students examine the activity. Point out the sample answer. Explain that "Jan." is short for "January."

Then tell the students to fill in the blanks with the abbreviations.

Have the students compare answers with a partner. Go around the room and check their work.

Finally, write the answers on the board.

ANSWERS:

1. Jan.

2. Feb.

3. Mar.

4. Apr.

5. May

6. Jun.

7. Jul.

8. Aug.

9. Sept.

10. Oct.

11. Nov.

12. Dec.

EXPANSION ACTIVITY: Write the abbreviations.

Have the students write the abbreviation of each month on a piece of paper as you say the months in random order. Be sure to write down the months as you say them for later reference.

Call on a student to write the answers on the board.

4 What time is it?

STUDENT BOOK PAGE 58

LEARNING POINT
Asking and saying what time it is

NEW LANGUAGE
_____ o'clock
_____-fifteen
_____-thirty
_____ forty-five

What time is it?
It's _____.

Listen.

Have the students open their books and examine the illustrations. Have the students listen with their books closed.

1. Ten o'clock. It's ten o'clock.

2. Seven-fifteen. It's seven-fifteen.

3. One forty-five. It's one forty-five.

4. Three-thirty. It's three-thirty.

5. Two o'clock. It's two o'clock.

6. Four forty-five. It's four forty-five.

7. Twelve-thirty. It's twelve-thirty.

8. Eight-fifteen. It's eight-fifteen.

Have the students listen again as they follow along with their books open.

Explain the different ways of dividing time into quarters by drawing an analog clock on the board and placing the hands in the o'clock, fifteen, thirty, and forty-five positions as you say the different times.

Listen and say.

Have the students listen to and repeat each time separately.

1. ten o'clock

2. seven-fifteen

3. one forty-five

4. three-thirty

5. two o'clock

6. four forty-five

7. twelve-thirty

8. eight-fifteen

Stop the tape or CD after each item or read aloud the separate lines with pauses. Then call on individual students to listen and repeat after you.

Listen.

Have the students listen with their books closed.

Don: What time is it?

Leo: It's 10:00.

Have the students listen again as they follow along with their books open.

Listen and say.

Repeat the procedure from the previous **Listen and say.**

Talk with a partner. Look at the clocks.

Copy the open-ended conversation on the board. Pick a student to model the open-ended conversation with you in front of the class. Point to the first illustration as you ask "What time is it?"

4 What time is it?

STUDENT BOOK PAGE 58

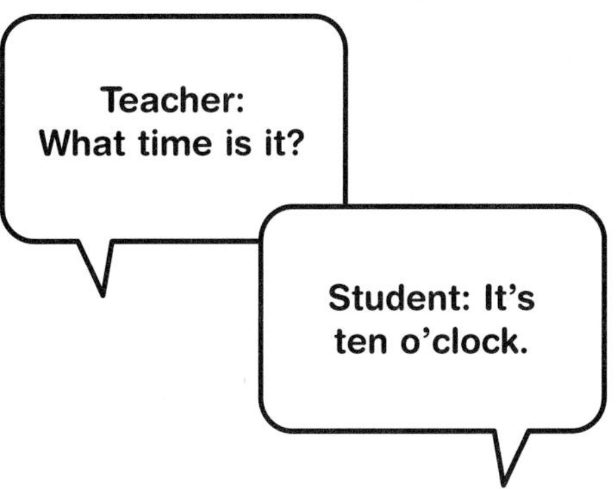

Teacher: What time is it?
Student: It's ten o'clock.

Have the students work in pairs to practice the conversation. Go around the room and check their work.

Finally, call on different pairs to share their conversations with the class.

EXPANSION ACTIVITY: Drawing and Telling the Time

Draw an analog clock on the board and prompt the class to say the time that's indicated.

Then have the students work in pairs to take turns drawing clocks and saying the time.

Finally, call on different students to draw random times on the clock on the board. Prompt the class or individual students to say the times.

5 It's 5:45.

STUDENT BOOK PAGE 59

LEARNING POINT
Saying what you do at different times of the day

NEW LANGUAGE
I get up at _____.
I go to school/work at _____.
I eat lunch at _____.
I go home at _____.
I go to bed at _____.

A Listen.

Have the students open their books and examine the illustrations. Have the students listen with their books closed.

1. Six o'clock. It's six o'clock.

2. Eight-fifteen. It's eight-fifteen.

3. Three-thirty. It's three-thirty.

4. Five forty-five. It's five forty-five.

Then have them open their books, look at the illustrations, and listen again as they follow along.

Listen and say.

Have the students listen to and repeat each line separately. Stop the tape or CD after each line or read aloud the separate lines with pauses.

1. six o'clock

2. eight-fifteen

3. three-thirty

4. five forty-five

Then call on individual students to listen and repeat after you.

B Listen and circle.

Have the students listen with their books closed.

1. It's seven-thirty.

2. She eats breakfast at eight-thirty.

3. She goes to school at twelve forty-five.

4. They study at two-fifteen.

5. Carlos reads the newspaper at four o'clock.

6. He goes to sleep at nine-fifteen.

Copy the first item on the board. Play or say the first item Tell the students to listen for a time. Circle "7:30."

Then, have the students listen again and complete the activity. Stop the tape or CD, or pause after each line, so students have time to circle the appropriate choice.

Have the students compare their answers with a partner.

Then have them listen again as they check their work.

Finally, call on individual students to read aloud the items they circled.

ANSWERS:

1. 7:30

2. 8:30

3. 12:45

4. 2:15

5. 4:00

6. 9:15

Complete. Read your sentences to classmates.

To help the students understand the new language, write the following sentences on the board:

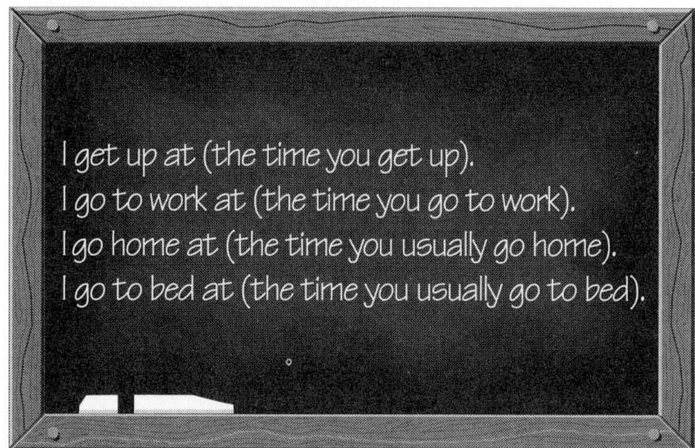

I get up at (the time you get up).
I go to work at (the time you go to work).
I go home at (the time you usually go home).
I go to bed at (the time you usually go to bed).

Next act out each sentence as you say it. For example, make the motions of waking up for the first sentence.

Copy the first item on the board and fill in the blank with your own information as you say the sentence.

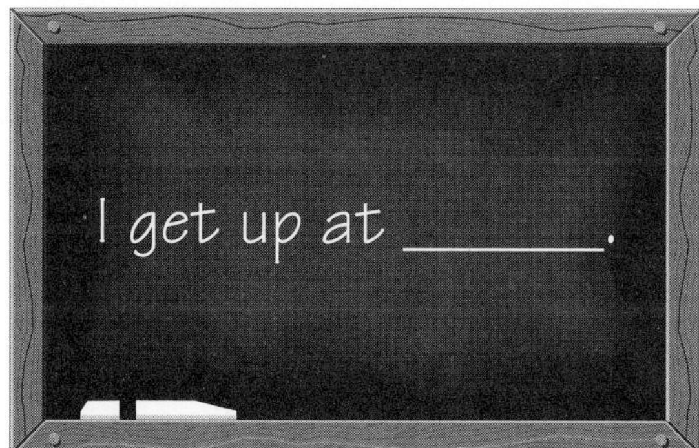

Explain to the students that they should write down their own personal information for each item. Go around the room and check their work.

Next have them share their sentences with different classmates by reading them aloud. Go around and listen in.

Finally, have different students volunteer to read their sentences to the class.

6 Making an appointment

STUDENT BOOK PAGE 60

LEARNING POINT
Making an appointment

NEW LANGUAGE
a cleaning
a tune-up
a haircut

I'd like to make an appointment for _____.
Can you come on _____ at _____?
_____ at _____? That's fine.

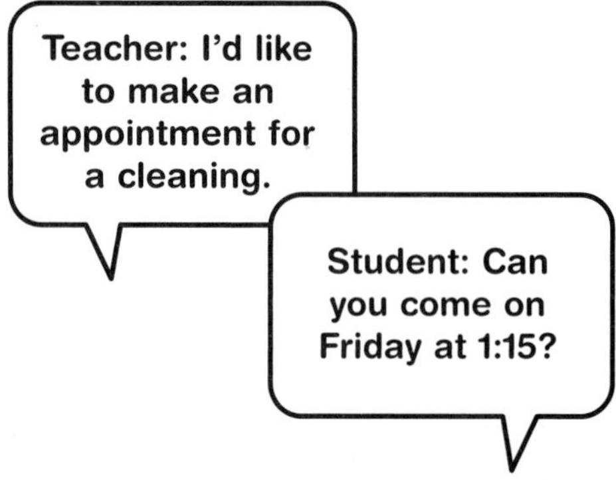

Teacher: I'd like to make an appointment for a cleaning.
Student: Can you come on Friday at 1:15?

Listen.

Have the students listen with their books closed.

Grace:	I'd like to make an appointment for a haircut.
Receptionist:	Can you come on Friday at 11:45?
Grace:	Friday at 11:45? That's fine.

Have the students listen again as they follow along with their books open.

Listen and say.

Have the students listen to and repeat each line of the conversation separately. Stop the tape or CD after each line or read aloud the separate lines with pauses.

Then call on individual students to listen and repeat after you.

Talk with a partner.

Copy the open-ended conversation on the board. Pick a student to model the open-ended conversation with you in front of the class.

Have the students work in pairs to practice the conversation. Go around and the room and check their work.

Finally, call on different pairs to share their conversations with the class.

Listen and write the times.

Have the students listen with their books closed.

Grace:	I'd like to make an appointment for a haircut.
Man:	Can you come on Monday at five-thirty?
Grace:	Monday at five-thirty? That's fine.
Grace:	I'd like to make an appointment for a tune-up.
Woman:	Can you come on Wednesday at three o'clock?
Grace:	Wednesday at three o'clock? That's fine.
Grace:	I'd like to make an appointment for a cleaning.
Man:	Can you come on Friday at one-fifteen?
Grace:	Friday at one-fifteen? That's fine.

6 Making an appointment

Have the students open their books. Point out the page from the personal calendar and read the dates and the handwritten entries aloud. Play or say the first conversation. Tell the students to listen for a time. Point to the sample answer.

Then have the students listen again and complete the activity. Stop the tape or CD, or pause after each conversation, so students have time to write a response.

Have the students compare their answers with a partner. Then have them listen again as they check their work.

Finally, call on different students to read aloud the times as you write the answers on the board.

ANSWERS:

5:30, 3:00, 1:15

EXPANSION:
Write down the time.

Say a time and write it on the board. For example, say, "one-fifteen" and write "1:15" on the board. Dictate different times as the students write them down ("two o'clock, five-fifteen, three-thirty,..."). Be sure to write down the times as you say them for later reference.

Call on a student to write the times on the board.

7 How often do you study?

LEARNING POINT
Saying how often you do something

NEW LANGUAGE
cook breakfast/dinner
get a haircut
shop for food
study English
talk on the phone

How often do you _____?
Every day. / Once a week. / Once a month.

Listen and read.

Have the students open their books and examine the illustrations.

Have the students listen with their books closed.

1. I study English every day.

2. I shop for food once a week.

3. I get a haircut once a month.

Then have them open their books, look at the illustrations, and listen again as they follow along. Relate the sentences to their corresponding calendar pages.

Help the students understand the terms every day, once a week, and once a month by pointing to each day on the first calendar as you say: "every day," pointing to a day of each week on the second calendar as you say: "once a week," and pointing to the 18th of the month as you say: "once a month."

Listen.

Have the students listen with their books closed.

Sandy: How often do you cook dinner?

Leo: Every day.

Tien: Once a week.

Carlos: Once a month.

Have the students listen again as they follow along with their books open.

Listen and say.

Have the students listen to and repeat each line of the conversation separately. Stop the tape or CD after each line or read aloud the separate lines with pauses.

Then call on individual students to listen and repeat after you.

Talk with a partner.

Copy the open-ended conversation on the board. Pick a student to model the open-ended conversation with you in front of the class.

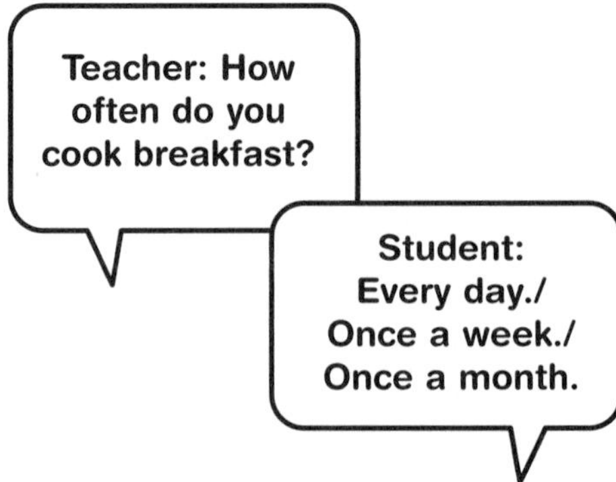

Teacher: How often do you cook breakfast?
Student: Every day./ Once a week./ Once a month.

Have the students work in pairs to practice the conversation. Tell them to use the words in the Word List. Go around the room and check their work.

Finally, call on different pairs to share their conversations with the class.

8 Ordinal numbers

LEARNING POINT
Recognizing and using ordinal numbers

NEW LANGUAGE

1st	first
2nd	second
3rd	third
4th	fourth
5th	fifth
6th	sixth
7th	seventh
8th	eighth
9th	ninth
10th	tenth
11th	eleventh
12th	twelfth
13th	thirteenth
14th	fourteenth

What is your date of birth?

Listen.

Have the students listen with their books closed.

first

second

third

fourth

fifth

sixth

seventh

eighth

ninth

tenth

eleventh

twelfth

thirteenth

fourteenth

Have the students listen again as they follow along with their books open. Point out that the -st, -nd, -rd, and –th endings in 1st and so on are abbreviations of the words first and so on.

Listen and say.

Have the students listen to and repeat each word. Stop the tape or CD after each word or read aloud the separate words with pauses.

Then call on individual students to listen and repeat after you.

Write the number.

Copy the sample item on the board and fill in the blank as you say the number fourteenth Then have the students follow your model and write the numbers in the blanks. Have the students compare answers with a partner.

Finally, call on a student to write the answers on the board.

ANSWERS:

1. 14th

2. 3rd

3. 12th

4. 1st

5. 10th

6. 2nd

Ordinal numbers

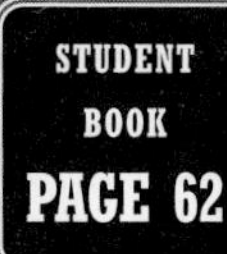
STUDENT
BOOK
PAGE 62

Listen and circle.

Have the students listen with their books closed.

1. Paul lives on Fifth Street.

2. Tien lives on Third Avenue.

3. Go to Twelfth Street.

4. The garage sale is on Fourteenth Street.

5. I live on Thirteenth Street.

6. Grace lives on First Avenue.

Copy the first item on the board. Play or say the first item. Tell the students to listen for numbers. Circle "5th."

Then have the students listen again and complete the activity. Stop the tape or CD, or pause after each sentence, so students have time to circle the appropriate choice.

Have the students compare their answers with a partner. Then have them listen again as they check their work.

Finally, call on individual students to write the answers on the board.

ANSWERS:

1. 5th

2. 3rd

3. 12th

4. 14th

5. 13th

6. 1st

Listen.

Repeat the procedure from the previous **Listen.**

Woman: What is your date of birth?

Grace: March sixteenth, 1964.

Listen and say.

Repeat the procedure from the previous **Listen and say.**

Point out the margin note and read the contents aloud. Then have the students repeat the pronunciation of the number in the box after you.

Ask three classmates.

Copy the open-ended conversation on the board.

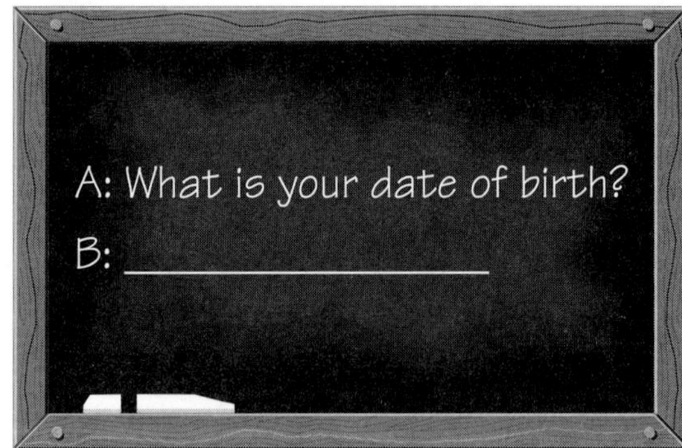
A: What is your date of birth?
B: ___

Pick a student to model the open-ended conversation with you in front of the class.

Have the students follow your model and interview three classmates. Go around the room and check their work.

8 Ordinal numbers

STUDENT BOOK PAGE 62

EXPANSION ACTIVITY: Say the numbers.

Say a cardinal number and prompt the class to respond with the corresponding ordinal number. For example, you say: "one," and the class says "first."

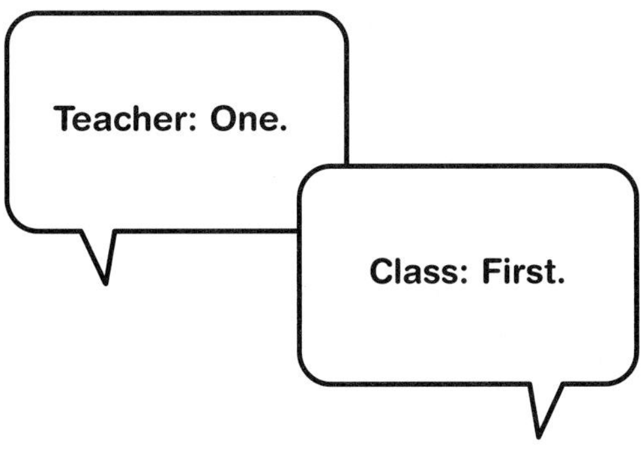
Teacher: One.
Class: First.

Say the numbers in sequence and have the class respond together.

Say the numbers randomly and have the class respond together. Then call on individual students to respond.

9 Completing a form

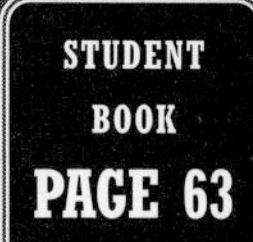

LEARNING POINT
Writing down personal information

NEW LANGUAGE
date of birth
medical history

Read.

Have the students follow along in their books as you read aloud the information on the medical history form. Then explain that a medical history is information about one's health—past and present.

Finally, have the students read over the medical history again.

Complete the form.

Point out the form and tell the students to fill in their own information. Point out the margin box and remind them to write their birth date—month/day/year. Review that MI stands for "Middle Initial."

Go around the room and check the students' work. Then have a student copy the blank form onto the board and fill in his or her information.

Write information about your class and appointments for this week.

Read the directions aloud as the students follow along in their books. Demonstrate how to complete the calendar by copying part of it on the board and filling in information as you explain what you are doing. Then read the information aloud.

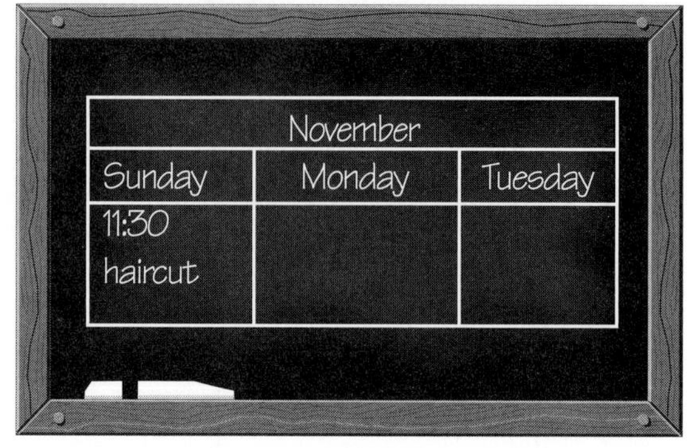

Have the students follow your model and write information in the calendar in their books. Remind them to write in the current month. Tell them to use their imaginations if they cannot think of actual personal information. Go around the room and check their work.

Have the students compare and share their work with a partner.

Finally, have a student copy the blank calendar on the board. Ask another student to fill in his or her information.

10 Review

A Listen and write.

Have students listen with their books closed.

1. My birthday is October twelfth.
2. Paul's birthday is July fourth.
3. My class is at four-thirty.
4. I study on Tuesday.

Copy the first sentence on the board. Play or say the first item. Write "October." Have the students listen again and complete the exercise. Stop the tape or CD, or pause after each sentence, so students have time to write a response.

Have the students compare their answers with a partner. Then have them listen again as they check their work.

Finally, call on different students to read the completed sentences aloud as you write the answers on the board.

ANSWERS:

1. October
2. July
3. 4:30
4. Tuesday

B Listen and √ check the answer.

Have the students listen with their books closed.

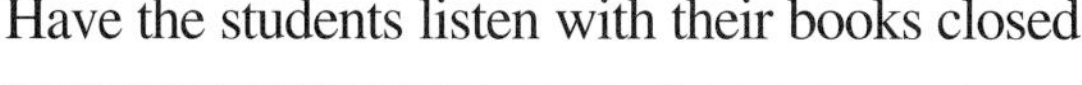

1. How often do you shop for food?
2. When do you go to garage sales?
3. What do you do every day?
4. What time is it?
5. Can you come on Sunday at five o'clock?
6. What is your date of birth?

Copy the first exercise item on the board. Play or say the first sentence. Write a check mark in the blank next to "Once a week."

Then have the students listen again and complete the exercise. Stop the tape or CD, or pause after each question, so students have time to check the appropriate response.

Have the students compare their answers with a partner. Then have them listen again to check their work.

Finally, ask a student to write the items on the board and check √ the answers.

ANSWERS:

1. Once a week.
2. Saturday.
3. I read the newspaper.
4. 3:00.
5. Sunday at 5:00?
6. February 18, 1991.

10 Review

STUDENT BOOK PAGES 64-65

Listen and circle.

Have the students listen with their books closed.

1. Can you come at seven o'clock?

2. He lives on Sixth Street.

3. The house is on Eleventh Street.

4. I go to school at two-thirty.

5. My birthday is May thirteenth.

6. I go to school at nine forty-five.

Copy the first item on the board. Play or say the first item. Tell students to listen for a number. Circle "7:00"

Then have the students listen again and complete the activity. Stop the tape or CD, or pause after each sentence, so students have time to circle the appropriate response.

Have the students compare their answers with a partner. Then have them listen again as they check their work.

Finally, call on individual students to read aloud the items they circled.

ANSWERS:

1. 7:00

2. 6th

3. 11th

4. 2:30

5. 13th

6. 9:45

D Listen and write.

Have the students listen with their books closed.

Cleaning Appointment
On Monday, April 21st at eight a.m.

Edward J. Weiss, D.D.S.
517 Old Road
Santa Cruz, California

Jane's Haircuts
Hours
Tuesday to Saturday
nine thirty a.m. to six p.m.
310 Cook Road, Middletown, Michigan

Copy the first appointment card on the board. Play or say the first item. Fill in the first blank with "Monday."

Then have the students listen again and complete the activity. Stop the tape or CD, or pause after each line, so students have time to write an appropriate response.

Have the students compare their answers with a partner. Then have them listen again as they check their work.

Finally, call on individual students to read aloud the items they circled.

ANSWERS:

Monday

April

8:00 a.m.

6:00

10 Review

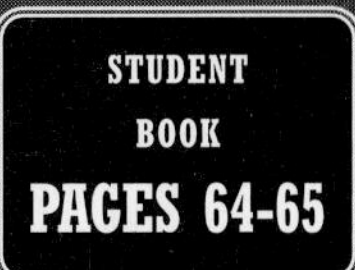

Learning Log

Write five words you remember.

Review the purpose of a learning log.

Tell the students to try to fill in the log without looking back in their books for words. Then have them compare answers with a partner.

Finally, copy the Learning Log on the board. Call several students to the board and have them write one word in each column of the log. Check their work.

SAMPLE ANSWERS:

Days	Months	Ordinal Numbers
Sunday	June	fifth
Monday	July	second
Tuesday	August	thirteenth
Wednesday	September	twentieth
Thursday	October	thirty-first

√ Check what you can do.

Tell the students to complete the checklist. Go around the room and check their work.

Finally, call on different students to read aloud the items they checked and what they filled in for item No. 5.

1. I can ask for and say the time. _____

2. I can name the days of the week and the months of the year. _____

3. I can make appointments. _____

4. I can say and write ordinal numbers from 1-14. _____

5. I can ____________________. _____

Looking Back

Look at page 54. What do you do every day? Write three more words in your Learning Log.

Have the students look at the illustration on page 54 and add three words to their Learning Logs. Then have them compare their additions with a partner.

Finally, call on different students to read aloud the headings and the words they added.

See Color Transparencies package for unit wrap-up activity. This task can be used as an oral assessment tool. Many unit wrap-up activities include a reproducible blackline master.

Unit 6 Let's go shopping.

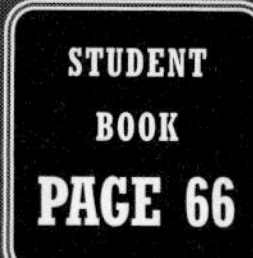
STUDENT BOOK PAGE 66

UNIT OVERVIEW

	LESSON:	LEARNING POINTS:	SB#
1.	**I'm looking for a shirt.**	Asking for merchandise in a store	**p. 67**
2.	**May I help you?**	Asking for help in a store	**p. 68**
3.	**What color is your jacket?**	Identifying colors	**p. 69**
4.	**What are you wearing?**	Talking about what people are wearing	**p. 70**
5.	**What's your favorite color?**	Talking about clothing and favorite colors	**p. 71**
6.	**What size are you?**	Identifying clothing sizes	**p. 72**
7.	**The jacket is too small.**	Identifying and writing about clothing sizes	**p. 73**
8.	**Money**	Recognizing denominations of American money	**p. 74**
9.	**Writing a check**	Writing a check	**p. 75**
10.	**Review**	Review Unit 6	**p. 76**

Suggestions for Unit Opener (Student Book page 66)

Brainstorm. Have students look at the unit-opening illustration. Ask them for words related to department stores and shopping that they already know. Write the words on the board as students say them.

Model the language. Begin by reading the caption aloud —"Where are the students? What do you see?" Point to the signs and read them, and point to the items of clothing and name them. Write the words on the board.

Model the language again. This time have the class repeat the words after you. Then go around the room and have individual students repeat different words.

Point and say. Point to the words you've written on the board as you say them. Have the students repeat them after you.

Initiate pair work. Have the students work in pairs. Tell them to take turns pointing to the different people, floors, and items in the illustration and naming them. Demonstrate this by asking a student to point to someone or something and by saying the name yourself, then pointing yourself and asking the same student to say the name. Go around the room and check students' work.

See Color Transparencies package for additional unit-opening activity. Many of these tasks include a reproducible blackline master.

1 I'm looking for a shirt.

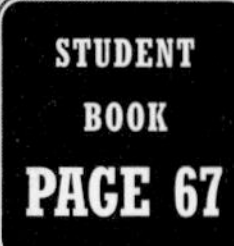

LEARNING POINT
Asking for merchandise in a store

NEW LANGUAGE

coat	shoes
dress	sweater
pants	suit
shirt	watch

Excuse me. I'm looking for _____.
Follow me, please.
Thank you.

A Listen.

Have the students open their books and examine the illustrations. Have the students listen with their books closed.

1. A shirt. Don is looking for a shirt.

2. A coat. Maria is looking for a coat.

3. A sweater. Isabel is looking for a sweater.

4. Shoes. Grace is looking for shoes.

5. A watch. Leo is looking for a watch.

6. A dress. Maria is looking for a dress.

7. Pants. Don is looking for pants.

8. A suit. Paul is looking for a suit.

Then have them open their books, look at the illustrations, and listen again as they follow along.

Listen and say.

Have the class listen to and repeat each word separately. Stop the tape or CD after each word or read aloud the separate words with pauses.

1. a shirt

2. a coat

3. a sweater

4. shoes

5. a watch

6. a dress

7. pants

8. a suit

Then call on individual students to listen and repeat after you.

B Listen.

Have the students listen with their books closed.

Maria: Excuse me. I'm looking for a coat.

Clerk: Follow me, please.

Maria: Thank you.

Write the new language on the board.

Next, act out *looking for (something)* by making the motions of looking for something. Then act out *follow me* by pointing to a student, and saying "Follow me." Prompt the student to follow you.

1 I'm looking for a shirt.

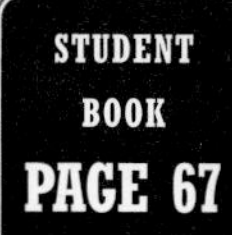
STUDENT
BOOK
PAGE 67

Demonstrate that *Excuse me* is used to get someone's attention by tapping a student on the shoulder and saying: "Excuse me. I'm looking for a (a familiar classroom object such as the student's book)." Prompt the student to hand you the object.

Have the students listen again as they follow along with their books open.

Listen and say.

Repeat the procedure from the previous **Listen and say.**

C Talk with a partner.

Copy the open-ended conversation on the board. Pick a student to model the open-ended conversation with you in front of the class.

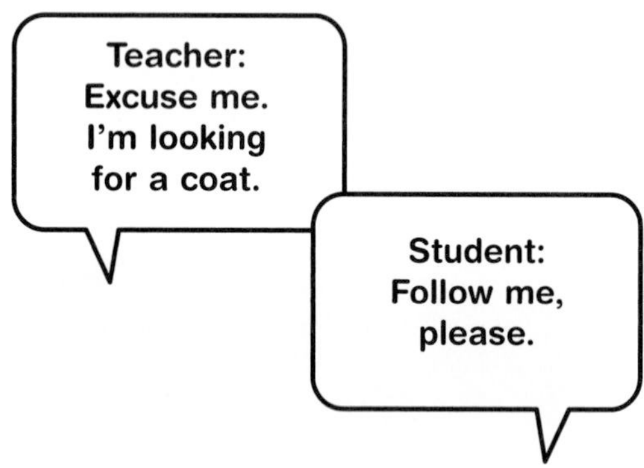
Teacher:
Excuse me.
I'm looking
for a coat.
Student:
Follow me,
please.

Have the students work in pairs to practice the conversation. Tell them to use the words in the Word List. Go around the room and check their work.

Finally, call on different pairs to share their conversations with the class.

EXPANSION ACTIVITY:
Play *Garage Sale.*

Divide the class into two groups—"the buyers" and "the sellers." Tell them to pretend they are at a garage sale. Have the sellers use a long table or several desks pushed together to display their "merchandise." Explain that they can display things from the classroom, including clothing items and illustrations of things that can represent real items. Give the sellers ten to fifteen minutes to make their drawings and assemble their merchandise.

Next have the buyers move around the table and act out the conversation from Activity C with the sellers. Join in the activity as you check the students' work.

Match.

Have the students examine the illustrations. Point out the sample answer. Then tell the students to match the pictures to the words.

Have the students compare answers with a partner. Go around the room and check their work.

Finally, call on a student to say the answers as you write them on the board.

ANSWERS:

1. d

2. a

3. c

4. b

2 May I help you?

STUDENT BOOK PAGE 68

LEARNING POINT
Asking for help in a store

NEW LANGUAGE
bathing suit
blouse
jacket
skirt
sneakers

May I help you?
Yes, I'm looking for _____.
_____ is looking for_____.

A Listen.

Have the students open their books and examine the illustrations.

Have the students listen with their books closed.

1. A blouse. Isabel is looking for a blouse.
2. A bathing suit. Carlos is looking for a bathing suit.
3. A skirt. Grace is looking for a skirt.
4. A jacket. Paul is looking for a jacket.
5. Sneakers. Leo is looking for sneakers.

Then have them open their books, look at the illustrations, and listen again as they follow along.

Listen and say.

Have the students listen to and repeat each word separately. Stop the tape or CD after each word or read aloud the separate words with pauses.

1. a blouse
2. a bathing suit
3. a skirt
4. a jacket
5. sneakers

Then call on individual students to listen and repeat after you.

B Listen.

Have the students listen with their books closed.

Clerk: May I help you?

Carlos: Yes, I'm looking for a bathing suit.

Have the students listen again as they follow along with their books open.

Listen and say.

Repeat the procedure from the previous **Listen and say.**

C Talk with a partner.

Copy the open-ended conversation on the board. Pick a student to model the open-ended conversation with you in front of the class.

Teacher:
May I help you?
Student: Yes,
I'm looking
for a bathing suit.

Have the students work in pairs to practice the conversation. Tell them to use the illustrations and the words from the Word List. Go around the room and check their work.

Finally, call on different pairs to share their conversations with the class.

2 May I help you?

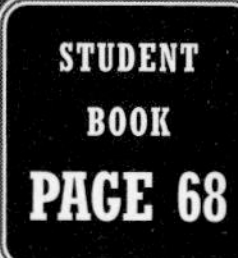

Complete.

Have the students look at the illustrations and the sentences. Then have the students fill in the blanks with the appropriate words.

Finally, call on a student to write the answers on the board for you to check.

ANSWERS:

1. sweater

2. pants

3 What color is your jacket?

STUDENT BOOK PAGE 69

LEARNING POINT
Identifying colors

NEW LANGUAGE

black	purple
blue	red
brown	white
green	yellow
pink	

What color is/are your ____?

A Listen.

Have the students open their books and examine the colors.

Have the students listen with their books closed.

1. white

2. black

3. brown

4. pink

5. red

6. yellow

7. green

8. blue

9. purple

Then have them open their books, look at the colors, and listen again as they follow along.

Listen and say.

Have the students listen to and repeat each word separately. Stop the tape or CD after each word or read aloud the separate words with pauses.

Then call on individual students to listen and repeat after you.

B Listen and circle.

Have the students listen with their books closed.

1. yellow sneakers

2. a blue sweater

3. a green blouse

4. a purple jacket

5. a pink bathing suit

6. a black skirt

Point out the pairs of illustrations. Play or say the first item and point out the example. Then hold up your book and make a circling gesture around the sample answer as you say: "yellow sneakers."

Then have the students listen again, and complete the exercise. Stop the tape or CD, or pause after each item, so students have time to circle the appropriate choice.

Have the students compare their answers with a partner. Then have them listen again as they check their work.

Finally, hold up your book and point to each correct illustration as you say the corresponding phrase.

ANSWERS:

1. illustration on the right

2. illustration on the left

3. illustration on the left

4. illustration on the left

5. illustration on the right

6. illustration on the left

3 What color is your jacket?

STUDENT
BOOK
PAGE 69

C Listen.

Have the students listen with their books closed.

Sandy: What color is your jacket?

Grace: Purple.

Sandy: What color are your sneakers?

Grace: Yellow.

Have the students listen again as they follow along with their books open.

Listen and say.

Repeat the procedure from the previous **Listen and say.**

D Talk with a partner about clothes.

Copy the open-ended conversation on the board. Pick a student to model the open-ended conversation with you in front of the class.

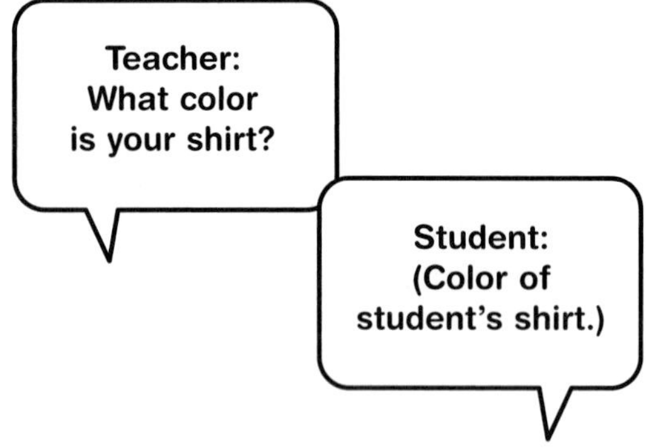
Teacher:
What color
is your shirt?
Student:
(Color of
student's shirt.)

Have the students work in pairs to practice the conversation. Tell them to use the words in the Word List. Go around the room and check their work.

Finally, call on different pairs to share their conversations with the class.

EXPANSION ACTIVITY:
Say the color.

Using the colors taught in this lesson, point to different clothing items and objects in the classroom and prompt the class to say the colors. For example, point to the board and say "green" (or "black"). Then point to objects and have individual students say the colors.

Next have the students work in pairs to take turns pointing to objects and saying the colors. You can also call on different students to lead the activity with the class.

4 What are you wearing?

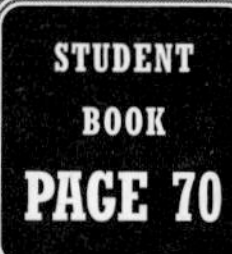

LEARNING POINT
Talking about what people are wearing

NEW LANGUAGE
What are you wearing?
I'm wearing _____.
What is _____ wearing?
He's/She's wearing _____.

Listen.

Have the students listen with their books closed.

Grace: What are you wearing to the party?

Maria: I'm wearing a blue dress.
What is Carlos wearing?

Grace: He's wearing a blue suit.

Help the students understand the meaning of the word *wearing*. On the board write "I'm wearing _____." Then say what you are wearing.

Teacher:
I'm wearing
(item of clothing).

Provide another example by repeating the procedure with a student. Point to an item of clothing the student is wearing as you say: "(Student's name) is wearing (item of clothing)."

Listen and say.

Have the students listen to and repeat each line of the conversation separately. Stop the tape or CD after each line or read aloud the separate lines with pauses.

Then call on individual students to listen and repeat after you.

Talk with a partner.

Copy the open-ended conversation on the board. Pick a student to model the open-ended conversation with you in front of the class.

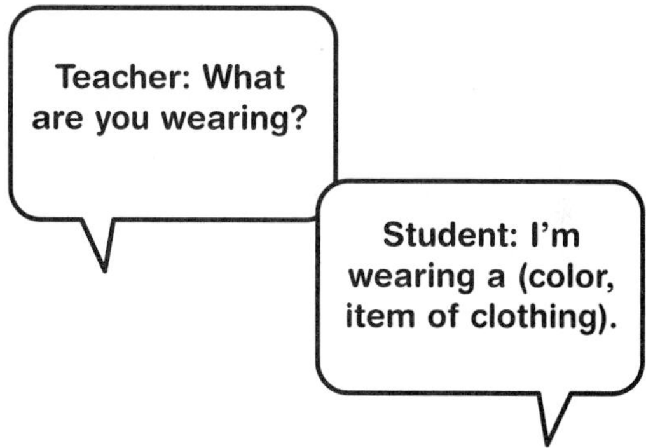

Teacher: What are you wearing?
Student: I'm wearing a (color, item of clothing).

Have the students work in pairs to practice the conversation. Go around the room and check their work.

Finally, call on different pairs to share their conversations with the class.

Talk with a partner. Look at the picture on page 66.

Point out the illustration on page 66. Then model the open-ended conversation with a student in front of the class. Point to the different characters in the illustration as you do so.

Have the students work in pairs to practice the conversation. Go around the room and check their work.

Finally, call on different pairs to share their conversations with the class.

5 What's your favorite color?

STUDENT BOOK PAGE 71

LEARNING POINT
Talking about clothing and favorite colors

NEW LANGUAGE
favorite

What's your favorite color?

Listen.

Have the students listen with their books closed.

Isabel: What's your favorite color?

Tien: Red. And you?

Isabel: Blue.

To help students understand the meaning of "favorite," take a piece of clothing or an object with the color you've just specified and hold it up to your chest and smile as you say: "My favorite color is (the name of the color)."

Have the class listen again as they follow along.

Listen and say.

Have the class listen to and repeat each line of the conversation separately. Stop the tape or CD after each line or read aloud the separate lines with pauses.

Then call on individual students to listen and repeat after you.

Talk with a partner.

Copy the open-ended conversation on the board. Pick a student to model the open-ended conversation with you in front of the class.

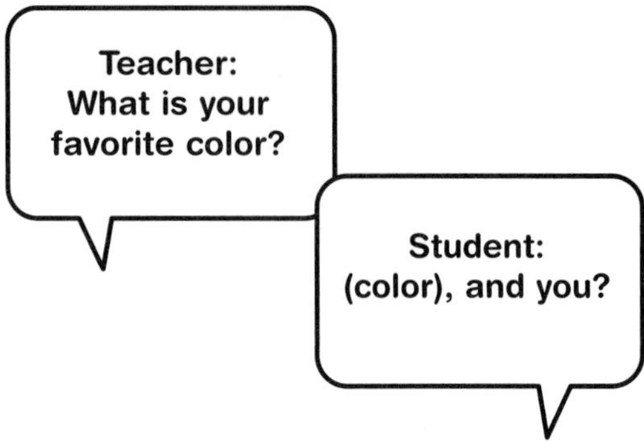
Teacher: What is your favorite color?
Student: (color), and you?

Have the students work in pairs to practice the conversation. Go around the room and check their work.

Finally, call on different pairs to share their conversations with the class.

Ask classmates.

Copy the chart on the board. Ask a student, "What's your favorite color?" After the student tells you his/her favorite color, say: "Please sign here," as you point to the appropriate place in the chart.

Have the students walk around the room to talk to their classmates. Go around the room and check their work.

Finally, call on different students to share their answers with the class.

6 What size are you?

LEARNING POINT
Identifying clothing sizes

NEW LANGUAGE
small
medium
large

What size are you?
I'm a _____.

 **Listen.**

Have the students open their books and examine the illustrations. Have the students listen with their books closed.

1. Small. The red shirt is small.

2. Medium. The blue shirt is medium.

3. Large. The green shirt is large.

Then have them open their books, look at the illustrations, and listen again as they follow along.

Listen and say.

Have the class listen to and repeat each word of the conversation separately. Stop the tape or CD after each word or read aloud the separate words with pauses.

1. small

2. medium

3. large

Then call on individual students to listen and repeat after you.

 √ **Check.**

Point out the illustrations of the clothing items and the sample answer. Then tell the students to refer to the circled items to check √ the appropriate columns.

Have them compare answers with a partner. Go around the room and check their work.

Finally, ask a student to copy the three right columns of the chart on the board and fill in the correct check marks.

ANSWERS:

1. medium

2. small

3. large

 **Listen and circle.**

Have the students listen with their books closed.

1. Paul is a large.

2. Tien is a small.

3. Carlos is a large.

4. Isabel is a medium.

Copy the first line on the board. Play or say the first item. Tell the students to listen for size words. Circle "large."

Then have the students listen again and complete the activity. Stop the tape or CD, or pause after each sentence, so students have time to circle the appropriate choice.

Have the students compare their answers with a partner. Then have them listen again as they check their work.

WORKBOOK PAGE 52

Finally, call on individual students to read aloud the items they circled.

ANSWERS:

1. large

2. small

3. large

4. medium

D Listen.

Have the students listen with their books closed.

Salesclerk:	What size are you?
Leo:	I'm a large.

Have the students listen again as they follow along with their books open.

Listen and say.

Repeat the procedure from the previous **Listen and say.**

E Talk with a partner.

Copy the open-ended conversation on the board. Pick a student to model the open-ended conversation with you in front of the class.

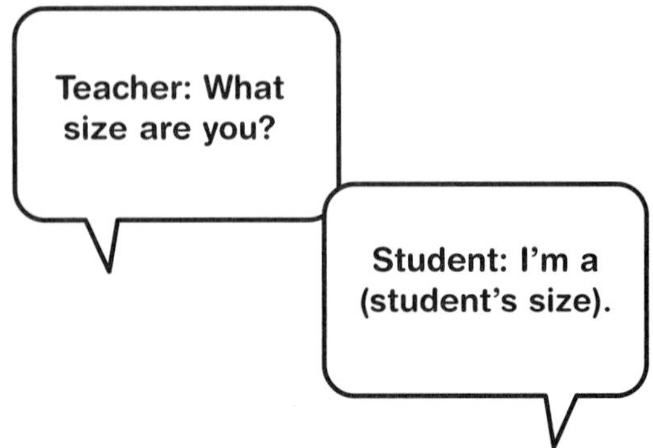

Have the students work in pairs to practice the conversation. Go around the room and check their work.

Finally, call on different pairs to share their conversations with the class.

 WORKBOOK PAGE 52

7 The jacket is too small.

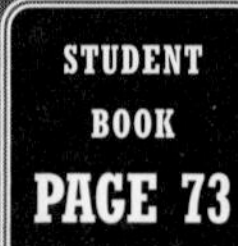

LEARNING POINT
Identifying and writing about clothing sizes

NEW LANGUAGE
big
long
short
small
too big/long/short/small

The _____ is/are too _____.

Listen.

Have the students open their books and examine the illustrations. Have the students listen with their books closed.

1. Too short. The pants are too short.

2. Too long. The sweater is too long.

3. Too small. The jacket is too small.

4. Too big. The blouse is too big.

Then have them them open their books, look at the illustrations, and listen again as they follow along.

Listen and say.

Have the students listen to and repeat each line separately. Stop the tape or CD after each line or read aloud the separate lines with pauses.

Then call on individual students to listen and repeat after you.

1. too short

2. too long

3. too small

4. too big

B Look at Activity A. Match.

Have the students examine the illustrations in Activity A. Point out the sample answer. Then tell the students to use the illustration to match the columns.

Have the students compare answers with a partner. Go around the room and check their work.

Finally, write the answers on the board.

ANSWERS:

1. b

2. d

3. a

4. c

Write two sentences about Leo's clothes.

Point out the illustration of Leo. Tell the students to write sentences to describe Leo and his clothes. Go around the room and check their work. Then have them compare answers with a partner.

Finally, call on a pair of students to write the answers on the board.

ANSWERS:

1. His pants are too long.

2. His shirt is too small.

8 Money

STUDENT BOOK PAGE 74

LEARNING POINT
Recognizing denominations of American money

NEW LANGUAGE
penny
nickel
dime
quarter
cent
dollar

A Listen.

Have the students open their books and examine the illustrations. Have the students listen with their books closed.

1. A penny. One cent.

2. A nickel. Five cents.

3. A dime. Ten cents.

4. A quarter. Twenty-five cents.

Then have them open their books, look at the illustrations, and listen again as they follow along.

Listen and say.

Have the students listen to and repeat each line separately. Stop the tape or CD after each line or read aloud the separate lines with pauses.

Then call on individual students to listen and repeat after you.

B Listen.

Repeat the procedure from the previous **Listen.**

1. One dollar.

2. Five dollars

3. Ten dollars.

4. Twenty dollars.

Listen and say.

Repeat the procedure from the previous **Listen and say.**

EXPANSION ACTIVITY: Identify real money.

Bring to class the different coin and dollar denominations practiced in this lesson—a penny, a nickel, a dime, a quarter, a one-dollar bill, a five-dollar bill, a ten-dollar bill, and a twenty-dollar bill. Place the money on your desk and have the students gather around as you point to the different denominations in order of their value (from lesser to greater) and say the names. Then have the students repeat as you point again. Next point in a random order and have the students repeat after you.

Finally, prompt the students to say the names as you point. You can also call on individual students to say the names as you point.

To prepare students for the next activity, have them practice adding the coins and dollar bills. You will have to put additional coins and bills on the desk. For example, point to two five-dollar bills and say: "ten dollars." Next point to a nickel and four pennies and say: "nine cents" and so on. Then point and prompt the students to reply.

STUDENT BOOK PAGE 74

C Match.

Have the students examine the illustrations. Then tell the students to match the pictures to the dollar amounts.

Have the students compare answers with a partner. Go around the room and check their work.

Finally, write the answers on the board.

ANSWERS:

1. b

2. c

3. a

9 Writing a check

STUDENT BOOK PAGE 75

LEARNING POINT
Writing a check

NEW LANGUAGE
check
Pay to the order of _____.

Read.

Have the students examine the check. Read the sentences and the words on the check and have the class follow along.

Use gestures and words the students already know to explain the purpose of a check and to indicate the parts of the check that a person must fill out. Read aloud the information on Isabel's check as the students follow along in their books. Explain that "Memo" is to remind the check-writer why he or she wrote the check.

Write a check.

Have the students examine the check. Read the sentences and have the class follow along.

Copy the blank check on the board. Fill out the first three lines with your name and address.

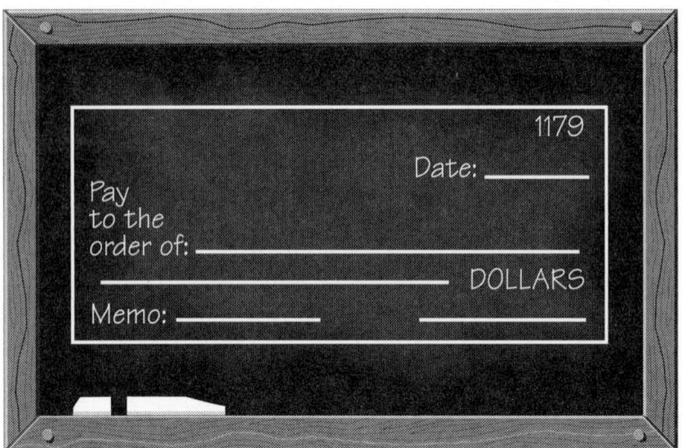

Explain to the students that they will fill the check out with their own information and the information from the paragraph.

Have the students fill out the check.
Then have them compare their work with a partner. Go around the room and check their work. Next have a student fill in his or her information on the blank check on the board.

10 Review

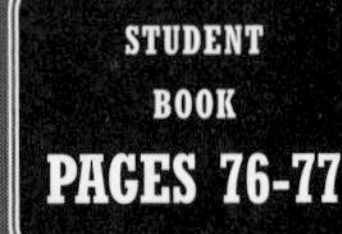

Match.

Have the students examine the illustrations. Point out the sample answer and read aloud the corresponding sentence. Then have the students match the remaining items. Have them compare their answers with a partner.

Draw the blanks on the board and have a student fill in the correct numbers.

ANSWERS:

2, 3, 4, 1,

Listen and √ check.

Have the students listen with their books closed.

1. What size are you?

2. May I help you?

3. What is he wearing?

4. What is your favorite color?

Copy the first item on the board. Play or say the first item. Write a check mark next to "I'm a medium."

Then have the students listen again. Stop the tape or CD, or pause after each question, so students have time to check the appropriate response.

Have the students compare their answers with a partner. Have them listen again to check their work.

Finally, ask a student to write the items on the board and check √ the answers.

ANSWERS:

1. I'm a medium.

2. Yes, I'm looking for a dress.

3. He's wearing a brown suit.

4. Yellow.

Play *Guess Who!*

Have the students read the conversation. Explain that Leo and Sandy are playing a game. Tell the students that they will play the same game.

On the board write the following:

With a student in mind, read aloud the sentence as you fill in the missing information. Have the class guess who the student is.

Next tell the students to copy the open-ended sentence on separate piece of paper and then to think about a classmate and complete the sentence with information about that student.

Have the students play the game with a partner. Go around the room and check their work.

Next have different students stand up and play the game with the class. Have them read aloud the sentences they used with partners and prompt the class to guess.

10 Review

STUDENT BOOK PAGES 76-77

What are you wearing today?

Read the question aloud and then write three sentences on the board about what you are wearing today.

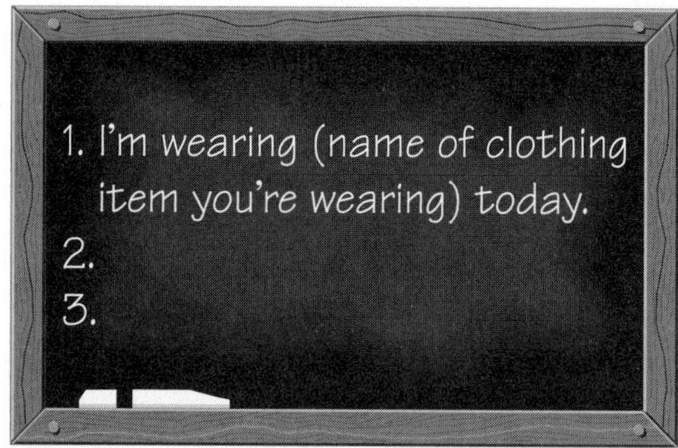

1. I'm wearing (name of clothing item you're wearing) today.
2.
3.

Tell the students to follow your model and write their own sentences.

Next have them read their sentences with a partner. Go around the room and check their sentences.

Finally, call on different students to write their sentences on the board.

Learning Log

Write five words you remember.

Review the purpose of a learning log.

Tell the students to try to fill in the log without looking back in their books for words. Then have them compare answers with a partner.

Finally copy the Learning Log on the board. Call several students to the board and have them write one word in each column of the log. Check their work.

SAMPLE ANSWERS:

Colors	Clothing	Money
purple	a dress	a penny
yellow	pants	five cents
blue	a shirt	a dime
green	shoes	a quarter
red	a skirt	ten dollars

√ Check what you can do.

Tell the students to complete the checklist. Go around the room and check their work.

Finally, call on different students to read aloud the items they checked and what they filled in for item No. 5.

1. I can ask for help in a store. _____

2. I can name colors and sizes. _____

3. I can say what I'm wearing. _____

4. I can write a check. _____

5. I can ____________________. _____

Looking Back

Look at page 66. Now write three more words in your Learning Log.

Have the students look at the illustration on page 66 and add three words to their Learning Logs. Then have them compare their additions with a partner.

Finally, call on different students to read aloud the headings and the words they added.

4-6 Grammar Spotlight for Units 4-6

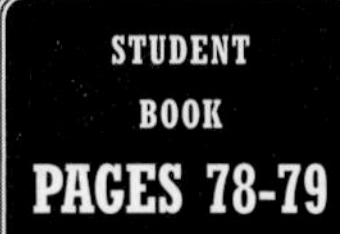

Singular and Plural Nouns

Copy the chart on the board.

	Singular	Plural
Most nouns	a coat a room	two coat**s** four room**s**
Nouns that end in-ch, -sh, -s, or -x	a watch a dress	12 watc**hes** 200 dress**es**

Review singular and plural with the students by holding up one finger and saying "singular, one coat / a coat." Then hold up two fingers, then three fingers as you say: "plural, two coats/three coats."

Next go over the chart with the students. Explain the rule for formation of plurals: add -s to most nouns and –es to nouns that end in -ch, -sh, -s, or –x. Ask the students for other examples (class, brush, six).

Circle the plural nouns.

Point out the circled answer and tell the students to circle only plural nouns. Go around the room and check their work. Then have the students compare answers with a partner.

Finally, call on a student to write the circled items on the board.

ANSWERS:

chairs

books

dresses

coats

watches

rooms

bedrooms

bathrooms

A/an

Copy the chart on the board.

Paul lives in **a** house.	Use **a** for one noun.
Maria lives in **an** apartment.	Use **an** before ***a, e, i, o, u.***

Go over the chart with the students. Read the contents aloud as they follow along in their books. Then answer any questions students may have about the use of *a/an*.

Write *a* or *an*.

Point out the sample item and read the sentence aloud. Tell the students to read over the paragraph and then write "a" or "an" in the blanks. Have them compare their work with a partner.

Finally, ask a student to write the paragraph on the board. Then read aloud the completed paragraph as the students follow along in their books.

ANSWERS:

a, an, a, a, an, an

4-6 Grammar Spotlight for Units 4-6

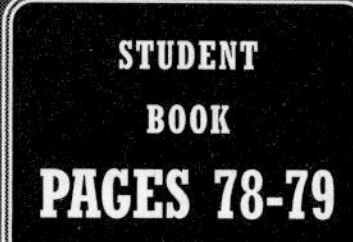

C Simple Present Tense

Copy the charts on the board and read the sentences aloud.

I	**read** books.
You	**speak** English.
We	**eat** breakfast.
They	**work** every day.

He	**reads** books.
She	**speaks** English.
It	**eats** breakfast.

Explain that we use the simple present tense to talk about things we do every day, once a week, once a month. Answer any questions students may have about the formation of the simple present tense.

Write.

Point out the sample answer and read the completed sentence aloud. Have the students complete the activity and compare their answers with a partner.

Have the pairs take turns reading their answers aloud. Check their work.

Finally, call on a student to write the answers on the board and read them aloud.

ANSWERS:

1. read
2. works
3. play
4. eats
5. cook
6. talks
7. need
8. sleep
9. speak
10. lives

4-6 Review for Units 4-6

Match.

Point out the sample item and read aloud the question and answer. Explain to the students that they will match questions with the appropriate answers.

Then have the students complete the activity. Go around the room and check their work.

Have the students compare their work with a partner. Then call on a pair to read the questions and the corresponding answers aloud so that the class can check their work.

Have a student write the answers on the board.

ANSWERS:

1. c

2. e

3. d

4. a

5. f

6. b

What does Carlos need?

Talk with a partner. Draw the furniture Carlos needs.

Have the class brainstorm words for furniture items as you write them on the board.

Have the students examine the illustration as you read the directions aloud. Then, draw a sample piece of furniture on the board that Carlos probably needs—for example, a sofa.

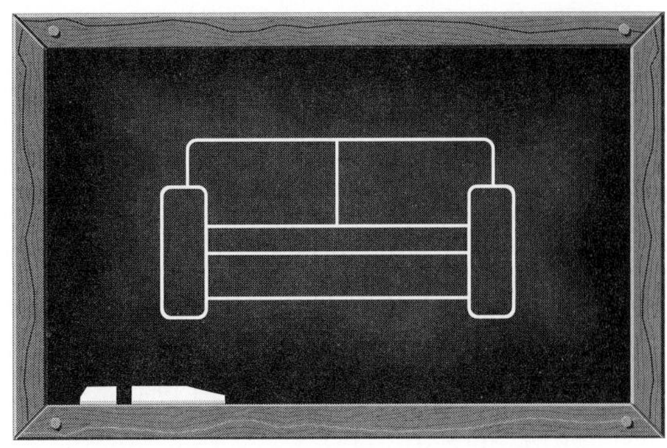

Then tell the students to work in pairs and to draw the furniture Carlos needs in the different rooms in the drawing.

Go around the room and check the pairs' work. Then ask different pairs to draw their answers on the board and to say the names of the furniture.

C Write three sentences about Carlos's new furniture on page 80.

On the board write "There is a _____ in the _____." Then point out the sample answer in the book. Tell the students to write sentences about Carlos's new furniture. Remind them to use their drawings for information.

Go around the room and check the students' work. Then have them work in pairs to share and compare sentences.

Finally, call on different students to write their sentences on the board.

SAMPLE ANSWERS:

1. There is a desk in the bedroom.

2. There are chairs in the living room.

4-6 Review for Units 4-6

STUDENT BOOK PAGES 80-81

D Community Challenge

Read.

Read the two sentences aloud and then point out the different features of the check-out page. Next have the students read through the information. Then read it aloud as the students follow along in their books. Answer any questions students may have about the information, its purpose and place on the check-out page, and so on.

√ Check *True* or *False*.

Demonstrate the difference between *True* and *False* by making a true statement about your clothes and then writing the word *True* on the board. Then make an obviously false statement about your clothes and write the word *False* on the board as you say the word.

> **Teacher:**
> **My shirt is (false color) False.**

Point out the sample answer in the exercise. Indicate the information in the check-out page that makes the sentence true.

Tell the students to use the check-out page to do the exercise.

Have the students complete the exercise and then compare answers with a partner. Go around the room and check their work.

Finally, call on different students to read the statements aloud and say the answers as you write them on the board.

ANSWERS:

1. T

2. T

3. F

4. F

5. T

EXPANSION ACTIVITY: Correct the false statements.

Write a false statement about your clothes on the board.

Cross out the false sentence and write a true sentence about your clothes on the board.

Have the students work in pairs to correct the false statements from Exercise 2.

Have the pairs compare their work with other pairs. Then call on a pair to write the corrected statements on the board.

ANSWERS:

1. She needs a small sweater.
2. The shirts are medium.

Unit 7 I'm so hungry!

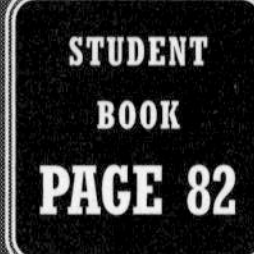

UNIT OVERVIEW

	LESSON:	LEARNING POINTS:	SB#
1.	**We need eggs.**	Talking about what food you need	**p. 83**
2.	**Do we need cake?**	Asking what food you need	**p. 84**
3.	**I'm looking for apples.**	Categorizing and asking for food in a supermarket	**p. 85**
4.	**Breakfast, lunch, and dinner**	Talking about breakfast, lunch, and dinner	**p. 86**
5.	**Let's have lunch.**	Talking about breakfast, lunch, and dinner	**p. 87**
6.	**I'll have a tuna sandwich, please.**	Ordering food in a restaurant	**p. 88**
7.	**Do you have eggs for lunch?**	Asking what people have for different meals	**p. 89**
8.	**Containers**	Identifying and using words for food containers	**p. 90**
9.	**A potluck dinner**	Talking about a potluck dinner	**p. 91**
10.	**Review**	Review Unit 7	**p. 92**

Suggestions for Unit Opener (Student Book page 82)

Brainstorm. Have students look at the unit-opening illustration. Ask them for words related to food that they already know. Write the words on the board as students say them.

Model the language. Begin by reading the caption aloud —"What food do you see?" Point to the food items in the illustration and name them. Write the words on the board.

Model the language again. This time have the class repeat the words after you. Then go around the room and have individual students repeat different words.

Point and say. Point to the words you've written on the board as you say them. Have the students repeat them after you.

Initiate pair work. Have the students work in pairs. Tell them to take turns pointing to the different people and food items in the illustration and naming them. Demonstrate this by asking a student to point to someone or something and by saying the name yourself, then pointing yourself and asking the same student to say the name. Go around the room and check students' work.

See Color Transparencies package for additional unit-opening activity. Many of these tasks include a reproducible blackline master.

1 We need eggs.

STUDENT BOOK PAGE 83

LEARNING POINT
Talking about what food you need

NEW LANGUAGE
apples
carrots
eggs
ice cream
milk
potatoes

We need _____.
That's right. We need _____ , too.

A Listen.

Have the students open their books and examine the illustrations. Have the students listen with their books closed.

1. Eggs. We need eggs.
2. Ice cream. We need ice cream.
3. Carrots. We need carrots.
4. Apples. We need apples.
5. Potatoes. We need potatoes.
6. Milk. We need milk.

Then have them open their books, look at the illustrations, and listen again as they follow along.

Listen and say.

Have the class listen to and repeat each word separately. Stop the tape or CD after each word or read aloud the separate words with pauses.

1. eggs
2. ice cream
3. carrots
4. apples
5. potatoes
6. milk

Then call on individual students to listen and repeat after you.

B Listen.

Have the students listen with their books closed.

Carlos: We need eggs.

Antonio: That's right. We need apples, too.

Have the students listen again as they follow along with their books open.

Listen and say.

Repeat the procedure from the previous **Listen and say.**

C Talk with a partner.

Copy the open-ended conversation on the board. Pick a student to model the open-ended conversation with you in front of the class.

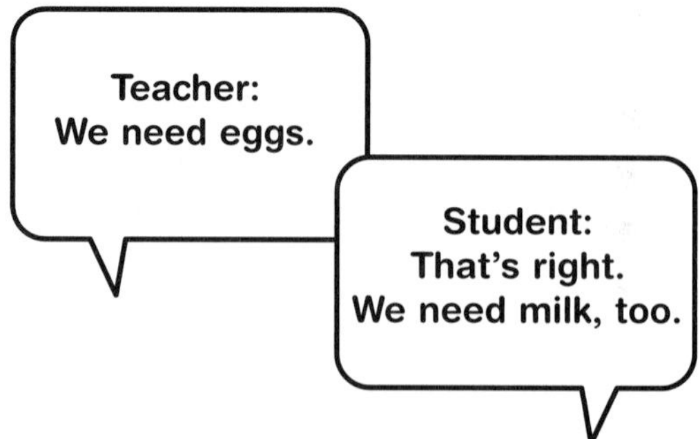
Teacher:
We need eggs.
Student:
That's right.
We need milk, too.

Have the students work in pairs to practice the conversation. Tell them to use the words in the Word List.

Go around the room and check their work.

Finally, call on different pairs to act out the exchange for the class.

Do we need cake?

LEARNING POINT
Asking what food you need

NEW LANGUAGE

beef	cheese
bread	chicken
butter	oranges
cake	

Do we need _____?
Yes, we do./No, we don't.

Listen.

Have the students open their books and examine the illustrations.

Have the students listen with their books closed.

1. Cake. Do we need cake?

2. Bread. Do we need bread?

3. Beef. Do we need beef?

4. Chicken. Do we need chicken?

5. Oranges. Do we need oranges?

6. Butter. Do we need butter?

7. Cheese. Do we need cheese?

Then have them open their books, look at the illustrations, and listen again as they follow along.

Listen and say.

Have the students listen to and repeat each word separately. Stop the tape or CD after each word or read aloud the separate words with pauses.

1. cake

2. bread

3. beef

4. chicken

5. oranges

6. butter

7. cheese

Then call on individual students to listen and repeat after you.

Listen.

Repeat the procedure from the previous **Listen.**

Grace: Do we need butter?

Ben: Yes, we do.

Grace: Do we need oranges?

Ben: No, we don't.

Listen and say.

Repeat the procedure from the previous **Listen and say.**

Talk with a partner.

Copy the open-ended conversation on the board. Pick a student to model the open-ended conversation with you in front of the class. Point to the refrigerator in Activity B as you ask the question.

WORKBOOK PAGE 61

2 Do we need cake?

STUDENT BOOK PAGE 84

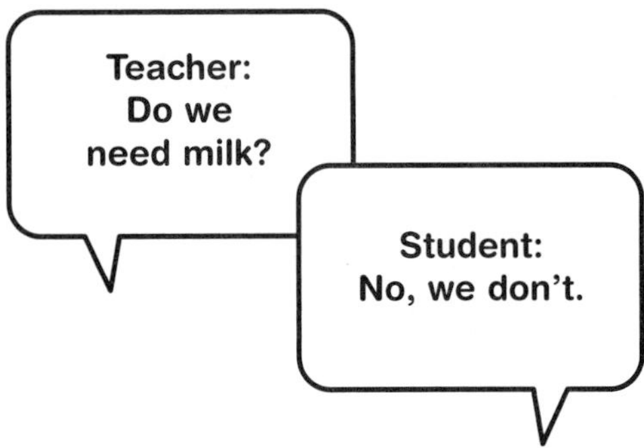
Teacher:
Do we
need milk?
Student:
No, we don't.

Have the students work in pairs to practice the conversation. Tell them to use the illustration in Activity B and the words in the Word List. Go around the room and check their work.

Finally, call on different pairs to share their conversations with the class.

EXPANSION ACTIVITY: Draw and Guess Game

Divide the class into two teams—Team A and Team B.

On small slips of paper, write down words for food items. For a list of words, see the New Language lists for Lessons 1 and 2.

Put the slips of paper into a bowl. Demonstrate how to play the game by choosing a slip and drawing the item on the board. Prompt the class to guess what you're drawing.

Have a student from Team A choose a slip and draw the item on the board. Explain that the other members of Team A have to guess what their teammate is drawing, and that Team B must not guess. Tell Team A that they have one minute to draw and guess as many items as they can. Then give Team B a turn. Keep track of the number of items each team guesses correctly.

Keep playing until all the slips are used. The team that has guessed more words correctly wins.

3 I'm looking for apples.

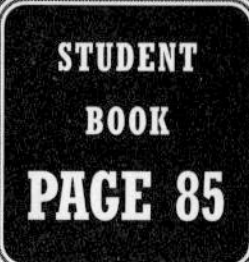

LEARNING POINT
Categorizing and asking for food in a supermarket

NEW LANGUAGE
aisle
bakery
dairy
fruits and vegetables
meat

Excuse me. I'm looking for _____.
Let's see. Aisle _____.

Listen.

Have the students open their books and examine the illustration.

Have the students listen with their books closed.

Grace: Excuse me. I'm looking for apples.

Clerk: Let's see. Aisle 1.

Then have them open their books, look at the illustration, and listen again as they follow along.

Listen and say.

Have the students listen to and repeat each line of the conversation separately. Stop the tape or CD after each line or read aloud the separate lines with pauses.

Then call on individual students to listen and repeat after you.

Listen and complete the chart.

Have the students listen with their books closed.

1. Apples are in Aisle 1.

2. Beef is in Aisle 2.

3. Chicken is in Aisle 2.

4. Cheese is in Aisle 4.

5. Cake is in Aisle 3.

6. Oranges are in Aisle 1.

7. Milk is in Aisle 4.

Have the students open their books. Help them understand the new vocabulary words—fruits, vegetables, dairy, meat, and bakery—by writing them on the board, saying the words, and pointing the items out in the illustration on page 82.

Play or say the first sentence as you point to the first column in the chart in your book. Tell students to listen carefully for aisle numbers.

Then have the students listen again and complete the activity. Stop the tape or CD, or pause after each sentence, so students have time to check the appropriate column.

Have the students compare their answers with a partner. Then have them listen again to check their work.

Finally, call on a pair of students to copy the chart on the board and fill in the check marks.

I'm looking for apples.

STUDENT BOOK PAGE 85

ANSWERS:

1. Aisle 1

2. Aisle 2

3. Aisle 2

4. Aisle 4

5. Aisle 3

6. Aisle 1

7. Aisle 4

Talk with a partner. Use the chart.

Copy the open-ended conversation on the board. Pick a student to model the open-ended conversation with you in front of the class.

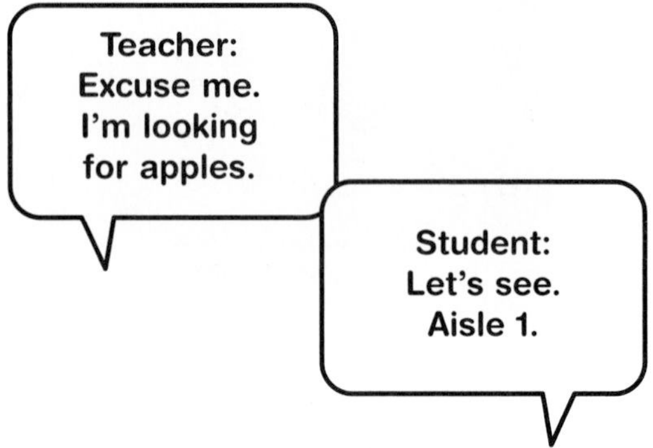
Teacher: Excuse me. I'm looking for apples.
Student: Let's see. Aisle 1.

Have the students work in pairs to practice the conversation. Go around the room and check their work.

Finally, call on different pairs to share their conversations with the class.

 WORKBOOK PAGE 61

4 Breakfast, lunch, and dinner

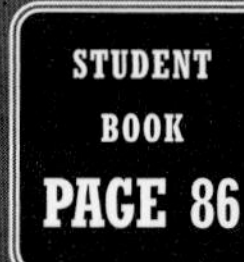

LEARNING POINT
Talking about breakfast, lunch, and dinner

NEW LANGUAGE
breakfast
lunch
dinner
sometimes
usually

What do you have for breakfast?
I usually have _____. Sometimes I have _____.

A Listen.

Have the students open their books and examine the illustrations.

Have the students listen with their books closed.

1. Breakfast. At seven o'clock, I eat breakfast.

2. Lunch. At twelve-thirty, I eat at lunch.

3. Dinner. At six forty-five, I eat dinner.

Then have them open their books, look at the illustrations, and listen again as they follow along.

Listen and say.

Have the students listen to and repeat each word separately. Stop the tape or CD after each word or read aloud the separate words with pauses.

1. breakfast

2. lunch

3. dinner

Then call on individual students to listen and repeat after you.

Listen.

Repeat the procedure from the previous **Listen.**

Leo: What do you have for breakfast?

Sandy: I usually have bread and cheese. Sometimes I have eggs.

Explain that "usually" means more than half of the time and point out the number of times Sandy has bread and cheese for breakfast. Explain that "sometimes" means less than half of the time, and point out the number of times Sandy has eggs for breakfast.

Listen and say.

Repeat the procedure from the previous **Listen and say.**

Talk with a partner.

Copy the open-ended conversation on the board. Pick a student to model the open-ended conversation with you in front of the class.

Teacher: What do you have for breakfast?
Student: I usually have (food item). Sometimes I have (food item).

Have the students work in pairs to practice the conversation. Go around the room and check their work.

Finally, call on different pairs to share their conversations with the class.

4 Breakfast, lunch, and dinner

EXPANSION ACTIVITY: What's for breakfast?

At the top of the board, write BREAKFAST. Have the students work in groups to write the names of food items that people eat for breakfast. Remind them that not everyone eats the same things for breakfast.

Call on different students to copy their lists on the board.

5 Let's have lunch.

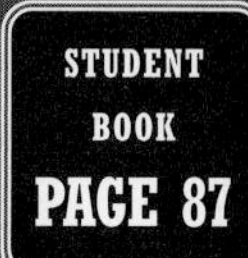
STUDENT
BOOK
PAGE 87

LEARNING POINT
Talking about breakfast, lunch, and dinner

NEW LANGUAGE
It's _____. I'm so hungry!
Me, too. Let's have _____.

Listen.

Have the students open their books and examine the illustration. Have the students listen with their books closed. Use gestures and related body language to help students understand the sentence "I'm so hungry!"

Don: It's 12:30. I'm so hungry!

Paul: Me, too. Let's have lunch.

Then have them open their books, look at the illustrations, and listen again as they follow along.

Listen and say.

Have the students listen to and repeat each line of the conversation separately. Stop the tape or CD after each line or read aloud the separate lines with pauses.

Then call on individual students to listen and repeat after you.

Talk with a partner.

Copy the open-ended conversation on the board. Pick a student to model the open-ended conversation with you in front of the class.

Teacher:
It's 8:00.
I'm so hungry!
Student:
Me too. Let's
have breakfast.

Have the students work in pairs to practice the conversation. Tell them to use the words in the Word List. Go around the room and check their work.

Finally, call on different pairs to share their conversations with the class.

Complete.

Copy the sentences and blanks on the board.

Then read the sentences aloud as you fill in the blanks with personal information.

I usually have breakfast at ______.
Then I have lunch at ________. I go
home and have dinner at ________.
I usually have ________ for dinner.
(food)

Have the students write their own information in the blanks in their books. Then have them work in groups of three or four to take turns reading their sentences to each other.

Finally, call on volunteers to read their sentences to the class.

SAMPLE ANSWERS:

I usually have breakfast at 6:30. Then I have lunch at 12:30. I go home and have dinner at 6:00. I usually have chicken for dinner.

6 I'll have a tuna sandwich, please.

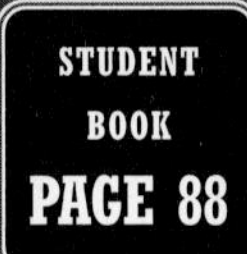

LEARNING POINT
Ordering food in a restaurant

NEW LANGUAGE

cherry pie	soda
coffee	tea
hamburger	tuna sandwich
pizza	

May I help you?
Yes. I'll have _____, please.
Anythinng else?
Yes. I'll have _____, too.

 **Listen.**

Have the students open their books and examine the illustration.

Have the students listen with their books closed.

pizza
tuna sandwich
hamburger
cherry pie
coffee
tea
soda

Then have them open their books, look at the illustration, and listen again as they follow along.

Listen and say.

Have the students listen to and repeat each word of the conversation separately. Stop the tape or CD after each word or read aloud the separate words with pauses.

Then call on individual students to listen and repeat after you.

 **Listen.**

Have the students listen with their books closed. Use gestures, body language, and words the students already know to help them understand unfamiliar language such as "May I help you?" and "Anything else?"

Server: May I help you?
Paul: Yes. I'll have a tuna sandwich, please.
Server: Anything else?
Paul: Yes. I'll have a coffee, too.

Have the students listen again as they follow along with their books open.

Listen and say.

Repeat the procedure from the previous **Listen and say**.

 **Talk with a partner.**

Copy the open-ended conversation on the board. Pick a student to model the open-ended conversation with you in front of the class.

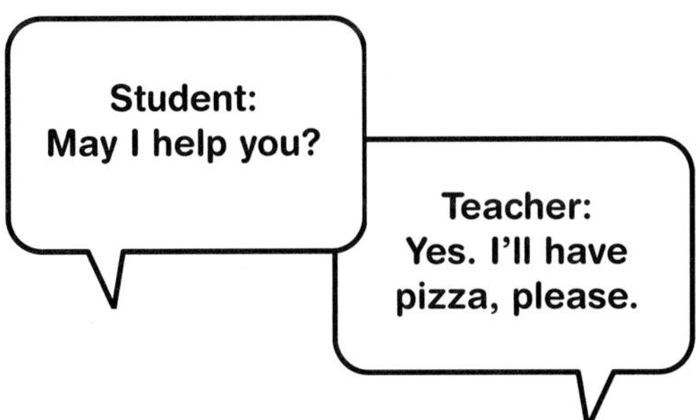

Student:
May I help you?
Teacher:
Yes. I'll have pizza, please.

6 I'll have a tuna sandwich, please.

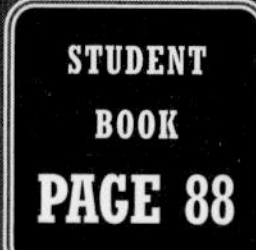

Have the students work in pairs to practice the conversation. Tell them to use the words in the Word List. Go around the room and check their work.

Finally, call on different pairs to share their conversations with the class.

EXPANSION ACTIVITY: What's for lunch?

At the top of the board, write LUNCH. Have the students work in groups to write the names of food items that people eat for lunch. Remind them that not everyone eats the same things for lunch.

Call on different students to copy their lists on the board.

7 Do you have eggs for lunch?

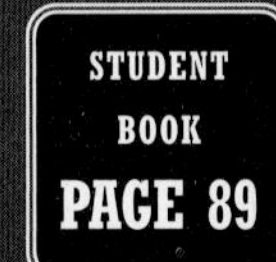

LEARNING POINT
Asking what people have for different meals

NEW LANGUAGE
Do you have _____ for _____?
I have _____ for _____.
I sometimes have _____ for _____.

Listen.

Have the students listen with their books closed.

Leo: Do you have eggs for lunch?

Grace: Yes, I do.

Paul: No, I don't.

Have the students listen again as they follow along with their books open.

Listen and say.

Have the students listen to and repeat each line of the conversation separately. Stop the tape or CD after each line or read aloud the separate lines with pauses.

Then call on individual students to listen and repeat after you.

Talk with four classmates.

Copy the open-ended conversation on the board. Pick a student to model the open-ended conversation with you in front of the class.

Teacher:
Do you have coffee for breakfast?
Student: Yes, I do./Sometimes/ No, I don't.

Have the students work in pairs to practice the conversation. Tell them to use the words in the Word List. Go around the room and check their work.

Finally, call on different pairs to share their conversations with the class.

C Write three questions.

Write the open-ended questions on the board. Then read them aloud as you fill in the blanks.

Have the students write their own questions. Go around the room and check their work.

SAMPLE ANSWERS:

1. Do you have eggs for breakfast?

2. Do you have hamburgers for lunch?

3. Do you have pizza for dinner?

Ask a classmate your questions.

Ask a student one of the questions you wrote on the board.

Teacher: Do you have (food item) for breakfast?

Tell the students to follow your model and interview a classmate. Go around the room and check their work.

Write.

Copy the first item on the board and fill in the blank with your own information.

Have the students complete the activity.

Go around the room and check their work.

Finally, call on different students to read aloud their completed sentences.

EXPANSION ACTIVITY: What's for dinner?

At the top of the board, write DINNER. Have the students work in groups to write the names of food items that people eat for dinner. Remind them that not everyone eats the same things for dinner.

Call on different students to copy their lists on the board.

8 Containers

LEARNING POINT
Identifying and using words for food containers

NEW LANGUAGE

bag	can
bottle	jar
box	package
bunch	

A Listen.

Have the students open their books and examine the illustrations.

Have the students listen with their books closed.

1. A bottle. This is a bottle of oil.

2. A can. This is a can of tomato soup.

3. A bag. This is a bag of rice.

4. A package. This is a package of sugar.

5. A box. This is a box of cereal.

6. A bunch. This is a bunch of grapes.

7. A jar. This is a jar of peanut butter.

Then have them open their books, look at the illustrations, and listen again as they follow along.

Listen and say.

Have the students listen to and repeat each word separately. Stop the tape or CD after each word or read aloud the separate words with pauses.

1. a bottle

2. a can

3. a bag

4. a package

5. a box

6. a bunch

7. a jar

Then call on individual students to listen and repeat after you.

B Listen and circle.

Have the students listen with their books closed.

1. I need a bunch of grapes.

2. We need a bag of rice.

3. Do we need a can of soup?

4. They need a package of sugar.

5. She needs a box of cereal.

6. Paul needs a bottle of oil.

Copy the first item on the board. Play or say the first sentence. Tell the students to listen for container words. Circle "a bunch."

Then have the students listen again and complete the activity. Stop the tape or CD, or pause after each sentence, so students have time to circle the appropriate choice.

Have the students compare their answers with a partner. Then have them listen again as they check their work.

Finally, call on individual students to read aloud the items they circled.

ANSWERS:

1. bunch	**4.** package
2. bag	**5.** box
3. can	**6.** bottle

8 Containers

STUDENT BOOK PAGE 90

Play *What Do We Need?*

Have the students examine the illustration.

Demonstrate how to play the game with a small group of students. Point to a food item in the shopping cart in the book and say a complete sentence. Then prompt another student to add to the sentence, and so on.

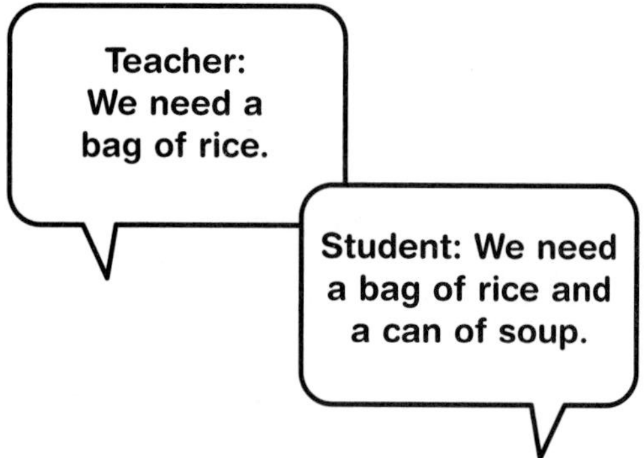

Teacher: We need a bag of rice.
Student: We need a bag of rice and a can of soup.

Divide the class into groups of four or five students. Have the groups play the game. Go around the room and check their work.

Finally, call on different groups to play the game in front of the class.

EXPANSION ACTIVITY: Match the cards.

This game requires the use of index cards. On seven of the cards, write down types of containers ("a bottle," "a can," "a bag,"...). On seven other cards, write down words for food items that belong in the containers ("oil," "soup," "rice,"...). For a list of container and food words, see the illustration in Activity A. If you have more than 14 students, prepare more cards, repeating some of the container and food words.

Give each student a card. Tell the students to walk around the classroom to find the person or people with the card that matches theirs. For example, the card with "a bottle" written on it matches the card with "oil" written on it.

 WORKBOOK PAGE 65

9 A potluck dinner

STUDENT BOOK PAGE 91

LEARNING POINT
Talking about a potluck dinner

NEW LANGUAGE

bring
different
fun
interesting
make
potluck dinner
special

A Listen and read.

Have the students read the paragraph. Then have them listen as they read a long.

A Potluck Dinner

Once a month Sandy's class has a potluck dinner. The students bring different foods. They bring fruits, vegetables, meat, drinks, or desserts. Sandy's students make special foods from their countries. The potluck dinners are fun, and the food is interesting.

Have the students listen again as they follow along.

B √ Check *True* or *False*.

Review the meaning of true and false with the students. Then point out the sample item. Explain that it is false because Sandy's class has a potluck dinner once a month, not once a week.

Have the students complete the exercise.

Finally, have the students compare answers with a partner as you go around the room and check their work. Then have a student write the answers on the board.

ANSWERS:

1. False

2. False

3. True

4. True

5. False

C Write.

Tell the class what you would make for a potluck.

Have the students write down the food that they would bring to a potluck.

Go around the room and check their work.

Finally, call on individual students to read aloud the items they wrote down.

9 A potluck dinner

EXPANSION ACTIVITY: A Potluck Dinner

Have a potluck dinner in your class. Write a list of words from this unit on the board that students will need to talk about the different dishes. See the New Language boxes for each lesson in this unit for relevant words.

Have the students describe for the class or for members of a group what they will bring to class for the potluck.

At the actual potluck, write the following open-ended sentences on the board and have the students use them to describe their dishes.

This is (name of the dish).
It's from (name of the student's country).
It is made of (names of the ingredients).

10 Review

STUDENT BOOK PAGES 92-93

Listen and √ check the food Maria needs to buy.

Have the students listen with their books closed.

1. I need to buy chicken.

2. I need milk for breakfast.

3. I need apples for lunch.

4. I need oranges, too.

5. I need cheese.

Have the students open their books. Read the directions aloud and explain to the class that Maria is talking about food she needs to buy. Tell the students to listen carefully for the different food words. Point out the checklist and read the words aloud.

Copy the first item on the board. Play or say the first sentence. Write a check next to "chicken."

Then have the students listen again and complete the activity. Stop the tape or CD, or pause after each sentence, so students have time to check the appropriate response.

Have the students compare their answers with a partner. Have them listen again to check their work.

Finally, ask a student to write the items on the board and check √ the answers.

ANSWERS:

1. chicken

2. milk

3. apples

4. oranges

5. cheese

B Listen and circle the answer.

Have the students listen with their books closed.

1. Where's the bread?

2. What do you usually have for breakfast?

3. Excuse me. Where are the oranges?

4. What do we need?

5. May I help you?

6. Anything else?

Copy the first line on the board. Play or say the first item. Circle "Let's see. Aisle 2."

Then have the students listen again and complete the activity. Stop the tape or CD, or pause after each question, so students have time to circle the appropriate response.

Have the students compare their answers with a partner. Then have them listen again as they check their work.

Finally, call on individual students to read aloud the items they circled.

ANSWERS:

1. Let's see. Aisle 2.

2. Cereal, juice, and fruit.

3. Oranges are in Aisle 5.

4. A bottle of oil.

5. Yes, I'll have a hamburger.

6. Yes, I'll have a coffee.

Review

STUDENT BOOK PAGES 92-93

Ask three classmates.

Copy the chart on the board and interview a student as you fill in his or her information.

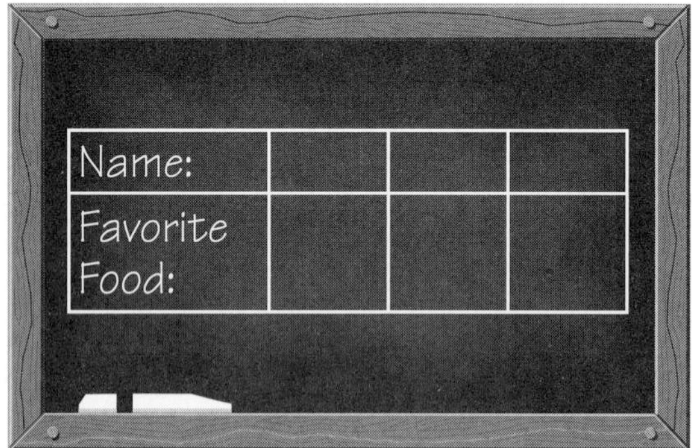

Have the students follow your model and ask three classmates, "What is your favorite food?"

Finally, call on different students to copy their charts on the board.

Tell a partner what food you need.

Point out the illustration and tell the students to talk about what they need based on what they see in the illustration. To help them get started, point out the coffee jar and say: "I don't need coffee." Then point to the sugar container and say: "I need sugar."Have the students work with a partner to talk about what food they need.

ANSWERS:

sugar

tea

bread

oil

Write.

Copy the first sentence on the board and complete it with your own information. Then have the students complete the activity.

Have them read their sentences with a partner.

Finally, call on different students to share their sentences with the class.

Learning Log

Write five words you remember.

Review the purpose of a learning log.

Tell the students to try to fill in the log without looking back in their books for words. Then have them compare answers with a partner.

Copy the Learning Log on the board. Call several students to the board and have them write one word in each column of the log. Check their work.

SAMPLE ANSWERS:

Food	Meals	Containers
apples	lunch	a bag
oranges	dinner	a can
eggs	breakfast	a box
hamburger		a jar
rice		a package

10 Review

STUDENT BOOK PAGES 92-93

√ Check what you can do.

Tell the students to complete the checklist. Go around the room and check their work.

Finally, call on different students to read aloud the items they checked and what they filled in for item No. 5.

1. I can name foods. _____

2. I can talk about containers. _____

3. I can ask for help in a supermarket. _____

4. I can order food. _____

5. I can ____________________. _____

Looking Back

What food do you see on page 82? Now write three more words in your Learning Log.

Have the students look at the illustration on page 82 and add three words to their Learning Logs. Then have them compare their additions with a partner.

Finally, call on different students to read aloud the headings and the words they added.

See Color Transparencies package for unit wrap-up activity. This task can be used as an oral assessment tool. Many unit wrap-up activities include a reproducible blackline master.

Unit 8 How's the weather?

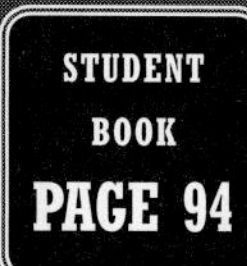

UNIT OVERVIEW

	LESSON:	LEARNING POINTS:	SB#
1.	**It's rainy.**	Talking about the weather	**p. 95**
2.	**It's hot!**	Identifying different kinds of weather	**p. 96**
3.	**What's your favorite season?**	Talking about the seasons	**p. 97**
4.	**I'm playing soccer.**	Talking about what people are doing	**p. 98**
5.	**What's Grace doing?**	Talking about what people are doing	**p. 99**
6.	**What do you like doing in the spring?**	Talking about what you like to do in different seasons	**p. 100**
7.	**It's hot and cloudy.**	Talking and writing about the weather	**p. 101**
8.	**What's the temperature?**	Talking and writing about temperatures	**p. 102**
9.	**A weather map**	Reading a weather map	**p. 103**
10.	**Review**	Review Unit 8	**p. 104**

Suggestions for Unit Opener (Student Book page 94)

Brainstorm. Have students look at the unit-opening illustration. Ask them for words related to the weather that they already know. Write the words on the board as students say them.

Model the language. Begin by reading the caption aloud—"Where is Tien? Where is Carlos?" Point to the two scenes and describe the weather. Write the words on the board.

Model the language again. This time have the class repeat the words after you. Then go around the room and have individual students repeat different words.

Point and say. Point to the words you've written on the board as you say them. Have the students repeat them after you.

Initiate pair work. Have the students work in pairs. Tell them to take turns pointing to the different people, sites, and situations in the illustration and naming them. Demonstrate this by asking a student to point and by saying the name yourself, then pointing yourself and asking the same student to say the name. Go around the room and check students' work.

See Color Transparencies package for additional unit-opening activity. Many of these tasks include a reproducible blackline master.

1 It's rainy.

STUDENT BOOK PAGE 95

LEARNING POINT
Talking about the weather

NEW LANGUAGE

cold	snowy
hot	sunny
rainy	windy

How's the weather?
It's _____.

A Listen.

Have the students open their books and examine the illustrations.

Have the students listen with their books closed.

1. Sunny. It's sunny.

2. Snowy. It's snowy.

3. Hot. It's hot.

4. Cold. It's cold.

5. Windy. It's windy.

6. Rainy. It's rainy.

Then have them open their books, look at the illustrations, and listen again as they follow along.

Listen and say.

Have the class listen to and repeat each sentence separately. Stop the tape or CD after each line or read aloud the separate lines with pauses.

1. It's sunny.

2. It's snowy.

3. It's hot.

4. It's cold.

5. It's windy.

6. It's rainy.

Then call on individual students to listen and repeat after you.

EXPANSION ACTIVITY: Guess the weather.

Write "It's _____." and the weather words from the New Language list on the board. Tell the class that you are going to act out reactions to weather and they are going to guess the weather.

Use gestures, realia, and mime to pretend to react to different kinds of weather as you have the class guess the weather. For example, pretend to be sweating and thirsty from the heat as you prompt the class to say: "It's hot." For "It's rainy," you can draw raindrops on the board and open an imaginary umbrella.

Next have the students work in pairs to take turns miming and guessing the weather.

Finally, have different students mime for the entire class.

B Listen.

Have the students listen with their books closed.

Tien: How's the weather?

Carlos: It's sunny.

Have the students listen again as they follow along with their books open.

Listen and say.

Repeat the procedure from the previous **Listen and say.**

1 It's rainy.

Talk with a partner about the pictures in Activity A.

Copy the open-ended conversation on the board. Pick a student to model the open-ended conversation with you in front of the class. Point to item 1 in Activity A.

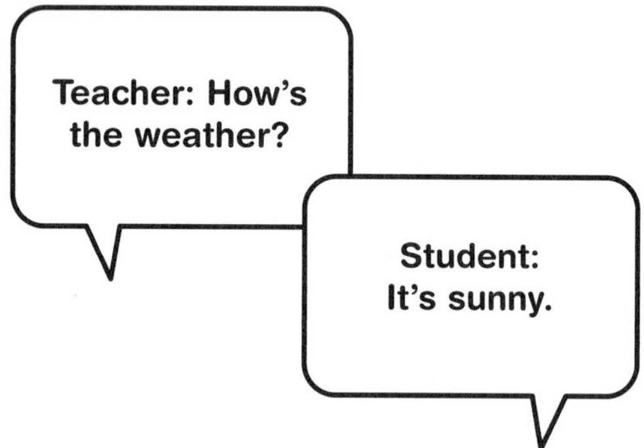

Teacher: How's the weather?
Student: It's sunny.

Have the students work in pairs to practice the conversation. Go around the room and check their work.

Finally, call on different pairs to share their conversations with the class.

2 It's hot!

STUDENT BOOK PAGE 96

LEARNING POINT
Identifying different kinds of weather

NEW LANGUAGE
Language from Lesson 1

Listen and circle.

Have the students open their books and examine the illustrations.

Have the students listen with their books closed.

1. It's rainy.

2. It's hot.

3. It's cold.

4. It's windy.

Point to the first item in your book. Play or say the first sentence. Point to the illustration on the right.

Then have the students listen again and complete the activity. Stop the tape or CD, or pause after each sentence, so students have time to circle the appropriate choice.

Have the students compare their answers with a partner. Then have them listen again as they check their work.

Finally, call on individual students to point to the items they circled.

ANSWERS:

1. illustration on the right

2. illustration on the left

3. illustration on the right

4. illustration on the right

Match.

Have the students examine the illustrations. Point out the sample answer. Then tell the students to match the illustrations to the sentences.

Have them compare answers with a partner. Go around the room and check their work.

Finally, write the answers on the board.

ANSWERS:

1. d

2. f

3. e

4. a

5. c

6. b

EXPANSION ACTIVITY: Draw your favorite kind of weather.

Have the students draw illustrations of their favorite kind of weather. To provide a model, draw a scene on the board showing your favorite weather—for example, draw a sun for "sunny."

2 It's hot!

STUDENT BOOK PAGE 96

Have the students write sentences about their illustrations on the backs of their drawings. Write a sentence under your drawing on the board—for example, write, "It's sunny." Go around the room and check the students' work.

Call on different students to show their drawings to the class. Prompt the class members to guess the sentences. Then have the students read their sentences aloud.

WORKBOOK PAGE 69

3 What's your favorite season?

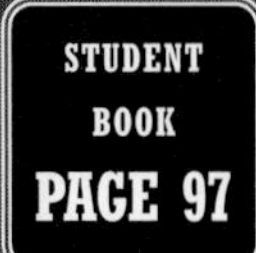

LEARNING POINT
Talking about the seasons

NEW LANGUAGE
winter
spring
summer
fall
season

Listen.

Have the students open their books and examine the illustrations.

Have the students listen with their books closed.

1. Winter. It's winter.

2. Spring. It's spring.

3. Summer. It's summer.

4. Fall. It's fall.

Then have them open their books, look at the illustrations, and listen again as they follow along.

Listen and say.

Have the class listen to and repeat each line of the conversation separately. Stop the tape or CD after each line or read aloud the separate lines with pauses.

1. winter

2. spring

3. summer

4. fall

Then call on individual students to listen and repeat after you.

Complete.

Point out the illustrations and talk about each one. Use language the students are already familiar with. For example, say: "How's the weather? It's cold."

Teacher: How's the weather? It's cold.

Tell the students to complete the activity by writing the appropriate seasons in the blanks.

Have them compare answers with a partner.

Finally, call on a student to write the answers on the board.

ANSWERS:

1. winter

2. summer

Listen.

Have the students listen with their books closed.

Grace: What's your favorite season?

Leo: Winter.

Have the students listen again as they follow along with their books open.

Listen and say.

Repeat the procedure from the previous **Listen and say**. Review the meaning of the word favorite with the students (see Unit 6, Lesson 5).

3 What's your favorite season?

STUDENT BOOK PAGE 97

D Talk with a partner.

Copy the open-ended conversation on the board. Pick a student to model the open-ended conversation with you in front of the class.

Have the students work in pairs to practice the conversation. Go around and the room and check their work.

Finally, call on different pairs to share their conversations with the class.

EXPANSION ACTIVITY: What's your favorite _____?

Write the following open-ended conversation on the board.

Brainstorm with the students different words to fill in the first blank—for example, "food," "movie," "month," "room," "class," "day," etc. Write the words on the board. Then act out a sample conversation with a student. Next have the students work in pairs to have conversations based on the language on the board. Go around the room and check the pairs' work.

Finally, call on different pairs to share conversations with the class.

4 I'm playing soccer.

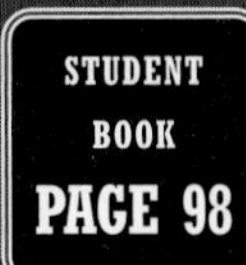
STUDENT BOOK PAGE 98

LEARNING POINT
Talking about what people are doing

NEW LANGUAGE

cooking	reading
dancing	swimming
listening to music	walking
playing soccer	watching TV

What are you doing?
I'm _____.
What about you?

A Listen.

Have the students open their books and examine the illustrations.

Have the students listen with their books closed.

1. Walking. She's walking.
2. Playing soccer. He's playing soccer.
3. Dancing. They're dancing.
4. Reading. She's reading.
5. Swimming. He's swimming.
6. Listening to music. She's listening to music.
7. Cooking. He's cooking.
8. Watching TV. He's watching TV.

Then have them open their books, look at the illustrations, and listen again as they follow along.

Listen and say.

Have the class listen to and repeat each line separately. Stop the tape or CD after each line or read aloud the separate lines with pauses.

1. walking
2. playing soccer
3. dancing
4. reading
5. swimming
6. listening to music
7. cooking
8. watching TV

Then call on individual students to listen and repeat after you.

B Listen.

Have the students listen with their books closed.

Will: What are you doing?
Sandy: I'm working. What about you?
Will: I'm cooking.

Have the students listen again as they follow along with their books open.

Listen and say.

Repeat the procedure from the previous **Listen and say.**

C Talk with a partner.

Copy the open-ended conversation on the board. Pick a student to model the open-ended conversation with you in front of the class.

4 I'm playing soccer.

STUDENT BOOK PAGE 98

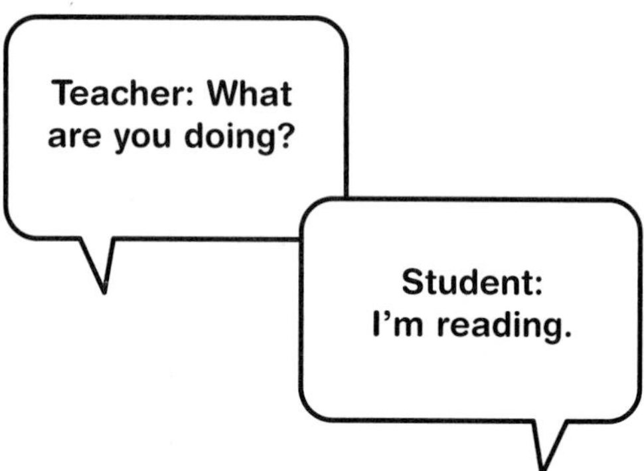

Teacher: What are you doing?
Student: I'm reading.

Have the students work in pairs to practice the conversation. Tell them to use the words in the Word List. Go around the room and check their work.

Finally, call on different pairs to share their conversations with the class.

 WORKBOOK PAGE 71

5 What's Grace doing?

LEARNING POINT
Talking about what people are doing

NEW LANGUAGE
What's _____ doing?
He's/She's _____.

Listen and circle.

Have the students listen with their books closed.

1. He's eating ice cream.

2. She's reading.

3. They're dancing.

4. He's swimming.

Point to the first item in your book. Play or say the first sentence. Point to the illustration on the right.

Then have the students listen again and complete the exercise. Stop the tape or CD, or pause after each sentence, so students have time to circle the appropriate choice.

Have the students compare their answers with a partner. Then have them listen again as they check their work.

Finally, call on individual students to point to the items they circled.

ANSWERS:

1. illustration on the right

2. illustration on the left

3. illustration on the left

4. illustration on the right

Listen.

Have the students listen with their books closed.

Sandy: What's Justin doing?

Will: He's playing basketball.

Have the students listen again as they follow along with their books open.

Listen and say.

Have the students listen to and repeat each line of the conversation separately. Stop the tape or CD after each line or read aloud the separate lines with pauses.

Then call on individual students to listen and repeat after you.

Talk with a partner.

Copy the open-ended conversation on the board. Pick a student to model the open-ended conversation with you in front of the class.

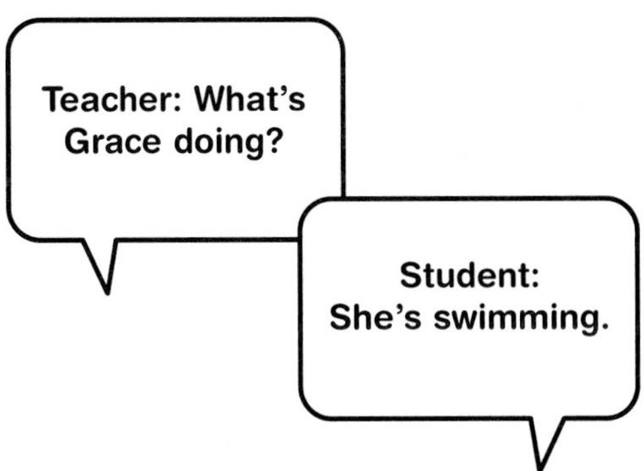

Teacher: What's Grace doing?
Student: She's swimming.

Have the students work in pairs to practice the conversation. Tell them to use the words in the Word List. Go around the room and check their work.

Finally, call on different pairs to share their conversations with the class.

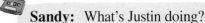

6 What do you like doing in the spring?

STUDENT BOOK PAGE 100

LEARNING POINT
Talking about what you like to do in different seasons

NEW LANGUAGE
What do you like doing in the _____?
I like _____.
What about in the _____?

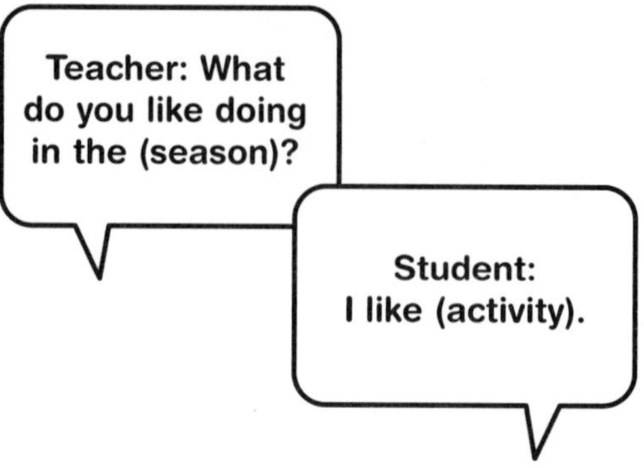

Teacher: What do you like doing in the (season)?
Student: I like (activity).

Listen.

Have the students listen with their books closed.

Isabel: What do you like doing in the spring?

Grace: I like playing soccer.

Isabel: What about in the winter?

Grace: I like listening to music.

Have the students listen again as they follow along with their books open.

Listen and say.

Have the students listen to and repeat each line of the conversation separately. Stop the tape or CD after each line or read aloud the separate lines with pauses.

Then call on individual students to listen and repeat after you.

Talk with a partner.

Copy the open-ended conversation on the board. Pick a student to model the open-ended conversation with you in front of the class.

Have the students work in pairs to practice the conversation. Go around the room and check their work.

Finally, call on different pairs to share their conversations with the class.

Ask four classmates.

Point out the chart and go over the sample entry with the students. Then copy the chart on the board. Invite a student to the board and ask the question. Write the student's name and the activity in the appropriate blanks on the chart.

Have the class follow your model. Tell them to go around the room and fill in all four sets of blanks. Go around and check their work.

Call on different students to copy their charts on the board. Point to different entries in the chart and talk about them: "Grace likes playing soccer in the spring."

 WORKBOOK PAGE 72

7 It's hot and cloudy.

STUDENT BOOK PAGE 101

LEARNING POINT
Talking and writing about the weather

NEW LANGUAGE
It's _____ and _____.

Listen and read.

Have the students open their books, examine the illustrations, and read the sentences.

Have the students listen as they read along.

1. It's summer. It's hot and cloudy.

2. It's fall. It's sunny and cool.

3. It's winter. It's rainy and windy.

Have the students listen again as they follow along.

Write.

Copy the first item on the board. Fill in the blanks with the appropriate words for your climate.

Have the students complete the activity.

Have them compare answers with a partner. Go around the room and check their work.

Finally, call on different students to write the sentences on the board.

8 What's the temperature?

STUDENT BOOK PAGE 102

LEARNING POINT
Talking and writing about temperatures

NEW LANGUAGE
Celsius
cool
degrees
Fahrenheit
temperature

It's _____ ° F.

A Listen and write the numbers.

Have the students open their books and examine the illustrations.

Have the students listen with their books closed.

1. It's very hot. It's 105 degrees Fahrenheit.

2. It's hot. It's 85 degrees Fahrenheit.

3. It's cool. It's 50 degrees Fahrenheit.

4. It's cold. It's 27 degrees Fahrenheit.

Have the students open their books. Play or say the first item and point out the example.

Have the students listen again and complete the activity. Stop the tape or CD, or pause after each line, so students have time to write a number. Go around the room and check their work.

Have the students compare their answers with a partner. Then have them listen again as they check their work.

Finally, call on different students to read aloud the completed sentences as you write the answers on the board.

ANSWERS:

1. 105

2. 85

3. 50

4. 27

 WORKBOOK PAGE 74

9 A weather map

LEARNING POINT
Reading a weather map

NEW LANGUAGE
cloudy
weather map
weather report

This is a weather report for _____.
The temperature is _____° F.
The weather is _____ and _____.

A Read the weather map.

Have the students study the weather map as you talk about it. Read aloud the names of the cities, the labeled icons, and the temperatures. Make sentences about the different places.

Teacher: It's sunny in Dallas.

B Complete the chart.

Point out the sample answer on the chart as you point to Seattle on the map. Then tell the students to use the weather map from the previous activity to complete the chart. Go around the room and check their work.

Next have them compare answers with a partner.

Finally, call on a pair of students to copy the chart on the board and fill in the answers.

ANSWERS:

Seattle: 40° F; cloudy

Los Angeles: 80° F; rainy

Dallas: 82° F; sunny

Portland: 20° F; snowy

New York: 40° F; cloudy

C Write a weather report for your city today.

Read the Chicago weather report aloud.

Have the students follow along in their books.

Write the following open-ended sentences on the board.

This is a weather report for
_______________.
The temperature is _____° F.
The weather is _______ and
_______________.

Tell the students to use the open-ended sentences to write their weather reports for your city. Go around the room and check their work. Then have them compare answers with a partner.

Finally, call on different students to write their reports on the board.

EXPANSION ACTIVITY: Draw a weather map.

Have the students draw weather maps for their home countries. Tell them to use the map in their books as a guide. Encourage them to use their imaginations.

Then have them share their maps with a partner and say sentences about different places on their maps. Go around the room and check their work.

Finally, call on different students to share their maps with the class.

10 Review

STUDENT BOOK PAGES 104-105

A Listen and write.

Have the students listen with their books closed.

1. How's the weather?

2. It's cold.

3. My favorite season is fall.

4. I'm playing soccer.

5. What are you doing?

6. They like reading.

Copy the first sentence on the board. Play or say the first item. Write "weather" in the blank.

Have the students listen again and complete the activity. Stop the tape or CD, or pause after each sentence, so students have time to write a response. Go around the room and check their answers.

Have the students compare their answers with a partner. Then have them listen again as they check their work.

Finally, call on different students to read aloud the completed sentences as you write the answers on the board.

ANSWERS:

1. weather

2. cold

3. fall

4. playing

5. doing

6. reading

B Listen and √ check.

Have the students listen with their books closed.

1. How's the weather?

2. How's the weather in New York?

3. What's your favorite season?

4. What are you doing?

5. What's Maria doing?

6. What do you like doing in the fall?

Have the students open their books. Copy the first item on the board. Play or say the first question. Write a check mark in the blank next to "It's hot and sunny."

Then have the students listen again and complete the activity. Stop the tape or CD, or pause after each question, so students have time to check the appropriate response.

Have the students compare their answers with a partner. Have them listen again to check their work.

Finally, ask a student to write the items on the board and check √ the answers.

ANSWERS:

1. It's hot and sunny.

2. It's snowy.

3. Summer.

4. I'm playing soccer.

5. She's working.

6. I like playing basketball.

10 Review

STUDENT BOOK PAGES 104-105

C Listen and circle.

Have the students listen with their books closed.

1. It's 60 degrees Fahrenheit.

2. Seattle is windy.

3. It's 55 degrees Fahrenheit in Miami.

4. Dallas is 40 degrees Fahrenheit.

5. It's cold in New York.

6. Los Angeles is rainy.

Copy the first item on the board. Play or say the first sentence. Circle "60° F."

Then have the students listen again and complete the activity. Stop the tape or CD, or pause after each sentence, so students have time to circle the appropriate choice.

Have the students compare their answers with a partner. Then have them listen again as they check their work.

Finally, call on individual students to read aloud the items they circled.

ANSWERS:

1. 60° F

2. windy

3. 55° F

4. 40° F

5. cold

6. rainy

Write.

Copy the first sentence on the board. Then fill in the blank with your own information as you read the completed sentence aloud.

Next tell the students to follow your model and complete their own sentences in their books.

Have the students work in small groups to compare their work.

Finally, call on different students to write their sentences on the board.

SAMPLE ANSWERS:

1. My favorite season is summer.

2. The weather is hot and sunny today.

3. The temperature is 80 ° F today.

Ask three classmates.

Copy the chart on the board. Then read aloud the sample conversation with a student as you point out the sample entries on the chart.

Next act out the conversation with a student as you write the student's name and information in the appropriate blanks on the chart.

Have the students follow your model. Tell them to go around the room and fill in all three sets of blanks. Go around and check their work.

Finally, call on three students to fill in one row in the chart on the board.

STUDENT BOOK PAGES 104-105

Learning Log

Write five words you remember.

Review the purpose of a learning log.

Tell the students to try to fill in the log without looking back in their books for words. Then have them compare answers with a partner.

Finally, copy the Learning Log on the board. Call several students to the board and have them write one word in each column of the log. Check their work.

SAMPLE ANSWERS:

Seasons	Weather	Activities
spring	cloudy	reading
summer	hot	watching TV
fall	rainy	playing soccer
winter	cold	listening to music
	snowy	dancing

√ Check what you can do.

Tell the students to complete the checklist. Go around the room and check their work.

Finally, call on different students to read aloud the items they checked and what they filled in for item No. 5.

1. I can ask about the weather. _____

2. I can talk about the seasons. _____

3. I can say what I'm doing. _____

4. I can read a weather map. _____

5. I can ____________________. _____

Looking Back

What's the weather on page 94? Now write three more words in your Learning Log.

Have the students look at the illustration on page 94 and add three entries to their Learning Logs. Then have them compare their additions with a partner.

Finally, call on different students to read aloud the headings and the language they added.

See Color Transparencies package for unit wrap-up activity. This task can be used as an oral assessment tool. Many unit wrap-up activities include a reproducible blackline master.

Unit 9 Where's the post office?

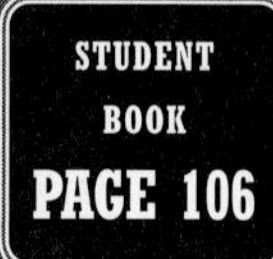

UNIT OVERVIEW

	LESSON:	LEARNING POINTS:	SB#
1.	**Places you see**	Talking about places in your community	**p. 107**
2.	**Neighborhood map**	Asking for and giving locations	**p. 108**
3.	**More places in the neighborhood**	Talking about places in your neighborhood	**p. 109**
4.	**Where's the bank?**	Asking and saying where people and places are	**p. 110**
5.	**It's on Lake Avenue.**	Saying where people and places are	**p. 111**
6.	**Do you live near a park?**	Talking about places that are near or far	**p. 112**
7.	**Where do you buy stamps?**	Talking about where you do different things	**p. 113**
8.	**Banking**	Making a deposit or a withdrawal	**p. 114**
9.	**Using an ATM**	Using an ATM	**p. 115**
10.	**Review**	Review Unit 9	**p. 116**

Suggestions for Unit Opener (Student Book page 106)

Brainstorm. Have students look at the unit-opening illustration. Ask them for words related to places and events in the community that they already know. Write the words on the board as students say them.

Model the language. Begin by reading the caption aloud—"What places do you see?" Point to the places and name them. Write the words on the board.

Model the language again. This time have the class repeat the words after you. Then go around the room and have individual students repeat different words.

Point and say. Point to the words you've written on the board as you say them. Have the students repeat them after you.

Initiate pair work. Have the students work in pairs. Tell them to take turns pointing to the different people, sites, and situations in the illustration and naming them. Demonstrate this by asking a student to point and by saying the name yourself, then pointing yourself and asking the same student to say the name. Go around the room and check students' work.

See Color Transparencies package for additional unit-opening activity. Many of these tasks include a reproducible blackline master.

1 Places you see

STUDENT BOOK PAGE 107

LEARNING POINT
Talking about places in your community

NEW LANGUAGE

bank	hospital
drugstore	library
fire station	police station
gas station	post office

Where are you going?
I'm going to the _____.

Listen. Look at page 106.

Have the students open their books and examine the illustration on page 106.

Have the students listen with their books closed.

1. Police station. I'm going to the police station.
2. Bank. I'm going to the bank.
3. Drugstore. I'm going to the drugstore.
4. Hospital. I'm going to the hospital.
5. Fire station. I'm going to the fire station.
6. Gas station. I'm going to the gas station.
7. Library. I'm going to the library.
8. Post office. I'm going to the post office.

Have students look at the illustration on page 106 and listen again as you point out and name the places.

Have the students return to the activity and listen again as they follow along.

Listen and say.

Have the class listen to and repeat each word separately. Stop the tape or CD after each word or read aloud the separate words with pauses.

1. police station
2. bank
3. drugstore
4. hospital
5. fire station
6. gas station
7. library
8. post office

Then call on individual students to listen and repeat after you.

Listen.

Have the students open their books and examine the illustration.

Have the students listen with their books closed.

Tien: Where are you going?

Grace: I'm going to the post office.

Then have them open their books, look at the illustration, and listen again as they follow along.

Listen and say.

Repeat the procedure from the previous **Listen and say.**

To explain the meaning of "I'm going to…," mimic the act of getting ready to go somewhere. For example, pick up some books and say "I'm going to the library."

Teacher:
I'm going to the library.

1 Places you see

STUDENT BOOK PAGE 107

C Talk with a partner.

Copy the open-ended conversation on the board. Pick a student to model the open-ended conversation with you in front of the class.

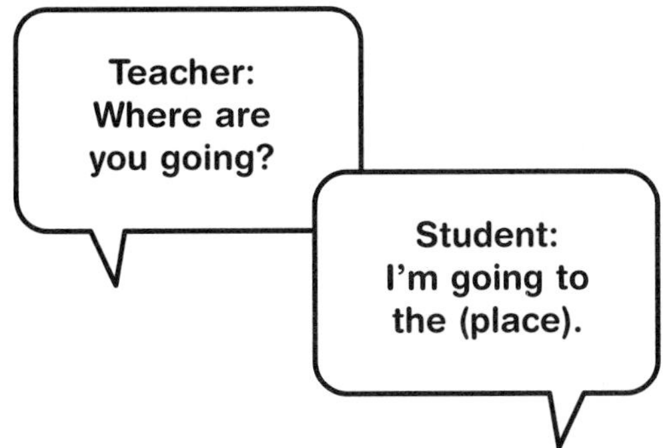

Have the students work in pairs to practice the conversation. Tell them to use the words in the Word List. Go around the room and check their work.

Finally, call on different pairs to share their conversations with the class.

D Match.

Have the students examine the illustrations. Point out the sample answer. Point out the bottle of aspirin  and the word *drugstore* and say: "This is from a drugstore." Then tell the students to match the illustrations to the places.

Have the students do the activity.

Have them compare answers with a partner. Go around the room and check their work.

Finally, call on a student to write the answers on the board as you point them out in the book.

ANSWERS:

1. b

2. a

3. d

4. c

2 Neighborhood map

STUDENT BOOK PAGE 108

LEARNING POINT
Asking for and giving locations

NEW LANGUAGE
Excuse me. Where's the _____?
It's on _____.

Look at page 106. Write the places.

Have the students look at the illustration on page 106. Point out the places and prompt the class to say the words.

Have the students look at the activity. Point out the sample answer.

Tell them to identify the places in the illustration and write the names in the blanks.

Have them compare answers with a partner. Go around the room and check their work.

Finally, ask a student to write the answers on the board.

ANSWERS:

1. fire station

2. drug store

3. hospital

4. gas station

Listen.

Have the students listen with their books closed.

Woman: Excuse me. Where's the gas station?

Grace: It's on 20th Street.

Woman: Thanks.

Have the students listen again as they follow along with their books open.

Listen and say.

Have the class listen to and repeat each line of the conversation separately. Stop the tape or CD after each line or read aloud the separate lines with pauses.

Then call on individual students to listen and repeat after you.

Talk with a partner.

Copy the open-ended conversation on the board. Pick a student to model the open-ended conversation with you in front of the class.

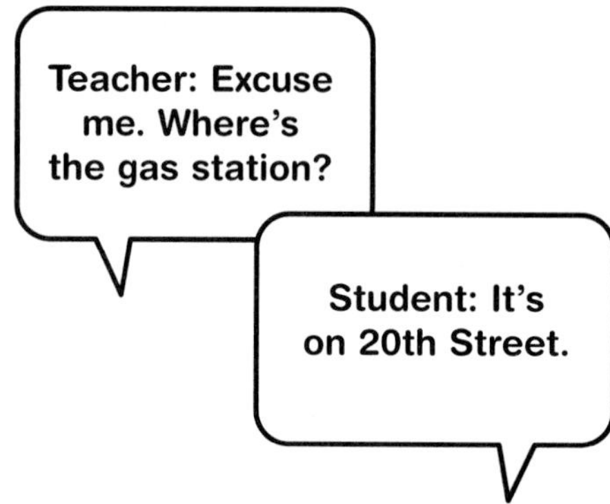

Teacher: Excuse me. Where's the gas station?
Student: It's on 20th Street.

Have the students work in pairs to practice the conversation. Tell them to use the words in the Word List. Go around the room and check their work.

Finally, call on different pairs to share their conversations with the class.

2 Neighborhood map

EXPANSION ACTIVITY:
Draw a map.

Have the students work in groups to draw maps of familiar community areas where local services are provided. Tell them to use the illustration on page 106 of the Student Book as a model. If all or certain groups share the same community area, have these groups work together.

3 More places in the neighborhood

STUDENT BOOK PAGE 109

LEARNING POINT
Talking about places in your neighborhood

NEW LANGUAGE

bus stop
laundromat
movie theater
neighborhood
park
restaurant
supermarket

Is there a _____ in your neighborhood?
Yes, there is./No, there isn't.

Listen.

Have the students open their books and examine the illustrations.

Have the students listen with their books closed.

1. laundromat

2. movie theatre

3. supermarket

4. bus stop

5. park

6. restaurant

Then have them open their books, look at the illustrations, and listen again as they follow along.

Listen and say.

Have the students listen to and repeat each word separately. Stop the tape or CD after each word or read aloud the separate words with pauses.

Then call on individual students to listen and repeat after you.

Listen.

Introduce the word "neighborhood." Use the illustrations in this unit to help you.

Review the structure Is there…? Yes, there is./ No, there isn't. Turn to the unit-opening illustration and point to the bank. Ask, "Is there a bank in the neighborhood?" and answer "Yes, there is." Ask, "Is there a school in the neighborhood?" and answer "No, there isn't."

Have the students listen with their books closed.

Isabel: Is there a restaurant in your neighborhood?

Leo: Yes, there is.

Maria: No, there isn't.

Have the students listen again as they follow along with their books open.

Listen and say.

Repeat the procedure from the previous **Listen and say.**

Talk with a partner.

Copy the open-ended conversation on the board. Pick a student to model the open-ended conversation with you in front of the class.

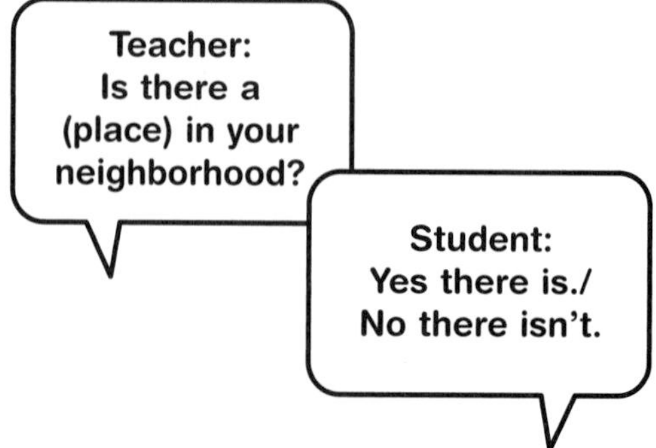

Teacher: Is there a (place) in your neighborhood?
Student: Yes there is./ No there isn't.

 WORKBOOK PAGE 80

3 More places in the neighborhood

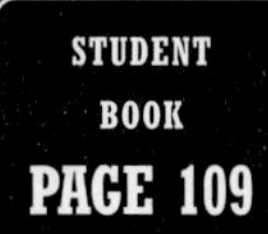

Have the students work in pairs to practice the conversation. Tell them to use the words in the Word List. Go around the room and check their work.

Finally, call on different pairs to share their conversations with the class.

4 Where's the bank?

STUDENT BOOK PAGE 110

LEARNING POINT
Asking and saying where people and places are

NEW LANGUAGE
between
in
next to

Where's the _____?
It's between/in/next to _____.

A Listen and read.

Have the students open their books, examine the illustration, and read the sentences.

Have the students listen with their books closed.

Maria is in the bank. The bank is between the drugstore and the supermarket. The drugstore is next to the bank.

Then have them open their books, look at the illustration, and listen again as they read along.

Hold up your book and point to the different locations as you say the sentences again. After each sentence, repeat the preposition and point to the corresponding location again. For example, say: "Maria is in the bank. In."

B Listen.

Have the students listen with their books closed.

Don: Where's the bank?

Paul: It's next to the drug store.

Tien: It's between the drugstore and the supermarket.

Have the students listen again as they follow along with their books open.

Listen and say.

Have the class listen to and repeat each line of the conversation separately. Stop the tape or CD after each line or read aloud the separate lines with pauses. Then call on individual students to listen and repeat after you.

C Talk with a partner.

Copy the open-ended conversation on the board. Pick a student to model the open-ended conversation with you in front of the class.

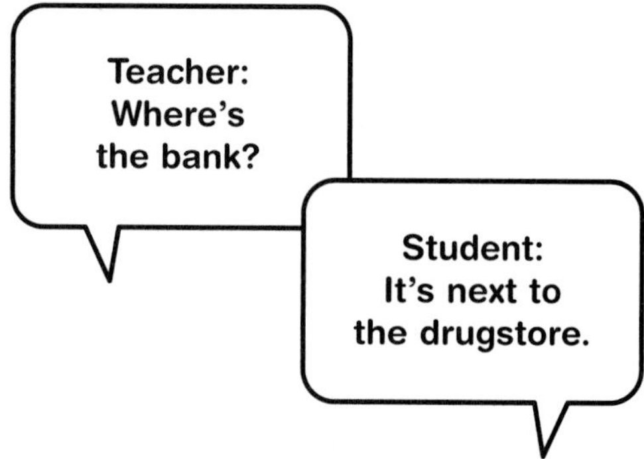

Teacher: Where's the bank?
Student: It's next to the drugstore.

Have the students work in pairs to practice the conversation. Tell them to use the illustration and the words in the Word List. Go around the room and check their work.

Finally, call on different pairs to share their conversations with the class.

4 Where's the bank?

STUDENT BOOK PAGE 110

EXPANSION ACTIVITY:
In, Between,* or *Next to

Write "in," "between," and "next to" on the board.

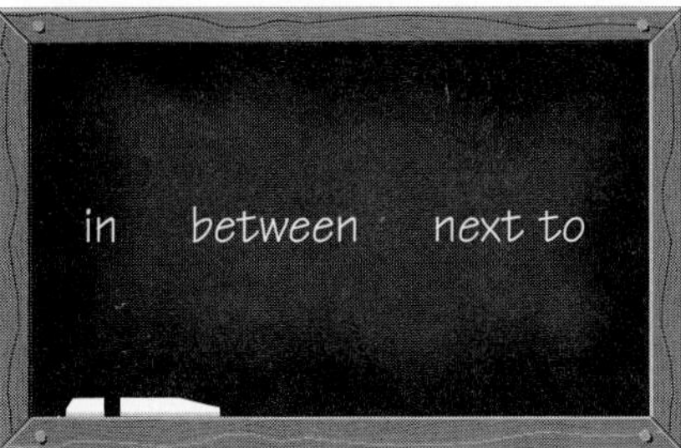

Use class members and objects in the classroom to practice the prepositions. Begin by pointing to a female student and saying, "(The student's name) is in the classroom." Then ask the question, "Where is (the student's name)?" Prompt the class to answer.

Next put a book on the floor between a desk and a chair. Ask "Where's the book?" Prompt the class to answer "It's between the desk and the chair." If the students have a difficult time responding, refer them to the prepositions on the board.

Continue to practice with students and with objects.

5 It's on Lake Avenue.

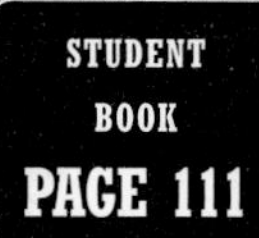
STUDENT BOOK PAGE 111

LEARNING POINT
Saying where people and places are

NEW LANGUAGE

between	next to
in	on

A Listen and write.

Have the students listen with their books closed.

1. The gas station is next to the library.
2. The hospital is between the gas station and the bank.
3. The hospital is on 19th Street.
4. The police station is next to the hospital.
5. The post office is between the library and the hospital.
6. Don and Sumin are in the bank.
7. Leo is in the drugstore.
8. The gas station is on South Avenue.

Copy the first sentence on the board. Play or say the first item. Write "next to" in the blank.

Have the students listen again and complete the activity. Stop the tape or CD, or pause after each sentence, so students have time to write an answer.

Have the students compare their answers with a partner. Then have them listen again as they check their work.

Finally, call on a student to write the answers on the board.

ANSWERS:

1. next to

2. between

3. on

4. next to

5. between

6. in

7. in

8. on

B Complete.

Point out the illustration and the box containing the prepositions. Then go over the sample answer with the class. Next have the students complete the sentences. Remind them to use the illustration and the words in the box to help them do the activity. Go around the room and check their work.

Have the students compare answers with a partner.

Finally, call on a student to write the complete sentences on the board.

ANSWERS:

1. on

2. between

3. next to

4. in

6 Do you live near a park?

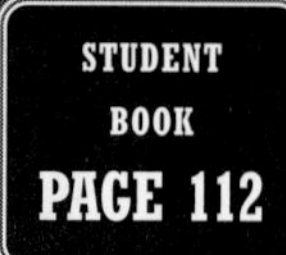

LEARNING POINT
Talking about places that are near or far

NEW LANGUAGE
near
far from

Do you live near/far from _____?
Yes, I do./No, I don't.

Listen.

Have the students open their books and examine the illustrations.

Have the students listen with their books closed.

1. Near. He's near the bus stop.

2. Far from. He's far from the bus stop.

Then have them open their books, look at the illustration, and listen again as they follow along.

Listen and say.

Have the students listen to and repeat each sentence separately. Stop the tape or CD after each sentence or read aloud the separate sentences with pauses.

1. He's near the bus stop.

2. He's far from the bus stop.

Then call on individual students to listen and repeat after you.

Listen and circle.

Have the students listen with their books closed.

1. The man lives near a bank.

2. She lives near a bus stop.

3. Sandy lives far from the city.

4. Paul lives near a fire station.

5. We live far from a movie theater.

6. Tien lives near a post office.

Copy the first item on the board. Play or say the first sentence. Tell the students to listen for the words "near" and "far from." Circle "near."

Then have the students listen again and complete the activity. Stop the tape or CD, or pause after each sentence, so students have time to circle the appropriate choice.

Have the students compare their answers with a partner. Then have them listen again as they check their work.

Finally, call on individual students to read aloud the items they circled.

ANSWERS:

1. near

2. near

3. far from

4. near

5. far from

6. near

Listen.

Have the students listen with their books closed.

Sandy: Do you live near a park?

Isabel: Yes, I do.

Paul: No, I don't.

6 Do you live near a park?

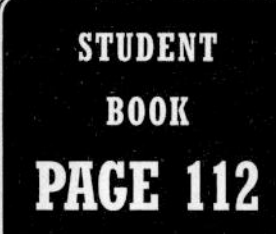

Have the students listen again as they follow along with their books open.

Listen and say.

Repeat the procedure from the previous **Listen and say.**

EXPANSION ACTIVITY:
***Near* or *Far From*?**

Have the students stand up. Point to a student standing next to another student and say: "(student's name) is near (another student's name)."

Teacher: (student's name) is near (another student's name).

Next, point to another student far away and say: "(student's name) is far from (another student's name)." Continue to practice, but this time pause and prompt the class to say the appropriate prepositions. For example, say: "(student's name) is (pause) (the other student's name)." You can also prompt individual students to respond.

Next, call on different students to make sentences about students in class.

D Ask classmates.

Copy the chart on the board. Pick a student to model the open-ended conversation with you in front of the class.

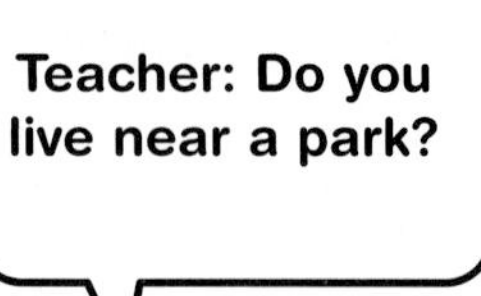

Continue to ask the student questions from the chart until he or she answers "yes" to a question. At that point, ask the student to sign his or her name in the appropriate space on the chart.

Have the students complete the activity. Go around the room and check their work.

Finally, call on different pairs to copy their charts on the board.

7 Where do you buy stamps?

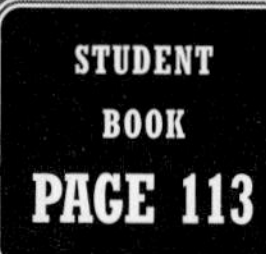

LEARNING POINT
Talking about where you do different things

NEW LANGUAGE
buy stamps
make a deposit
wash clothes
see a movie

Where do you _____?
At a _____.

Listen.

Have the students open their books and examine the illustrations.

Have the students listen with their books closed.

1. See a movie. Where do you see a movie?
2. Buy stamps. Where do you buy stamps?
3. Wash clothes. Where do you wash clothes?
4. Make a deposit. Where do you make a deposit?

Then have them open their books, look at the illustrations, and listen again as they follow along.

Listen and say.

Have the students listen to and repeat each line separately. Stop the tape or CD after each line or read aloud the separate lines with pauses.

1. see a movie
2. buy stamps
3. wash clothes
4. make a deposit

Then call on individual students to listen and repeat after you.

Listen.

Have the students listen with their books closed.

Carlos: Where do you buy stamps?

Grace: At a post office.

Have the students listen again as they follow along with their books open.

Listen and say.

Repeat the procedure from the previous **Listen and say.**

Talk with a partner.

Copy the open-ended conversation on the board. Pick a student to model the open-ended conversation with you in front of the class.

Teacher:
Where do you
buy stamps?
Student:
At a
post office.

Have the students work in pairs to practice the conversation. Tell them to use the words in the Word List. Go around the room and check their work.

Finally, call on different pairs to share their conversations with the class.

7 Where do you buy stamps?

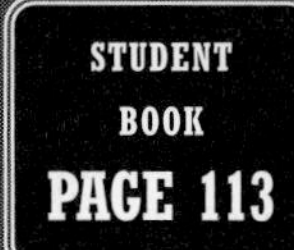
STUDENT BOOK PAGE 113

Write.

Read the first question and ask the class to respond.

Have the students write answers for the other questions. Go around the room and check their work.

Have them compare their work with a partner.

Finally, ask a pair of students to read the questions and answers in front of the class.

ANSWERS:

At a movie theater.

At a laundromat.

At a bank.

WORKBOOK PAGE 82

8 Banking

STUDENT BOOK PAGE 114

LEARNING POINT
Making a deposit or a withdrawal

NEW LANGUAGE

checking account	money
deposit	savings account

Listen and read.

Have the students open their books, examine the deposit slip, and read the sentences.

Have the students listen with their books closed.

> Tien is putting money in the bank. She is depositing money into her savings account. This is her deposit slip. She is depositing a check. She is also depositing cash.

Have the students listen again as they follow along with their books open.

Use gestures, mimes, realia, and words the students already know to help them understand the new language—putting money in the bank, depositing money.

Have the students follow along in their books as you read aloud the contents of Tien's deposit slip.

Write the numbers.

Point out the sample answer and read the sentence aloud as the students follow along in their books. Relate the sample answer to the date on the check.

> Teacher: The date is June 3, 2005.

Tell the students to use the information in Activity A to complete the sentences.

Have them compare answers with a partner.

Finally, call on a student to write the answers on the board.

ANSWERS:

1. June 3, 2005

2. 49-1916-03

3. 231.95

4. 42.00

Complete.

Point out the sample answer and read the sentence aloud as the students follow along.

Tell the students to use the information in Activity A to complete the sentences.

Have them compare answers with a partner.

Go around and check their work.

Finally, call on a student to write the answers on the board.

ANSWERS:

1. savings

2. one check

3. $189.95

4. $231.95

5. sixth

9 Using an ATM

STUDENT BOOK PAGE 115

LEARNING POINT
Using an ATM

NEW LANGUAGE
ATM = Automated Teller Machine
PIN
withdrawal

Insert your ATM card.
Enter your PIN.
Press "Enter."
Pick one.
Please take your money.

Listen and read.

Have the students open their books, examine the illustrations, and read the sentences.

Point out the illustrations and talk about them.

Explain that the illustrations show the steps for using an ATM.

Teacher: Don is using an ATM.

Have the students listen with their books closed.

Don is taking money from his checking account. He's making a withdrawal.

1. Insert your ATM card.

2. Enter your PIN. Press Enter.

3. Pick one: Withdrawal, Deposit, Balance.

4. Pick one. Savings, Checking, Credit.

5. Pick one: twenty dollars, forty dollars, sixty dollars, one hundred dollars, two hundred dollars.

6. Please take your money.

Have the students listen again as they follow along with their books open.

Circle. Work with a partner.

Tell the students to refer to the illustrations in Activity A to do this exercise. Go over the sample answer with them. Help students with unfamiliar language such as "taking money from" and "making a deposit and withdrawal" by using gestures, mime, and words students already know.

Have the students work with a partner to complete the activity.

Finally, call on a student to write the answers on the board.

ANSWERS:

1. 2-6-7-9

2. withdrawal

3. checking

4. $60

10 Review

STUDENT BOOK **PAGES 116-117**

A Listen and write.

Have the students listen with their books closed.

Isabel: Excuse me. Where is the police station?

Man: It's on 54th Street.

Isabel: Thanks.

Copy the first sentence on the board. Play or say the first item. Write "Excuse" in the blank.

Have the students listen again and complete the activity. Stop the tape or CD, or pause after each sentence, so students have time to write an answer.

Have the students compare their answers with a partner. Then have them listen again as they check their work.

Finally, call on a student to write the answers on the board.

ANSWERS:

1. Excuse

2. on

3. Thanks

B Listen and √ check.

Have the students listen with their books closed.

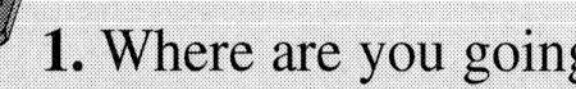

1. Where are you going?

2. Where's the bank?

3. Where's the library?

4. Do you live near a movie theater?

Copy the first sentence on the board. Play or say the first item. Write a check mark next to "To the library."

Then have the students listen again and complete the activity. Stop the tape or CD, or pause after each question, so students have time to check the appropriate columns.

Have the students compare their answers with a partner. Have them listen again to check their work.

Finally, call on a student to write the answers on the board.

ANSWERS:

1. To the library.

2. It's next to the fire station.

3. On 21st Avenue.

4. No, I don't.

C Listen and write.

Have the students listen with their books closed.

1. Waiter: Can I help you?

Sandy: Yes. I'll have a tuna sandwich.

2. Leo: This is a good movie.

Paul: Yes, it is.

3. Teller: May I help you?

Grace: I want to make a deposit, please.

4. Clerk: Good morning.

Don: Good morning. I want to buy some stamps.

10 Review

STUDENT BOOK PAGES 116-117

Copy the first sentence on the board. Play or say the first item. Write "restaurant" in the blank. Have the students listen again and complete the activity. Stop the tape or CD, or pause after each conversation, so students have time to write an answer.

Have the students compare their answers with a partner. Then have them listen again as they check their work.

Finally, call on a student to write the answers on the board.

ANSWERS:

1. restaurant

2. movie theatre

3. bank

4. post office

Complete the sentences about where you live.

Write the open-ended sentences on the board.

1. I live on ______________.
2. My address is ___________.
3. My house is near__________.

Now read the sentences on the board aloud as you fill the blanks with your own or fictitious information.

Have the students follow your model and complete the sentences with their own information. Then have them read their sentences with a group. Go around the room and check their work.

Finally, call on different students to write their answers on the board.

Learning Log

Write five words or phrases you remember.

Review the purpose of a learning log.

Tell the students to try to fill in the log without looking back in their books for words. Then have them compare answers with a partner.

Finally, copy the Learning Log on the board. Call several students to the board and have them write one word in each column of the log. Check their work.

SAMPLE ANSWERS:

Places	Banking	Activities
post office	deposit	buying stamps
bank	check	making a deposit
hospital	cash	washing clothes
restaurant	money	seeing a movie
drugstore	account	

10 Review

STUDENT BOOK PAGES 116-117

√ Check what you can do.

Tell the students to complete the checklist. Go around the room and check their work.

Finally, call on different students to read aloud the items they checked and what they filled in for item No. 5.

1. I can name places in my neighborhood. _____

2. I can ask for directions. _____

3. I can read a deposit slip. _____

4. I can use an ATM. _____

5. I can ____________________. _____

Looking Back

Look at page 106. What new places do you know? Now write three more words in your Learning Log.

Have the students look at the illustration on page 106 and add three words to their Learning Logs. Then have them compare their additions with a partner.

Finally, call on different students to read aloud the headings and the words they added.

See Color Transparencies package for unit wrap-up activity. This task can be used as an oral assessment tool. Many unit wrap-up activities include a reproducible blackline master.

7-9 Grammar Spotlight for Units 7-9

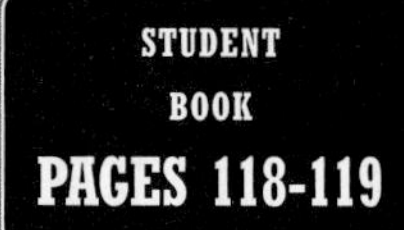

Present Continuous

Point out and read the chart, the headings, and the sentences aloud. Have the students repeat after you. Explain that contractions mean the same thing as full forms by writing an example on the board.

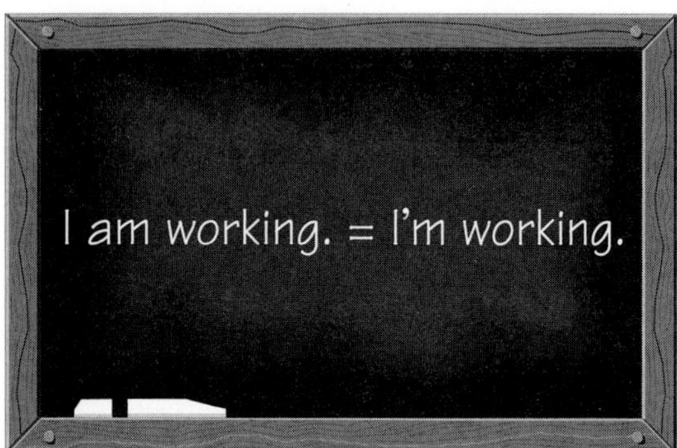

I **am** work**ing**	I**'m** work**ing**.
He **is** work**ing**.	He**'s** work**ing**.
She **is** work**ing**	She**'s** work**ing**.
It **is** work**ing**.	It**'s** work**ing**.
We **are** work**ing**.	We**'re** work**ing**.
You **are** work**ing**.	You**'re** work**ing**.
They **are** work**ing**.	They**'re** work**ing**.

If students want to know what the difference is between the two forms, explain that contractions are used in speech and informal writing and that full forms can be used for emphasis when speaking and in formal writing.

Write the present continuous.

Read the directions aloud and point out the sample answer. Relate "Leo" to "He" in the chart. Then have the students do the activity.

Go around the room and check their work. If they seem to be having trouble, write the second item on the board and prompt the class to give you the answer as you write it in the blank.

When the students finish, have them compare their answers with a partner.

Finally, call on a pair to write the answers on the board.

ANSWERS:

1. He's walking

2. They're eating

3. She's making

4. You're reading

5. I'm buying

What are you doing now? Write two sentences.

Read the directions aloud as the students follow along in their books. Write the following sentence on the board.

Have the students follow your model and write their own sentences.

Have the students compare sentences with a partner.

Finally, call on different students to write the sentences on the board.

Grammar Spotlight for Units 7-9

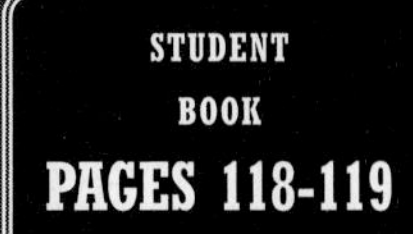

B Question Words

Point out and read the chart, the headings, and the sentences aloud. Have the students repeat after you.

Question Words	Questions	Answers
Where = places	**Where's** the bread? **Where are** Sandy and Will?	In Aisle 4. At the beach.
How = descriptions	**How's** the weather? **How are** your sons?	It's cold and rainy They're fine.
What = things	**What's** your favorite season? **What are** your favorite foods?	Winter. Bread and cheese.

Match.

Point out the sample question and corresponding answer and read them aloud as the students follow along in their books. Then have the students match the remaining items. Go around the room and check their work.

Have the students compare their answers with a partner.

Finally, read the questions aloud and ask for volunteers to read the matching answers.

ANSWERS:

1. c

2. d

3. e

4. a

5. b

Write *How, Where,* or *What.*

Go over the sample answer with the students by reading the question and answer aloud. Next review the meaning of *how*, *where*, and *what*. Then have the students do the activity.

Have them compare answers with a partner.

Finally, call on two students to write the full questions and answers on the board.

ANSWERS:

1. How

2. Where

3. What

4. How

5. Where

6. How

EXPANSION ACTIVITY: Matching Questions and Answers

Scramble the questions and answers from Activity B and write them in separate columns on the board under the appropriate headings.

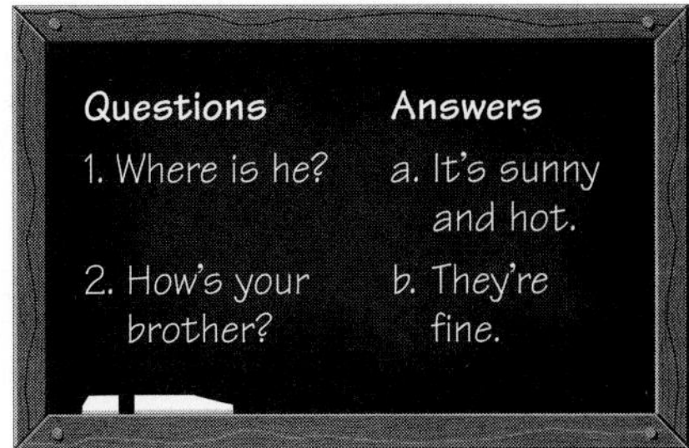

Questions
Answers
1. Where is he?
a. It's sunny and hot.
2. How's your brother?
b. They're fine.

Have the students match the questions with the appropriate answers. Have them write the exchanges on a separate piece of paper. Then have them work with a partner to compare answers and act out the exchanges.

7-9 Review for Units 7-9

STUDENT BOOK PAGES 120-121

Match.

Point out the sample question and corresponding answer and read them aloud as the students follow along in their books. Then have the students match the remaining items. Go around the room and check their work.

Have the students compare their answers with a partner.

Read the questions aloud and ask for volunteers to read the matching answers.

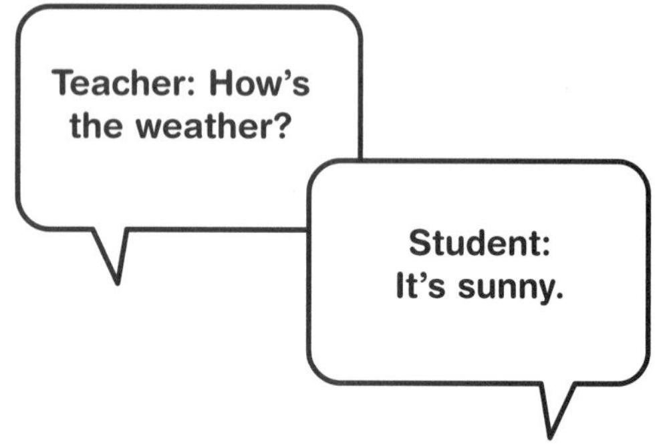

Teacher: How's the weather?
Student: It's sunny.

ANSWERS:

1. f	**4.** e
2. d	**5.** b
3. c	**6.** a

Listen and circle the correct answer.

Have the students examine the illustrations.

Have the students listen with their books closed.

1. Mother: Hello?

Isabel: Hi Mother. It's Isabel. How are you?

Mother: Hi Isabel. How's the weather in Los Angeles?

Isabel: It's rainy.

2. Grace: Hi, Maria.

Maria: Hi, Grace.

Grace: What are Carlos and Tien doing?

Maria: They're playing soccer.

3. Isabel: Hello?

Don: Hi Isabel.

Isabel: Hi, Don. How's the weather in Miami?

Don: It's cloudy.

Copy the first item on the board. Play or say the first conversation. Circle "It's rainy."

Then have the students listen again and complete the activity. Stop the tape or CD, or pause after each conversation, so students have time to circle the appropriate choice.

Have the students compare their answers with a partner. Then have them listen again as they check their work.

Finally, call on individual students to read aloud the items they circled.

ANSWERS:

1. b

2. b

3. a

Complete.

Point out the sample answer and read the sentence aloud as the students follow along.

7-9 Review for Units 7-9

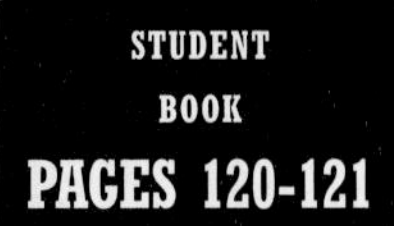

Tell the students to choose words from the box to complete the sentences.

Have them compare answers with a partner. Go around and check their work.

Finally, call on a pair of students to write the answers on the board.

ANSWERS:

1. bunch

2. jar

3. Aisle

4. laundromat

5. milk

6. summer

7. like

8. bank

D Community Challenge

Work with a partner. Find addresses and phone numbers in your city or town.

Make telephone or community yellow pages available so that the pairs can look up the information and write it in the chart.

Demonstrate in front of the class how to look up names in a directory. Explain that places are listed in alphabetical order. Refer the class to page 4 of the Student Book to see the alphabet in order.

Have the students complete the activity. Go around the room and check their work.

Have a pair of students copy the chart on the board and fill in the information. Call on different students to read the information aloud.

EXPANSION ACTIVITY: Use the yellow pages.

For this activity, have the students use the telephone directories they used for Activity D. Write the words "laundromat," "drugstore," "supermarket," and "movie theater" on the board. Tell the students they are going to find these places in the directories.

To model the activity, look up "laundromat" in the yellow pages. Locate a listing for a laundromat and write the laundromat's name and phone number on the board.

Tell the class to try to find two of each place in the yellow pages and to write down the name and phone number for each place.

Unit 10 You need to see a doctor.

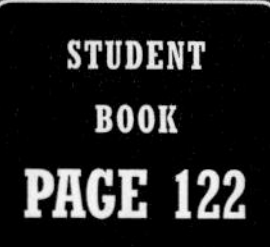

UNIT OVERVIEW

Suggestions for Unit Opener (Student Book page 122)

Brainstorm. Have students look at the unit-opening illustration. Ask them for words related to health and medical problems that they already know. Write the words on the board as students say them.

Model the language. Begin by reading the caption aloud—"Where are the people? What do you see?" Point to the items and medical problems in the illustration and name them. Write the words on the board.

Model the language again. This time have the class repeat the words after you. Then go around the room and have individual students repeat different words.

Point and say. Point to the words you've written on the board as you say them. Have the students repeat them after you.

Initiate pair work. Have the students work in pairs. Tell them to take turns pointing to the different people, sites, and situations in the illustration and naming them. Demonstrate this by asking a student to point and by saying the name yourself, then pointing yourself and asking the same student to say the name. Go around the room and check students' work.

See Color Transparencies package for additional unit-opening activity. Many of these tasks include a reproducible blackline master.

1 What's the matter?

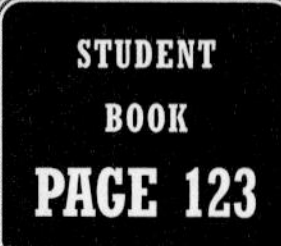

LEARNING POINT
Identifying health problems

NEW LANGUAGE

backache	headache
broken arm	sore throat
cold	stomachache
earache	toothache

What's the matter?
I have a/an _____.

A Listen.

Have the students open their books and examine the illustrations.

Have the students listen with their books closed.

1. An earache. I have an earache.

2. A sore throat. I have a sore throat.

3. A headache. I have a headache.

4. A broken arm. I have a broken arm.

5. A toothache. I have a toothache.

6. A stomachache. I have a stomachache.

7. A backache. I have a backache.

8. A cold. I have a cold.

Then have them open their books, look at the illustrations, and listen again as they follow along.

Listen and say.

Have the students listen to and repeat each line separately. Stop the tape or CD after each line or read aloud the separate lines with pauses.

1. an earache

2. a sore throat

3. a headache

4. a broken arm

5. a toothache

6. a stomachache

7. a backache

8. a cold

Then call on individual students to listen and repeat after you.

EXPANSION ACTIVITY: Charades

Tell the students that you are going to act out medical problems from this lesson. For a list of the medical problems, see the New Language list. Mime each medical problem as you say its name and write it on the board. For example, grimace as you clutch your ear for earache, your throat for sore throat, and so on. For a cold, sneeze into a tissue and put your hand to your head.

Next mime each problem again and prompt the class to say the name of the malady. Then call on individual students to name the malady as you act it out.

B Listen.

Have the students listen with their books closed.

Nurse: What's the matter?

Maria: I have a headache.

Have the students listen again as they follow along with their books open.

What's the matter?

STUDENT BOOK PAGE 123

Listen and say.

Repeat the procedure from the previous **Listen and say.**

C Talk with a partner.

Copy the open-ended conversation on the board. Pick a student to model the open-ended co front of the class.

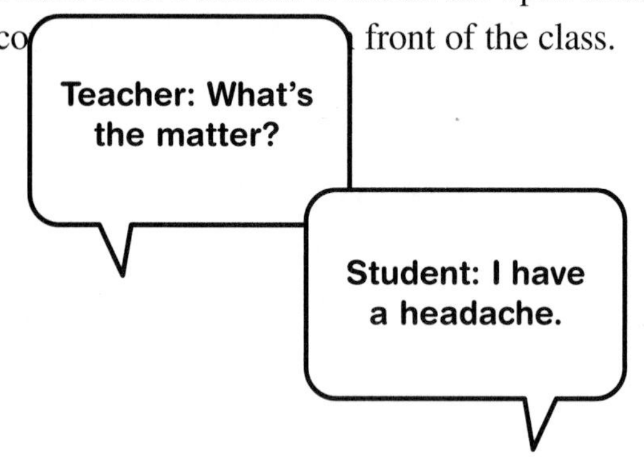
Teacher: What's the matter?
Student: I have a headache.

Have the students work in pairs to practice the conversation. Tell them to use the words in the Word List. Go around the room and check their work.

Finally, call on different pairs to share their conversations with the class.

 WORKBOOK PAGE 89

2 His hand hurts.

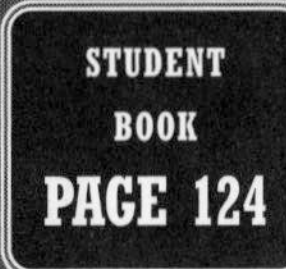

LEARNING POINT
Identifying parts of the body

NEW LANGUAGE

arm	head
eye	leg
finger	nose
foot	stomach
hand	

What's the matter with _____?
His/Her _____ hurts.

A Listen.

Have the students open their books and examine the illustration.

Have the students listen with their books closed.

1. head

2. eye

3. nose

4. stomach

5. arm

6. hand

7. finger

8. leg

9. foot

Then have them open their books, look at the illustrations, and listen again as they follow along.

Listen and say.

Have the students listen to and repeat each word separately. Stop the tape or CD after each word or read aloud the separate words with pauses.

Then call on individual students to listen and repeat after you. Have the students point to parts of their own bodies as they follow your model and say the words.

B Listen.

Repeat the procedure from the previous **Listen.**

Sandy: What's the matter with Don?

Leo: His hand hurts.

Listen and say.

Repeat the procedure from the previous **Listen and say.**

C Talk with a partner.

Help the students understand the pronoun/possessive adjective relationship by writing the words on the board.

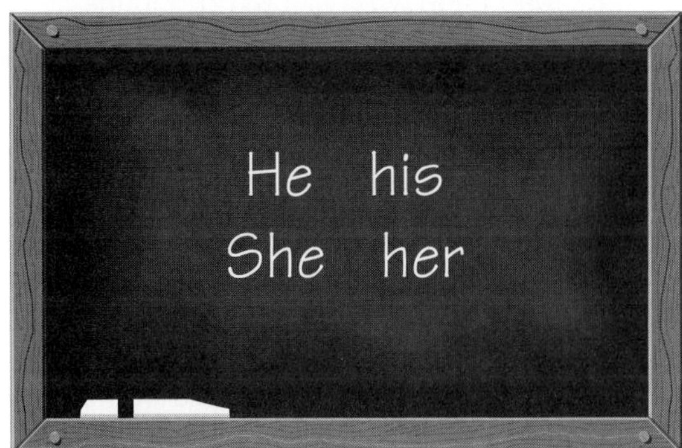

Copy the open-ended conversation on the board. Pick a student to model the open-ended conversation with you in front of the class.

2 His hand hurts.

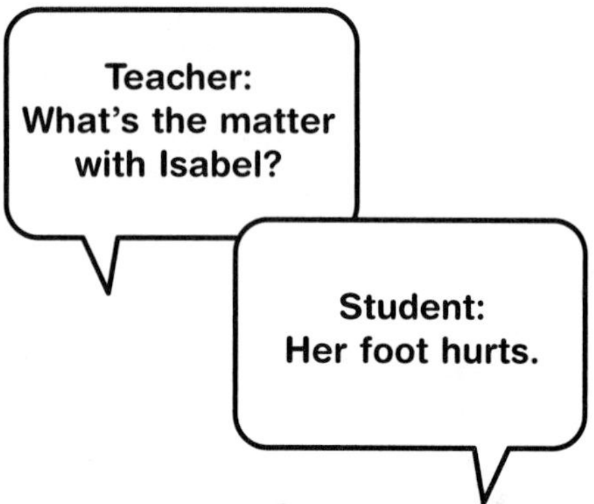

Teacher:
What's the matter with Isabel?
Student:
Her foot hurts.

Have the students work in pairs to practice the conversation. Tell them to use the words in the Word List. Go around the room and check their work.

Finally, call on different pairs to share their conversations with the class.

EXPANSION ACTIVITY: Point and say.

Write the words for body parts from the New Language list on the board. As you read each word aloud, point to the appropriate body part. Then point to the different parts of your body and prompt the class to say the names. Next point and prompt individual students to respond.

Have the student or students who name the most body parts correctly lead the class in a continuation of the activity.

Finally, have the students work in pairs and small groups to continue. Go around and check their work.

3 My daughter is sick.

STUDENT BOOK PAGE 125

LEARNING POINT
Talking about symptoms and making a doctor's appointment

NEW LANGUAGE
I feel bad.
_____ is sick.
You need to see a doctor.
Can Dr. _____ see _____ today?
Today at _____? That's fine.

Listen.

Have the students open their books and examine the illustration.

Have the students listen with their books closed.

Ana: I feel bad. My ear hurts.

Maria: You need to see a doctor.

Then have them open their books, look at the illustrations, and listen again as they follow along.

Listen and say.

Have the students listen to and repeat each line of the conversation separately. Stop the tape or CD after each line or read aloud the separate lines with pauses.

Then call on individual students to listen and repeat after you.

Talk with a partner.

Copy the open-ended conversation on the board. Pick a student to model the open-ended conversation with you in front of the class. Point to the body part as you name it.

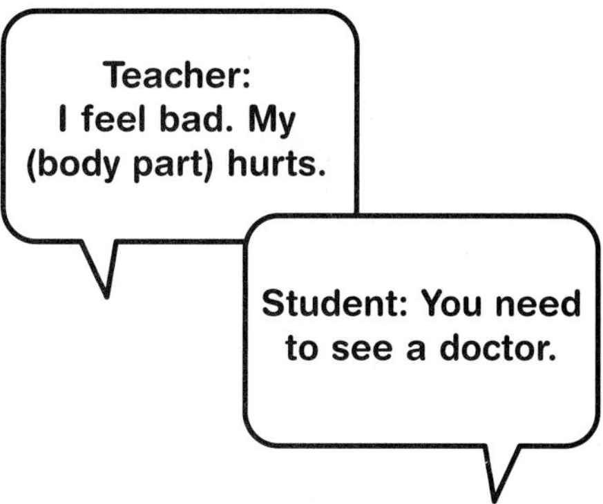
Teacher:
I feel bad. My
(body part) hurts.
Student: You need
to see a doctor.

Have the students work in pairs to practice the conversation. Tell them to use the words in the Word List. Go around and the room and check their work.

Finally, call on different pairs to share their conversations with the class.

Listen

Have the students listen with their books closed.

Maria: Hello. This is Maria Cruz. My daughter is sick. Can Dr. Brown see her today?

Man: Dr. Brown can see her at 10:00.

Maria: Today at 10:00? That's fine. Thank you.

Have the students listen again as they follow along with their books open.

Listen and say.

Repeat the procedure from the previous **Listen and say.**

Talk with a partner.

Repeat the procedure from the previous **Talk with a partner.**

4 Health problems

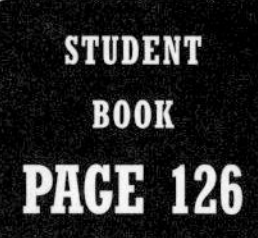
STUDENT BOOK PAGE 126

LEARNING POINT
Understanding problems and remedies

NEW LANGUAGE

antibiotic	cough syrup
aspirin	cut
bandage	fever
cough	infection

Listen.

Have the students open their books and examine the illustrations.

Have the students listen with their books closed.

1. a cut

2. a cough

3. an infection

4. a fever

Then have them open their books, look at the illustrations, and listen again as they follow along.

Listen and say.

Have the students listen to and repeat each word separately. Stop the tape or CD after each word or read aloud the separate lines with pauses.

Then call on individual students to listen and repeat after you.

Listen.

Repeat the procedure from the previous **Listen.**

1. a bandage

2. cough syrup

3. an antibiotic

4. aspirin

Listen and say.

Repeat the procedure from the previous **Listen and say.**

Listen and √ check.

Have the students listen with their books closed.

1. Isabel

Isabel: Ow! I have a cut on my hand.

Dr. Brown: You need a bandage.

2. Carlos

Carlos: I have a fever.

Dr. Brown: You need aspirin.

3. Don

Don: Ow! My foot hurts.
I have an infection.

Dr. Brown: You need an antibiotic.

4. Leo

Leo: Oh, my head is hot. I feel bad.
I have a fever.

Dr. Brown: Oh no. You need aspirin.

Copy the chart on the board. Tell the students that they should listen for the problem and for what the person needs. Play or say the first conversation. Put check marks in the columns for "a bandage" and "a cut."

Then have the students listen again and complete the activity. Stop the tape or CD, or pause after each conversation, so students have time to check the appropriate spaces.

 WORKBOOK PAGE 91

4 Health problems

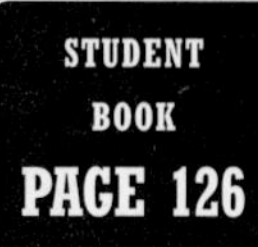

Have the students compare their answers with a partner. Have them listen again to check their work.

Finally, ask a student to check √ the answers on the chart on the board.

ANSWERS:

Isabel: a cut, bandage

Carlos: a fever, aspirin

Don: an infection, an antibiotic

Leo: a fever, aspirin

EXPANSION ACTIVITY: Be the patient. Be the doctor.

Divide the class in two. Provide one half with slips of paper with ailments written on them. Provide the other half with slips of paper with matching remedies written on them. Be sure that each ailment slip has a matching remedy slip.

Then have the students move around the room to find their matches by saying sentences, such as "I have a headache" and "You need aspirin." Tell the students to sit down once they find their matches.

Finally, call on each matched pair to act out their exchange for the class.

5 She needs a bandage.

STUDENT BOOK PAGE 127

LEARNING POINT
Talking about problems and remedies

NEW LANGUAGE
What's the matter?
That's too bad.
You need a _____.

Listen.

Have the students listen with their books closed.

Don: Sumin has a cut on her arm.

Grace: That's too bad. She needs a bandage.

Have the students listen again as they follow along with their books open.

Listen and say.

Have the students listen to and repeat each line of the conversation separately. Stop the tape or CD after each line or read aloud the separate lines with pauses.

Then call on individual students to listen and repeat after you.

Talk with a partner.

Copy the open-ended conversation on the board. Pick a student to model the open-ended conversation with you in front of the class.

Teacher: Paul has a cough. What should I do?
Student: That's too bad. He needs some cough syrup.

Have the students work in pairs to practice the conversation. Tell them to use the words in the Word List. Go around the room and check their work.

Finally, call on different pairs to share their conversations with the class.

Listen. Complete the chart.

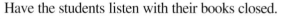

Have the students listen with their books closed.

1. Leo

Grace: What's the matter, Leo?

Leo: I have a cut on my finger.

Grace: That's too bad. You need a bandage.

2. Isabel

Carlos: What's the matter, Isabel?

Isabel: I have a headache. My head hurts.

Carlos: That's too bad. You need aspirin.

3. Paul

Leo: What's the matter, Paul?

Paul: I have an infection. My foot hurts.

Grace: That's too bad. You need an antibiotic.

Play or say the first conversation and point out the example. Tell the students that they should listen for the problem, where it is on the body, and what the person needs.

5 She needs a bandage.

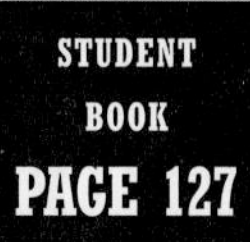

Have the students listen again and complete the activity. Stop the tape or CD, or pause after each conversation, so students have time to write a response.

Have the students compare their answers with a partner. Then have them listen again as they check their work.

Finally, call on different students to read the information in their charts.

ANSWERS:

1. Leo: a cut; finger; a bandage

2. Isabel: a headache; head; aspirin

3. Paul: an infection; foot; an antibiotic

6 I exercise.

STUDENT BOOK PAGE 128

LEARNING POINTS
Recognizing healthy habits

NEW LANGUAGE

drink water	Jump.
eat healthy food	Raise your arms.
exercise	Stretch.
get enough sleep	Touch your toes.

Listen.

Have the students open their books and examine the illustrations.

Have the students listen with their books closed.

1. Exercise. I exercise.

2. Drink water. I drink water.

3. Get enough sleep. I get enough sleep.

4. Eat healthy food. I eat healthy food.

Then have them open their books, look at the illustrations, and listen again as they follow along.

Listen and say.

Have the students listen to and repeat each line separately. Stop the tape or CD after each line or read aloud the separate lines with pauses.

1. exercise

2. drink water

3. get enough sleep

4. eat healthy food

Then call on individual students to listen and repeat after you.

√ Check what you do.

Copy the chart on the board.

__ I exercise.
__ I get enough sleep.
__ I drink water.
__ I eat healthy food.

Model the activity by checking the items that pertain to you as you say them aloud.

Next have the students complete their own charts and share them with a partner. Go around and check their work.

Finally, take a poll. Point to the first item, read it aloud, and ask how many people checked it. Raise your hand to indicate that you want those who checked the item to raise their hands. Do the same with the remaining items.

Listen.

Repeat the procedure from the previous **Listen.**

1. Raise your arms.

2. Touch your toes.

3. Stretch.

4. Jump.

Listen and say.

Repeat the procedure from the previous **Listen and say**. Act out each command as students listen and repeat.

6 I exercise.

Listen and follow the directions. Look at your teacher.

Have the students imitate your actions as you play or say the commands.

Teacher:
Stand up.

1. Stand up.
2. Raise your arms.
3. Stretch.
4. Touch your toes.
5. Jump.
6. Touch your toes.
7. Jump.
8. Stretch.
9. Raise your arms.
10. Sit down.

EXPANSION ACTIVITY: Charades

Write the words and phrases from the New Language list on the board. As you read each word or phrase aloud, act it out. Then mime the actions in random order and prompt the students to say them. For example, make the motions of drinking a glass of water and say: "I…" Prompt the students to say: "drink water."

Then invite different students to mime activities for the class.

7 They are healthy.

LEARNING POINT
Reading and writing about healthy habits

NEW LANGUAGE
healthy

I _____ every day/week.

Listen and read.

Have the students read the paragraphs. Have the students listen with their books closed.

The Goldman Sisters

Frances and Eleanor Goldman are sisters. They are healthy. Eleanor is 81 years old. Frances is 83. They exercise and eat healthy food every day. Frances likes apples. Eleanor likes oranges. They drink water. They get enough sleep.

Eleanor likes to swim. Frances likes to walk her dog. She has a large dog. Frances says, "Be healthy. Get a dog." Eleanor says, "Be healthy. Go swimming."

Have the students listen again as they follow along with their books open.

Complete.

Point out the Venn diagram and explain how it works—that the partial oval on the left is for things about Eleanor only, that the partial oval on the right is for things about Frances only, and that the center oval is for things about both Eleanor and Frances. Next point out the words in the box and read them aloud.

Point out the sample answer and say: "Eleanor is 81 years old," and "Eleanor and Frances are healthy." Then have the students complete the diagram.

Have them compare their work with a partner.

Finally, ask a pair to draw the diagram on the board and fill in the answers.

ANSWERS:

Eleanor	Both	Frances
81		83
swims	healthy	has a large dog
likes oranges	exercises	likes apples walks a lot

Write.

Point out the sample answer and read it aloud. Copy the sentence on the board and write in your own information as you read it aloud.

Brainstorm a list of words for the students to use and write them on the board.

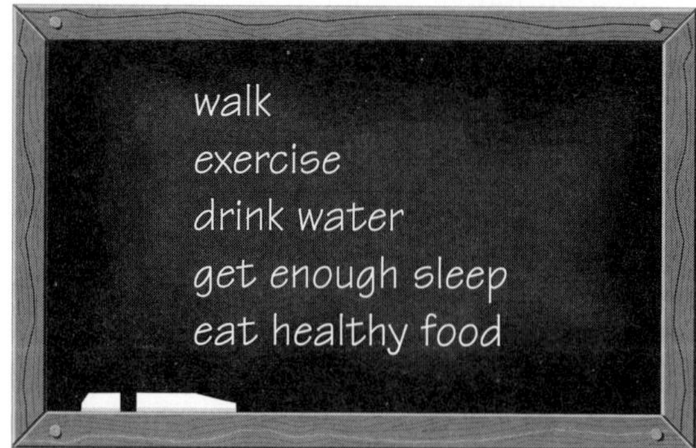

walk
exercise
drink water
get enough sleep
eat healthy food

Have the students write their own sentences.

When the students finish writing, have them read their sentences with a partner or with a small group. Go around and check their work.

Finally, call on different students to write their sentences on the board and read them aloud.

8 Taking medicine

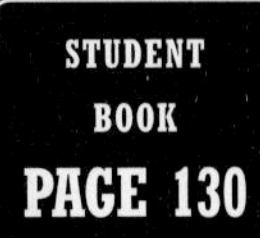

LEARNING POINT
Understanding instructions for taking medicine

NEW LANGUAGE
once
twice
three times
capsule
pill
teaspoon of medicine

Take _____ _____ a day.
Is that _____ _____ a day?
That's right.

A Listen.

Have the students open their books and examine the illustrations.

Have the students listen with their books closed.

1. a pill

2. a capsule

3. a teaspoon of medicine

Then have them open their books, look at the illustrations, and listen again as they follow along.

Listen and say.

Have the students listen to and repeat each line separately. Stop the tape or CD after each line or read aloud the separate lines with pauses.

Then call on individual students to listen and repeat after you.

B Listen.

Repeat the procedure from the previous **Listen.**

1. once

2. twice

3. three times

Listen and say.

Repeat the procedure from the previous **Listen and say.**

C Circle the answers in the chart.

Point out the illustrations and the chart. Then have the students use each illustration to circle the appropriate answer. Do the first item with the class to make sure they understand the procedure.

When they finish the activity, have the students compare answers with a partner. Go around and check their work.

Finally, ask a pair of students to copy the chart on the board and circle the answers.

ANSWERS:

1. pill; 3x

2. capsule; 2x

9 Health insurance

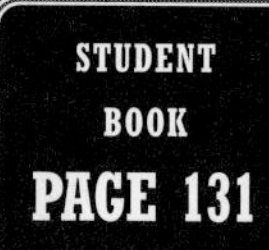

LEARNING POINT
Filling out an insurance form

NEW LANGUAGE
co-payment
health insurance

Listen and read.

Have the students open their books and examine the card.

Have the students listen with their books closed.

Grace has a health insurance card. She needs the card to see a doctor. Her health insurance is from her husband's work.

Have the students open their books and listen again as they read along.

Then answer any questions they have about unfamiliar language such as "plan" and "insurance card." Refer to the margin box and read the information aloud as you help the students understand the meaning of co-payment.

Fill in the form for Grace.

Refer the students to the insurance card from activity A. Tell them to use that information to fill out the form for Grace. Go around the room and check the students' work.

Have the students compare their work with a partner. Then call on a pair of students to copy the form on the board and to fill in the information.

ANSWERS:

Patient's name: Grace Lee

Today's date: (today's date)

Date of Birth: 3/16/64

Name of employee: Ben Lee

Type of plan: family

ID#: 90933MC

Co-payment: YES; $5.00

10 Review

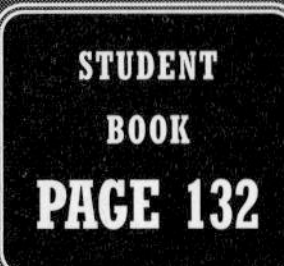

Write.

Point out the first item and the sample answer.

Then have the students complete the activity.

Have them compare answers with a partner. Go around the room and check their work.

Finally, ask a student to write the answers on the board.

ANSWERS:

1. a toothache

2. a stomachache

3. a headache

4. a sore throat

5. a cold

Listen and √ check the answer.

Have the students listen with their books closed.

1. What's the matter?

2. What's the matter with Don?

3. Can Dr. Wall see me today?

4. What's the matter with Sandy?

Copy the first item on the board. Play or say the first question. Write a check mark next to "I have a headache."

Then have the students listen again and complete the exercise. Stop the tape or CD, or pause after each question, so students have time to check the appropriate response.

Have the students compare their answers with a partner. Have them listen again to check their work.

Finally, ask a student to write the answers on the board.

ANSWERS:

1. I have a headache.

2. He feels bad.

3. Yes. Dr. Wall can see you at 3:00.

4. Her ear hurts.

Write.

Copy the open-ended conversation on the board. Then invite a student to help you fill in the missing information. Next act it out with the student.

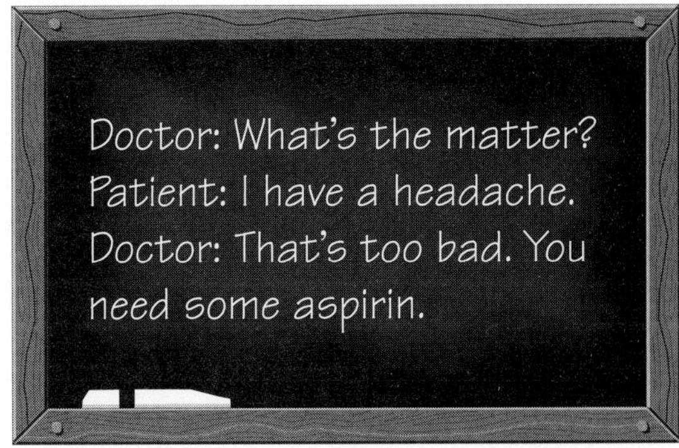

Doctor: What's the matter?
Patient: I have a headache.
Doctor: That's too bad. You need some aspirin.

Have the students fill in the blanks. Go around the room and check their work. When they are finished filling in the blanks, have them act out the conversations with partners.

Finally, call on different pairs to write their conversations on the board and act them out for the class.

SAMPLE ANSWERS:

You: headache, cut, infection

Doctor: aspirin, a bandage, an antibiotic

Cross out the wrong word.

Have the students look at the chart. Point out the sample. Explain that "a fever," "an infection," and "a cut" are different kinds of health problems and that "nose" is not.

Have the students complete the activity and cross out the word that doesn't belong in each column. Go around the room and check their work.

Have the students compare their work with a partner. Then call on a pair of students to copy the chart on the board and cross out the words that don't belong.

ANSWERS:

Health Problems: nose

Medicine: a backache

Body Parts: a capsule

Be Healthy: a cold

Learning Log

Write five words you remember.

Review the purpose of a learning log.

Tell the students to try to fill in the log without looking back in their books for words. Then have them compare answers with a partner.

Finally, copy the Learning Log on the board. Call several students to the board and have them write one word in each column of the log. Check their work.

SAMPLE ANSWERS:

Body	Health Problems	Be Healthy
leg	a cut	walking
arm	a broken arm	drinking water
foot	a cold	getting enough sleep
ear	an earache	exercising
head	a headache	eating healthy food

√ Check what you can do.

Tell the students to complete the checklist. Go around the room and check their work.

Finally, call on different students to read aloud the items they checked and what they filled in for item No. 5.

1. I can talk about a health problem. _____

2. I can name body parts. _____

3. I can make an appointment. _____

4. I can take medicine. _____

5. I can ____________________. _____

Looking Back

What health problems are on page 122? Now write three more words in the Learning Log.

Have the students look at the illustration on page 122 and add three words to their Learning Logs. Then have them compare their additions with a partner.

Finally, call on different students to read aloud the headings and the words they added.

Unit 11

What's your job?

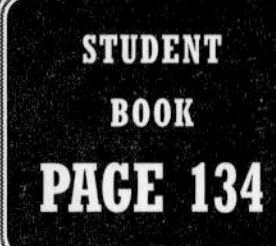

UNIT OVERVIEW

Suggestions for Unit Opener (Student Book page 134)

Brainstorm. Have students look at the unit-opening illustration. Ask them for words related to jobs that they already know. Write the words on the board as students say them.

Model the language. Begin by reading the caption aloud—"What jobs do you see?" Point to the people and say the names of the jobs they're doing. Write the words on the board.

Model the language again. This time have the class repeat the words after you. Then go around the room and have individual students repeat different words.

Point and say. Point to the words you've written on the board as you say them. Have the students repeat them after you.

Initiate pair work. Have the students work in pairs. Tell them to take turns pointing to the different people, scenes, and situations in the illustration and naming them. Demonstrate this by asking a student to point and by saying the name yourself, then pointing yourself and asking the same student to say the name. Go around the room and check students' work.

See Color Transparencies package for additional unit-opening activity. Many of these tasks include a reproducible blackline master.

1 Jobs

STUDENT BOOK PAGE 135

LEARNING POINT
Talking about what you do

NEW LANGUAGE

cashier	gardener
cook	receptionist
custodian	taxi driver
delivery person	waiter

What do you do?
I'm a _____. And you?

A Listen.

Have the students listen with their books closed.

1. A custodian. She's a custodian.

2. A delivery person. He's a delivery person.

3. A receptionist. He's a receptionist.

4. A taxi driver. She's a taxi driver.

5. A cashier. He's a cashier.

6. A cook. He's a cook.

7. A waiter. He's a waiter.

8. A gardener. He's a gardener.

Then have them open their books and look at the illustration on page 134 as you say the name of each job and point to the appropriate person.

Have the students listen again as they follow along with their books open.

Listen and say.

Have the students listen to and repeat each line separately. Stop the tape or CD after each line or read aloud the separate lines with pauses.

1. a custodian

2. a delivery person

3. a receptionist

4. a taxi driver

5. a cashier

6. a cook

7. a waiter

8. a gardener

Then call on individual students to listen and repeat after you.

EXPANSION ACTIVITY:
Draw the job.

Have the students work in pairs. Assign each pair a job from this lesson and tell each pair to draw an illustration representing the job. Have each pair write the name of the job on the back of their illustration.

Hold up each illustration, and have the class say the job. You can also have individual students say the jobs. When the correct job is given, verify it for the class by revealing the word on the back of the illustration.

B Listen.

Have the students listen with their books closed.

Paul: What do you do?

Tien: I'm a delivery person. And you?

Paul: I'm a custodian.

Have the students listen again as they follow along with their books open.

STUDENT BOOK PAGE 135

Listen and say.

Repeat the procedure from the previous **Listen and say.**

C Talk with a partner.

Copy the open-ended conversation on the board. Pick a student to model the open-ended conversation with you in front of the class.

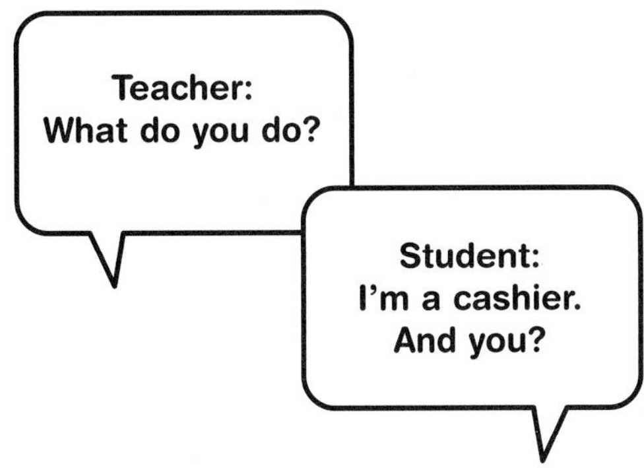

Teacher:
What do you do?
Student:
I'm a cashier.
And you?

Have the students work in pairs to practice the conversation. Tell them to use the words in the Word List. Go around the room and check their work.

Finally, call on different pairs to share their conversations with the class.

2 A cook uses pots and pans.

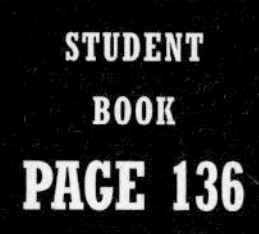

LEARNING POINT
Identifying things that people use on the job

NEW LANGUAGE

cash register	pots and pans
computer	taxi cab

 **Listen.**

Have the students open their books and examine the illustrations.

Have the students listen with their books closed.

1. A taxi cab. A taxi driver drives a taxi cab.

2. Pots and pans. A cook uses pots and pans.

3. A computer. A receptionist uses a computer.

4. A cash register. A cashier uses a cash register.

Then have them open their books, look at the illustrations, and listen again as they follow along.

Listen and say.

Have the students listen to and repeat each line separately. Stop the tape or CD after each line or read aloud the separate lines with pauses.

1. a taxi cab

2. pots and pans

3. a computer

4. a cash register

Then call on individual students to listen and repeat after you.

 √ **Check who uses it.**

Go over the chart with the students. Have them repeat the words after you. Then point out the sample answer and say a sentence about it.

Teacher:
A taxi driver drives a taxi cab.

Have the students complete the activity.

Have them compare answers with a partner. Go around the room and check their work.

Finally, ask a pair to copy the chart on the board and fill in the check marks.

ANSWERS:

taxi driver: A taxi cab

receptionist: A computer

cook: Pots and pans

cashier: A cash register

 **Listen and circle.**

Have the students listen with their books closed.

1. Woman:	I am a receptionist. I use a computer.
2. Man:	I am a cook. I use pots and pans.
3. Man:	I am a taxi driver. I drive a taxi cab.
4. Woman:	I am a cashier. I use a cash register.

 WORKBOOK PAGE 99

2 A cook uses pots and pans.

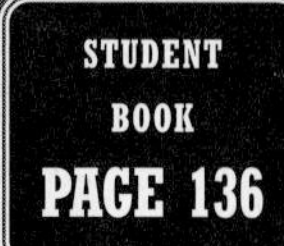

Copy the first line on the board. Play or say the first item. Circle "receptionist."

Then have the students listen again and complete the activity. Stop the tape or CD, or pause after each line, so students have time to circle the appropriate choice.

Have the students compare their answers with a partner. Then have them listen again as they check their work.

Finally, call on individual students to read aloud the items they circled.

ANSWERS:

1. receptionist

2. cook

3. taxi driver

4. cashier

3 Do you like to work outdoors?

STUDENT BOOK PAGE 137

LEARNING POINT
Understanding and talking about job environments

NEW LANGUAGE
indoors
outdoors
with machines
with people

Do you like to work _____?
Yes, I do./No, I don't.

Listen.

Have the students open their books and examine the illustrations.

Have the students listen with their books closed.

1. Indoors. Do you like to work indoors?
2. Outdoors. Do you like to work outdoors?
3. With people. Do you like to work with people?
4. With machines. Do you like to work with machines?

Then have them open their books, look at the illustrations, and listen again as they follow along.

Listen and say.

Have the students listen to and repeat each line separately. Stop the tape or CD after each line or read aloud the separate lines with pauses.

1. indoors
2. outdoors
3. with people
4. with machines

Then call on individual students to listen and repeat after you.

√ Check.

Point out the first item and talk about the sample answer. Refer to the illustration on page 134.

Teacher: Look at the cashier. He works indoors. He works with people.
Teacher: He uses a cash register. A cash register is a machine.

Have the students complete the chart and compare their work with a partner. Go around the room and check their work.

Finally, call on a pair of students to copy the chart on the board and check the appropriate columns.

ANSWERS:

1. cashier: Indoors, With People, With Machines
2. gardener: Outdoors, With Machines
3. waiter: Indoors, Outdoors, With People, With Machines
4. custodian: Indoors, With Machines
5. delivery person: Indoors, Outdoors, With People, With Machines

3 Do you like to work outdoors?

STUDENT BOOK PAGE 137

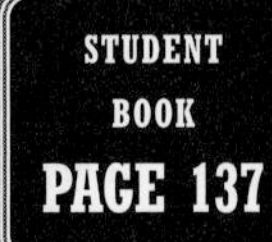

C Listen.

Have the students listen with their books closed.

Grace: Do you like to work indoors?

Don: Yes, I do. And you?

Grace: No, I don't.

Have the students listen again as they follow along with their books open.

D Talk with a partner.

Copy the open-ended conversation on the board. Pick a student to model the open-ended conversation with you in front of the class.

Teacher: Do you like to work indoors?

Student: Yes, I do./No, I don't.

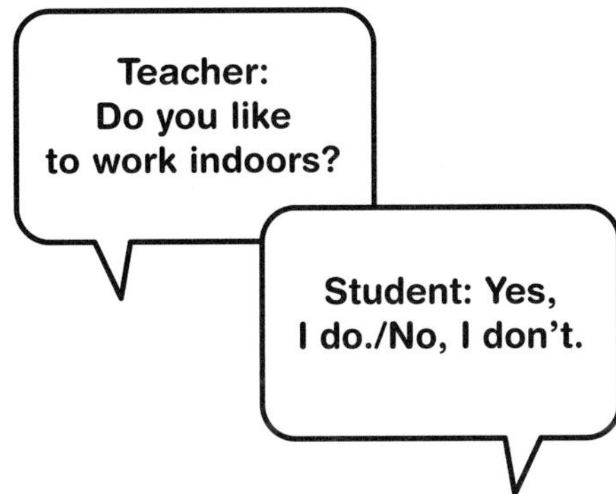

Have the students work in pairs to practice the conversation. Tell them to use the words in the Word List. Go around the room and check their work.

Finally, call on different pairs to share their conversations with the class.

4 I can use a computer.

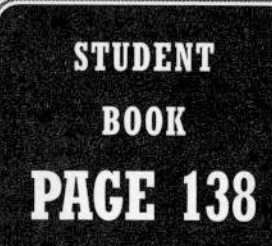

LEARNING POINT
Understanding and talking about job skills

NEW LANGUAGE

drive sell
fix use

What can you do?
I can _____.
_____ can _____.

Listen.

Have the students open their books and examine the illustrations.

Have the students listen with their books closed.

1. Drive. I can drive a car.

2. Fix. I can fix things.

3. Use. I can use a computer.

4. Sell. I can sell things.

Then have them open their books, look at the illustrations, and listen again as they follow along.

Listen and say.

Have the students listen to and repeat each line separately. Stop the tape or CD after each line or read aloud the separate lines with pauses.

1. drive

2. fix

3. use

4. sell

Then call on individual students to listen and repeat after you.

Complete with words from Activity A.

Copy the first sentence on the board and read it aloud.

Tell the students to read over the sentences and use the words from Activity A to fill in the blanks.

Go around the room and check the students' work.

Have them compare their answers with a partner.

Finally, call on a student to write the answers on the board.

ANSWERS:

1. drive

2. fix

3. use

4. sell

Listen.

Have the students listen with their books closed.

Leo: What can you do?

Paul: I can use a computer. And you?

Leo: I can drive a car.

Have the students listen again as they follow along with their books open.

Listen and say.

Repeat the procedure from the previous **Listen and say.**

4 I can use a computer.

STUDENT BOOK PAGE 138

D Write three things you can do.

On the board, write one thing you can do using the phrases from the lesson and/or other verbs.

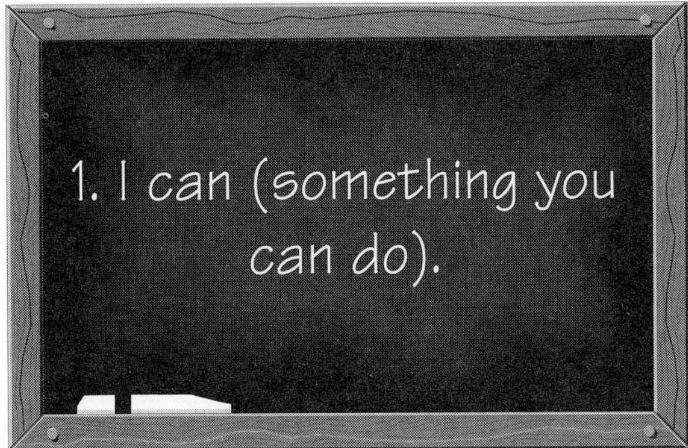
1. I can (something you can do).

Then have the students write their own sentences. Go around and check their work.

Finally, call on different students to write their sentences on the board.

EXPANSION ACTIVITY: Charades

Write the words "drive," "fix," "sell," and "use" on the board. Mime driving a car and say: "I can" to prompt the students to guess what you are doing—"drive a car." Write the sentence on the board to provide a model for future guesses. Continue by miming the other verbs from this lesson—fix (something), use (a machine), and sell (something). Next have the students work in pairs to take turns miming and guessing.

Finally, call on different students to mime for the class.

5 Yes, I can.

STUDENT BOOK PAGE 139

LEARNING POINT
Asking and answering questions about job skills

NEW LANGUAGE
cook food
use machines

Can you _____?

Listen.

Have the students open their books and examine the illustration.

Have the students listen with their books closed.

Man: Can you sell clothes?

Maria: Yes, I can.

Man: Can you drive a car?

Maria: No, I can't.

Then have them open their books, look at the illustration, and listen again as they follow along.

Listen and say.

Have the students listen to and repeat each line separately. Stop the tape or CD after each line or read aloud the separate lines with pauses.

Then call on individual students to listen and repeat after you.

Talk with a partner.

Copy the open-ended conversation on the board. Pick a student to model the open-ended conversation with you in front of the class.

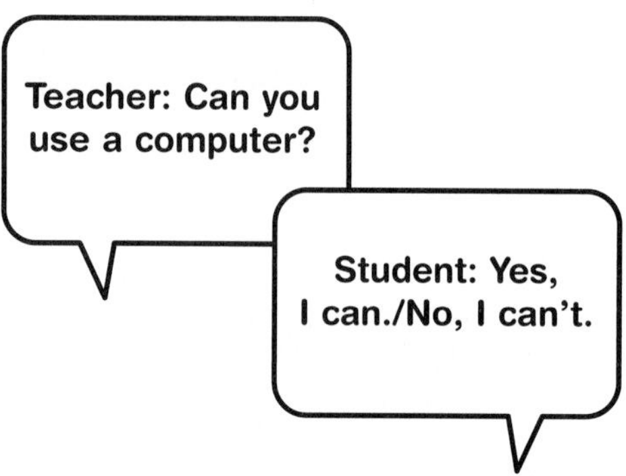

Teacher: Can you use a computer?
Student: Yes, I can./No, I can't.

Have the students work in pairs to practice the exchange. Tell them to use the words in the Word List. Go around the room and check their work.

Finally, call on different pairs to share their exchanges with the class.

Ask classmates.

Copy the chart on the board. Pick a student to model the open-ended conversation with you in front of the class.

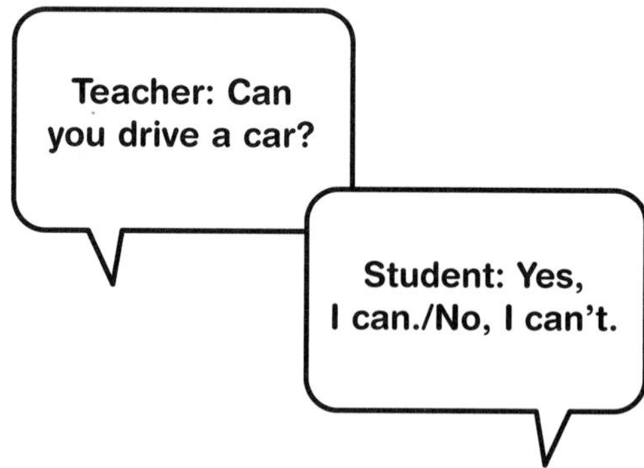

Teacher: Can you drive a car?
Student: Yes, I can./No, I can't.

Continue to ask the student questions from the chart until he or she answers "yes" to a question. At that point, have the student sign his or her name in the appropriate space on the chart.

Have the students complete the activity. Go around the room and check their work.

Finally, call on different students to copy their charts on the board.

 WORKBOOK PAGE 100

Reading want ads

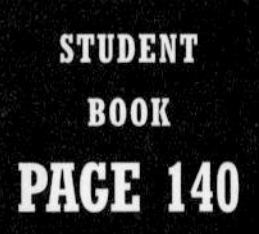

LEARNING POINT
Understanding and using want ads

NEW LANGUAGE
call
manager
pay

Read the want ads. Circle the jobs.

Have the students read the ads. Then read each ad aloud as the students follow along. Tell the students to find and circle the jobs in the ads.

ANSWERS:

1. cashiers

2. custodian

Match.

Have the students examine the want ads in Activity A. Point out the sample answer and the relevant information in the want ad. Then tell the students to match the questions to the answers.

Have them compare answers with a partner. Go around the room and check their work.

Finally, have a student write the answers on the board.

ANSWERS:

1. a

2. e

3. b

4. c

5. d

Listen and √ check the ad from Activity A.

Have the students listen with their books closed.

1. My name is Sara Holt. I am a cashier. I want to work at Wilder Men's Shop.

2. Hi, I'm Ben Lee. I want the custodian job. I can fix things.

3. My name is Frank Jones. I live in San Diego. I'm a good custodian.

4. Hi, I'm John Miller. I like to work with people. I'm a good cashier.

Copy the chart on the board. Play or say the first item. Tell the students to listen for key words, or important words, that tell what job the person wants. Write a check mark in the "Ad #1" column. Ask the students what the key words were and prompt them to reply, "cashier" and "Wilder Men's Shop."

Then have the students listen again and complete the activity. Stop the tape or CD, or pause after each item, so students have time to check the appropriate column.

Have the students compare their answers with a partner. Have them listen again to check their work.

Finally, ask a student to copy the chart on the board and check √ the answers.

ANSWERS:

Sara: Ad #1

Ben: Ad #2

Frank: Ad #2

John: Ad #1

WORKBOOK PAGE 101

7 I was a taxi driver.

STUDENT BOOK PAGE 141

LEARNING POINT
Talking about past jobs

NEW LANGUAGE
employer
work experience

What was your job before?
I was a/an _____ in _____.

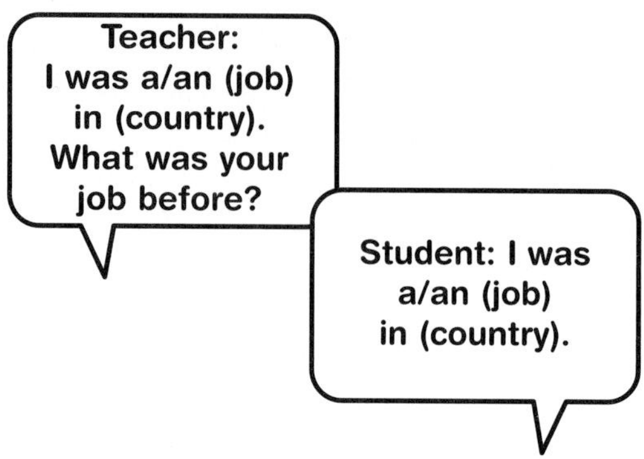

Teacher:
I was a/an (job) in (country). What was your job before?
Student: I was a/an (job) in (country).

A Listen.

Have the students open their books and examine the illustrations.

Have the students listen with their books closed.

Leo: I was a taxi driver in Russia. What was your job before?

Maria: I was a cashier in Mexico.

Then have them open their books, look at the illustrations, and listen again as they follow along.

Listen and say.

Have the students listen to and repeat each line separately. Stop the tape or CD after each line or read aloud the separate lines with pauses.

Then call on individual students to listen and repeat after you.

B Talk with a partner.

Copy the open-ended conversation on the board. Pick a student to model the open-ended conversation with you in front of the class.

Have the students work in pairs to practice the conversation. Go around the room and check their work.

Finally, call on different pairs to share their conversations with the class.

C Read. Answer the questions.

Have the students read the forms.

Have them follow along in their books as you read the information aloud. Explain that the term "work experience" means jobs from the past, before now. Explain that an employer is the person or company you work for.

Have the students complete the activity. Go around the room and check their work.

Have them compare their work with a partner.

Finally, call on different students to read their answers aloud.

ANSWERS:

1. 17 Apple Street, Los Angeles, CA, 90001

2. 213-555-8892

3. delivery person

4. taxi driver

 WORKBOOK PAGE 102

8 A paycheck

LEARNING POINT
Reading and understanding information on a paycheck

NEW LANGUAGE

deduction
federal taxes
gross pay
hours
paycheck
pay rate
state taxes

A Listen and read.

Begin by pointing out the paycheck and explaining that it is payment for work done. Write the new words on the board and explain the terms to the students.

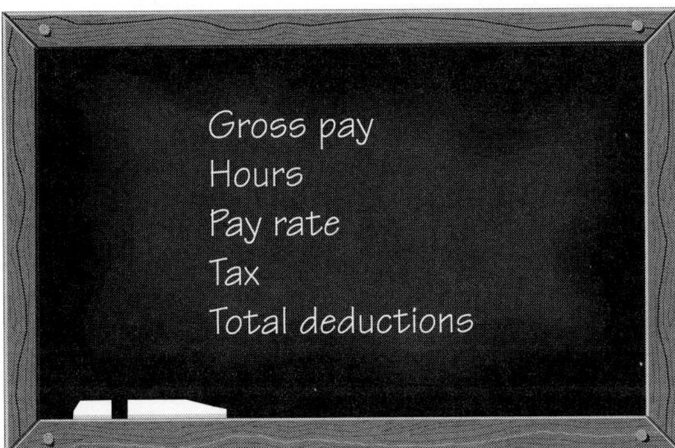

Provide general explanations of the words using gestures, realia, and language the students already know. Avoid trying to explain technical terms such as Federal, State, FICA, and Medicare; instead, simply make students aware that these words refer to different kinds of deductions.

Have the students follow along in their books as you read the paycheck information aloud. Then have them read the paragraphs.

Have them listen to the tape or CD with their books closed.

Don is a cashier. He works at Shop Rite Food Store. Don makes $10 an hour. Don works eight hours a week. He makes $80 a week.

Don has to pay taxes. He pays $7.09 in federal taxes. Don pays $2.95 in state taxes. Don pays other taxes, too. His paycheck is for $66.61.

Have them listen again as they follow along with their books open.

B Circle.

Refer the students to the paycheck in Activity A as you point out the sample answer. Then have them use the paycheck to complete the activity. Go around the room and check the students' work.

Have the students compare answers with a partner.

Finally, call on a student to write the answers on the board.

ANSWERS:

1. Don Park

2. $10 an hour

3. 8 hours

4. $7.09

5. $2.95

6. $66.61

8 A paycheck

STUDENT BOOK PAGE 142

Write.

Read the sentence aloud.

Teacher:
Don takes the check to the bank. He deposits ____.

Have the students complete the sentence.

Have the students compare their answers with a partner. Go around and check their work.

Finally, have a student write the complete sentence on the board.

ANSWER:

$66.61

EXPANSION ACTIVITY: Find a want ad.

Bring newspaper ads to class or have the students bring them in. Have the students work in pairs to find ads for the following jobs: receptionist, cook, and cashier. Have them circle the ads and underline the jobs, addresses, phone numbers, and pay rates.

Then have them look for jobs they're interested in. Ask them to circle these ads and underline the important information as they did with the other ads.

9 A job application

STUDENT BOOK PAGE 143

LEARNING POINT
Filling out a job application and talking about work experience

NEW LANGUAGE
application
years of experience

Read.

Have the students read the forms.

Have them follow along in their books as you read the information aloud. Explain the meaning of "Years of Experience" and the purpose of a job application.

B Complete the form.

Have the students fill in their own job applications. Go around the room and check their work. Then have them compare their work with a partner.

Finally, call on different students to copy their completed applications on the board.

EXPANSION ACTIVITY: Answer a want ad.

Refer students to the want ads in Lesson 6 on page 140 of the Student Book. Tell them to answer one of the ads. Have the students write their responses first, then say them with a partner. Tell them to say which job they want and then talk about their work experience and skills. Tell them to use their imaginations. Model some lines for the first ad and write them on the board.

I want to be a delivery person.
I was a delivery person from 1991 to 1995. I have 5 years of experience. I can drive a car and I can use a computer.

Finally, call on individual students to read their responses aloud to the class.

10 Review

STUDENT BOOK PAGES 144–145

Write the job.

Point out the first item and the sample answer.

Then have the students complete the exercise.

Have them compare answers with a partner. Go around and check their work.

Finally, ask a student to write the answers on the board.

ANSWERS:

1. delivery person

2. receptionist

3. cook

4. taxi driver

5. cashier

Listen and √ check the answer.

Have the students listen with their books closed.

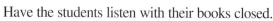

1. What do you do?

2. Do you like to work with machines?

3. What was your job before?

4. Can you drive a car?

5. What can you do?

Copy the first item on the board. Play or say the first question. Write a check mark next to "I'm a receptionist."

Then have the students listen again and complete the activity. Stop the tape or CD, or pause after each question, so students have time to check the appropriate response.

Have the students compare their answers with a partner. Have them listen again to check their work.

Finally, ask a student to copy the chart on the board and check √ the answers.

ANSWERS:

1. I'm a receptionist.

2. No, I don't.

3. I was a taxi driver.

4. Yes, I can.

5. I can fix machines.

Community Challenge: Want ad

Bring newspaper ads to class or have the students bring them in. Have each student choose an ad and use it to fill in the blanks. Then have them compare their work with a partner. Go around the room and check their work.

Finally, call on different students to read their ads to the class, write the information on the board, and read it aloud.

Write *What* or *Where*.

Go over the sample question and answer with the students. Explain that you use "What" for things and "Where" for places.

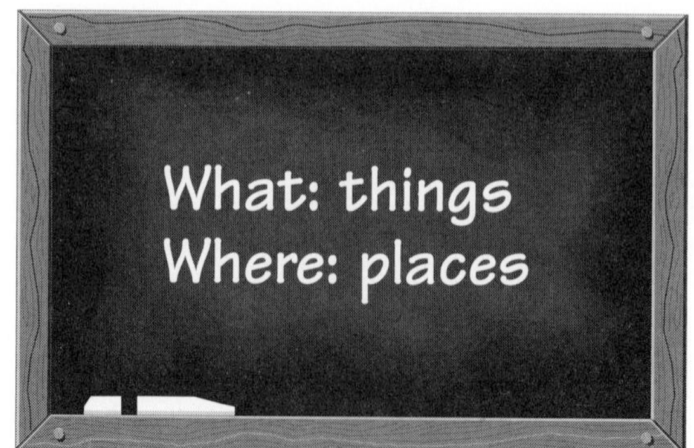

Then have the students complete the activity and share their work with a partner. Go around and check their work.

Finally, have a pair of students write the answers on the board. You can also have the pairs act out the exchanges.

ANSWERS:

1. What

2. Where

3. What

4. Where

5. What

Learning Log

Write five words you remember.

Review the purpose of a learning log.

Tell the students to try to fill in the log without looking back in their books for words. Then have them compare answers with a partner.

Finally, copy the Learning Log on the board. Call several students to the board and have them write one word in each column of the log. Check their work.

SAMPLE ANSWERS:

Jobs	Job Activities	Paychecks
gardener	cooking	federal taxes
taxi driver	driving	state taxes
receptionist	using computers	gross pay
custodian	selling clothes	net pay
cashier	fixing things	pay rate

√ Check what you can do.

Tell the students to complete the checklist. Go around the room and check their work.

Finally, call on different students to read aloud the items they checked and what they filled in for item No. 5.

1. I can talk about jobs. _____

2. I can say what my job was before. _____

3. I can understand a paycheck. _____

4. I can read want ads. _____

5. I can ____________________. _____

Looking Back

Talk about the jobs on page 134. Now write three more words in your Learning Log.

Have the students look at the illustration on page 134 and add three words to their Learning Logs. Then have them compare their additions with a partner.

Finally, call on different students to read aloud the headings and the words they added.

See Color Transparencies package for unit wrap-up activity. This task can be used as an oral assessment tool. Many unit wrap-up activities include a reproducible blackline master.

Unit 12 How do you get to class?

STUDENT BOOK PAGES 146

UNIT OVERVIEW

	LESSON:	LEARNING POINTS:	SB#
1.	**I take a bus.**	Asking and answering questions about modes of transportation	**p. 147**
2.	**It's on the left.**	Understanding, asking for, and giving directions	**p. 148**
3.	**It's next to the market.**	Asking for and giving directions	**p. 149**
4.	**How do I get to the airport?**	Asking for and giving directions	**p. 150**
5.	**When does the next train leave?**	Asking and answering questions about departure times	**p. 151**
6.	**Getting a learner's permit**	Applying for a learner's permit	**p. 152**
7.	**Road signs**	Understanding and reading road signs	**p. 153**
8.	**How often does the train leave?**	Understanding and asking about departure schedules	**p. 154**
9.	**Reading a schedule**	Reading a bus schedule	**p. 155**
10.	**Review**	Review Unit 12	**p. 156**

Suggestions for Unit Opener (Student Book page 146)

Brainstorm. Have students look at the unit-opening illustration. Ask them for words related to transportation that they already know. Write the words on the board as students say them.

Model the language. Begin by reading the caption aloud—"What do you see?" Point to the items in the illustration and name them. Write the words on the board.

Model the language again. This time have the class repeat the words after you. Then go around the room and have individual students repeat different words.

Point and say. Point to the words you've written on the board as you say them. Have the students repeat them after you.

Initiate pair work. Have the students work in pairs. Tell them to take turns pointing to the different people, scenes, and situations in the illustration and naming them. Demonstrate this by asking a student to point and by saying the name yourself, then pointing yourself and asking the same student to say the name. Go around the room and check students' work.

See Color Transparencies package for additional unit-opening activity. Many of these tasks include a reproducible blackline master.

1 I take a bus.

STUDENT BOOK PAGE 147

LEARNING POINT
Asking and answering questions about modes of transportation

NEW LANGUAGE

drive a car
ride a bike
take a bus
take a subway
walk

How do you get to school?
I drive a car.
I take a bus/subway.
I ride a bike.
I walk.

EXPANSION ACTIVITY: Say the sentence.

Practice the transportation expressions with the students. Begin by saying "bus," then write "I take a bus," on the board. Continue with the other nouns from the activity—subway, bike, and car.

Call on individual students to say complete sentences as you say nouns and verbs to them (bike, bus, car, subway, drive, ride, take). Start slowly and speed up as you continue.

A Listen.

Have the students open their books and examine the illustrations.

Have the students listen with their books closed.

1. Take a bus. I take a bus.

2. Take a subway. I take a subway.

3. Ride a bike. I ride a bike.

4. Drive a car. I drive a car.

Then have them open their books, look at the illustrations, and listen again as they follow along.

Listen and say.

Have the students listen to and repeat each line separately. Stop the tape or CD after each line or read aloud the separate lines with pauses.

1. take a bus

2. take a subway

3. ride a bike

4. drive a car

Then call on individual students to listen and repeat after you.

B Listen.

Have the students listen with their books closed.

Leo: How do you get to school?

Tien: I take a bus.

Have the students listen again as they follow along with their books open.

Listen and say.

Repeat the procedure from the previous **Listen and say.**

C Talk with a partner.

Copy the open-ended conversation on the board. Pick a student to model the open-ended conversation with you in front of the class.

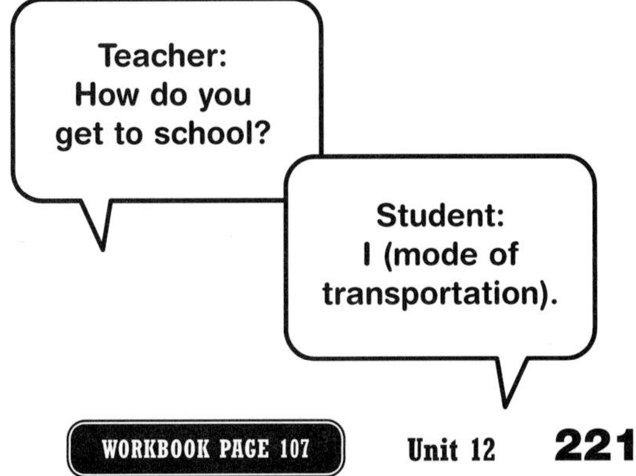
Teacher: How do you get to school?
Student: I (mode of transportation).

1 I take a bus.

STUDENT BOOK PAGE 147

Have the students work in pairs to practice the conversation. Go around and the room and check their work.

Finally, call on different pairs to share their conversations with the class.

D Ask classmates.

Copy the chart on the board. Pick a student to model the open-ended conversation with you in front of the class.

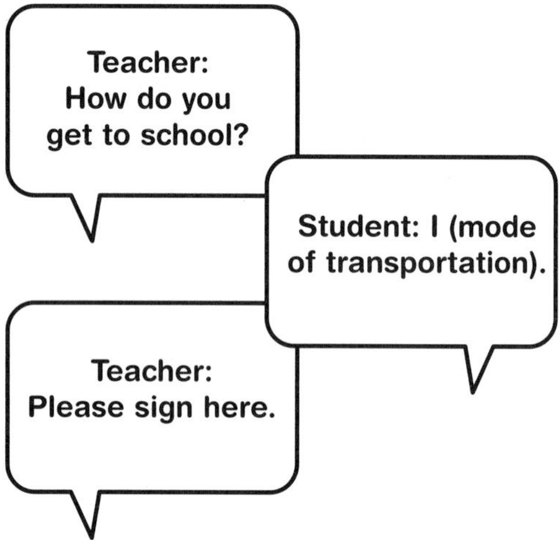
Teacher: How do you get to school?
Student: I (mode of transportation).
Teacher: Please sign here.

Have the student sign his or her name in the appropriate space on the chart.

Have the students complete the activity. Go around the room and check their work.

Finally, call on different students to copy their charts on the board.

2 It's on the left.

STUDENT BOOK PAGE 148

LEARNING POINT
Understanding, asking for, and giving directions

NEW LANGUAGE
on the left
on the right
straight ahead

Excuse me. Where is the _____?
It's on the left/on the right/straight ahead.

EXPANSION ACTIVITY: Point the way.

Mime the three directions (on the left, on the right, and straight ahead) as the class says the phrases after you. For example, point to your left and prompt the class to say: "on the left."

Next call on individual students to say the phrases as you point. Start slowly and speed up as you continue.

Listen.

Have the students open their books and examine the illustration.

Have the students listen with their books closed.

1. On the left. The movie theater is on the left.

2. Straight ahead. The post office is straight ahead.

3. On the right. The bank is on the right.

Then have them open their books, look at the illustration, and listen again as they follow along.

Listen and say.

Have the class listen to and repeat each line separately. Stop the tape or CD after each line or read aloud the separate lines with pauses.

1. on the left

2. straight ahead

3. on the right

Then call on individual students to listen and repeat after you.

Listen.

Have the students listen with their books closed.

Maria: Excuse me. Where is the movie theater?

Man: It's on the left.

Have the students listen again as they follow along with their books open.

Listen and say.

Repeat the procedure from the previous **Listen and say.**

Talk with a partner.

Copy the open-ended conversation on the board. Pick a student to model the open-ended conversation with you in front of the class.

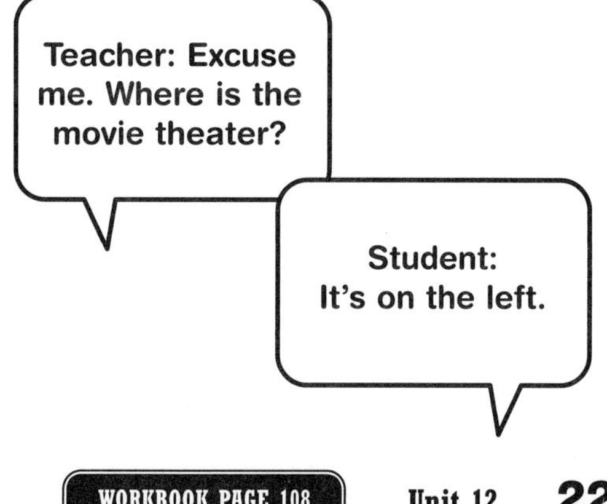

Teacher: Excuse me. Where is the movie theater?
Student: It's on the left.

It's on the left.

STUDENT BOOK PAGE 148

Have the students work in pairs to practice the conversation. Tell them to use the illustration in Activity A and the words in the Word List. Go around the room and check their work.

Finally, call on different pairs to share their conversations with the class.

Listen and circle.

Have the students listen with their books closed.

1. The bank is on the right.

2. The post office is straight ahead.

3. The movie theater is on the left.

4. The drugstore is on the right.

Copy the first line of the chart on the board. Play or say the first item. Tell them to listen for direction words. Circle "right."

Then have the students listen again and complete the activity. Stop the tape or CD, or pause after each sentence, so students have time to circle the appropriate choice. Go around the room and check their work.

Have the students compare their answers with a partner. Then have them listen again as they check their work.

Finally, call on individual students to read aloud the items they circled.

ANSWERS:

1. right

2. straight ahead

3. left

4. right

 WORKBOOK PAGE 108

3 It's next to the market.

STUDENT BOOK PAGE 149

LEARNING POINT
Asking for and giving directions

NEW LANGUAGE
between
next to
on the corner of

Listen.

Have the students open their books and examine the map. Point out and have students name the various buildings, streets, and vehicles.

Have the students listen with their books closed.

1. On the corner of. The bank is on the corner of 22nd Street and Pond Street.

2. Next to. The laundromat is next to the bank.

3. Between. The market is between the bank and the post office.

Then have them open their books, look at the illustration, and listen again as they follow along.

Listen and say.

Have the students listen to and repeat each line separately. Stop the tape or CD after each line or read aloud the separate lines with pauses.

1. on the corner of

2. next to

3. between

Then call on individual students to listen and repeat after you.

EXPANSION ACTIVITY: Where is...?

Write the prepositions from Units 9 and 12 on the board.

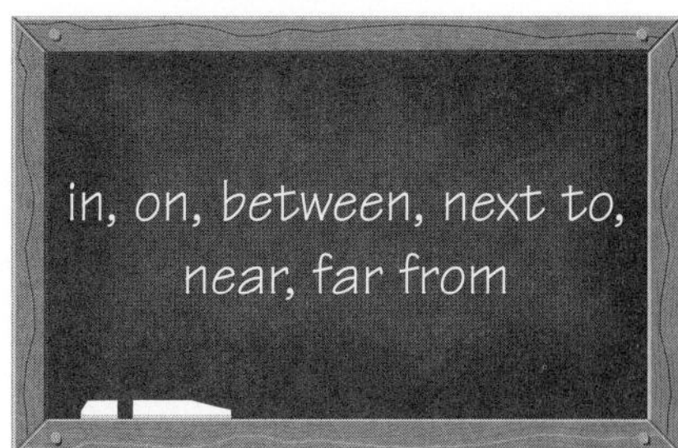

in, on, between, next to,
near, far from

Use the illustrations from this unit and from Unit 9 to point out people and things as you ask the question "Where is/are _____?" Have the students answer with the different prepositions. For example, point to the taxi on page 146 of the Student Book and say: "Where is the taxi?" Prompt the class to reply, "It's next to the bus."

Continue with other items in the illustrations.

Listen.

Have the students listen with their books closed.

Maria: Excuse me. Where is the post office?

Don: It's next to the market.

Have the students listen again as they follow along with their books open.

Listen and say.

Repeat the procedure from the previous **Listen and say.**

3 It's next to the market.

STUDENT BOOK PAGE 149

 **Talk with a partner.**

Copy the open-ended conversation on the board. Pick a student to model the open-ended conversation with you in front of the class.

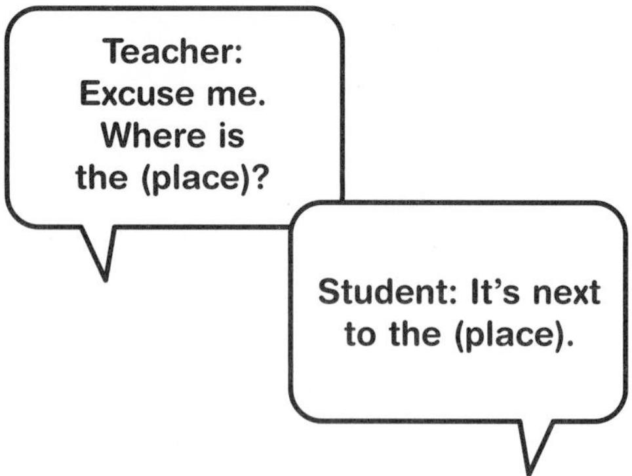
Teacher: Excuse me. Where is the (place)?
Student: It's next to the (place).

Have the students work in pairs to practice the conversation. Tell them to use the illustration in Activity A and the words in the Word List. Go around the room and check their work.

Finally, call on different pairs to share their conversations with the class.

4 How do I get to the airport?

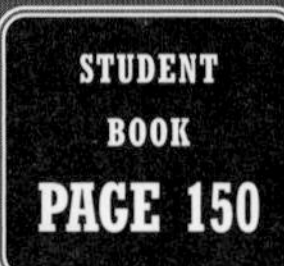

LEARNING POINT
Asking for and giving directions

NEW LANGUAGE
How do I get to _____?
Take the _____.
The _____? Thanks.

Match.

Point out the illustrations and read the information on the buses and subway trains aloud. Have the students repeat after you. Then go over the sample item with the students and have them complete the activity.

Have the students compare answers with a partner. Go around and check their work.

Finally, have a student write the answers on the board.

ANSWERS:

1. c

2. d

3. a

4. b

Listen.

Have the students listen with their books closed.

Paul: How do I get to Northway Airport?

Sandy: Take the D train.

Paul: The D train? Thanks.

Have the students listen again as they follow along with their books open.

Listen and say.

Have the students listen to and repeat each line separately. Stop the tape or CD after each line or read aloud the separate lines with pauses.

Then call on individual students to listen and repeat after you.

Talk with a partner.

Copy the open-ended conversation on the board. Pick a student to model the open-ended conversation with you in front of the class.

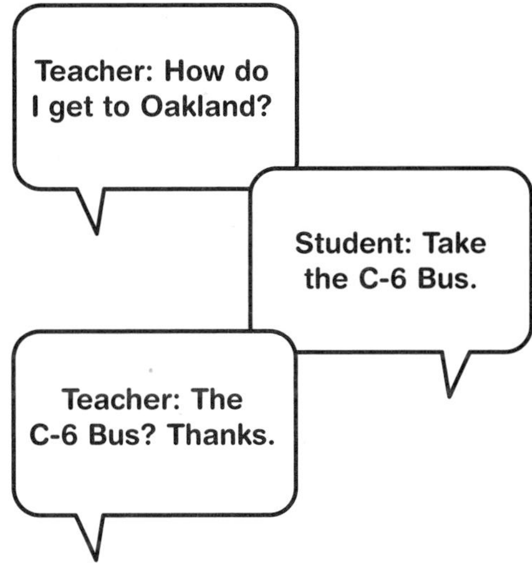

Teacher: How do I get to Oakland?
Student: Take the C-6 Bus.
Teacher: The C-6 Bus? Thanks.

Have the students work in pairs to practice the conversation. Tell them to use the words in the Word List. Go around and the room and check their work.

Finally, call on different pairs to share their conversations with the class.

5 When does the next train leave?

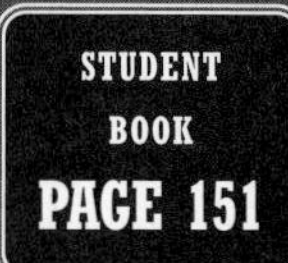

LEARNING POINT
Asking and answering questions about departure times

NEW LANGUAGE
leave
next
train

When does the next train to _____ leave?
It leaves at _____.
At _____? Thanks.

A Listen.

Have the students listen with their books closed.

Carlos: When does the next train to Miami leave?

Operator: It leaves at 4:20.

Carlos: At 4:20? Thanks.

Have the students listen again as they follow along with their books open.

Explain that the word *next* is different from the preposition *next to* in Lesson 2 of this unit. For example, say: "It's 4:00 now. When does the next plane to Miami leave? It leaves at 4:20."

Explain that the verb *leave* means to go away from a place. For example, say: "I leave work at 5:00. I go home at 5:00."

Listen and say.

Have the students listen to and repeat each line separately. Stop the tape or CD after each line or read aloud the separate lines with pauses.

Then call on individual students to listen and repeat after you.

B Talk with a partner.

Copy the open-ended conversation on the board. Pick a student to model the open-ended conversation with you in front of the class.

Teacher: When does the next train to Miami leave?
Student: It leaves at 4:20.
Teacher: At 4:20? Thanks.

Have the students work in pairs to practice the conversation. Tell them to use the words in the Word List. Go around and the room and check their work.

Finally, call on different pairs to share their conversations with the class.

When does the next train leave?

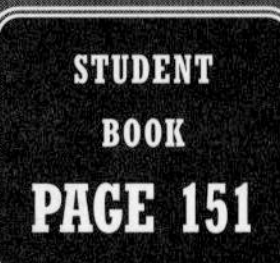

Listen and circle.

Have the students listen with their books closed.

1. Man: When does the next train to Chicago leave?

Woman: It leaves at six-fourteen.

Man: At six-fourteen? Thanks.

2. Man: When does the next train to Los Altos leave?

Woman: It leaves at ten o'clock.

Man: At ten o'clock? Thanks.

3. Woman: When does the next train to San Diego leave?

Man: It leaves at twelve o'clock.

Woman: At twelve o'clock? Thanks.

4. Woman: When does the next train to Newark leave?

Man: It leaves at ten oh two.

Woman: At ten oh two? Thanks.

Copy the first line of the chart on the board. Play or say the first item. Tell the students to listen for times and cities. Circle "6:14" and "Chicago."

Then have the students listen again and complete the activity. Stop the tape or CD, or pause after each conversation, so students have time to circle the appropriate response.

Have the students compare their answers with a partner. Then have them listen again as they check their work.

Finally, call on individual students to read aloud the items they circled.

ANSWERS:

1. Chicago 6:14

2. Los Altos 10:00

3. San Diego 12:00

4. Newark 10:02

6 Getting a learner's permit

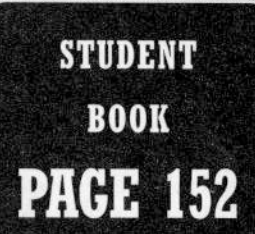

LEARNING POINT
Applying for a learner's permit

NEW LANGUAGE

female	male
learner's permit	test

Listen and read.

Have the students look at the illustration and read the paragraph.

Have them follow along in their books as you read the paragraph aloud.

Circle.

Copy the first item on the board. Circle "a learner's permit" and point to the relevant information in the paragraph.

Then have the students complete the activity.

Have the students compare their answers with a partner.

Finally, call on individual students to read the complete sentences aloud.

ANSWERS:

1. a learner's permit

2. appointment

3. Thursday

4. $25

C Complete the form.

Copy the blank application on the board. Then have the students follow along as you read the words aloud.

Explain the words *male* and *female*. Point to yourself and say your gender. Then point to various students and say their genders. Next, point to various students and prompt them to say their own genders.

Explain that MM/DD/YY means two numbers for the month/two numbers for the day/and two numbers for the year. Write an example on the board.

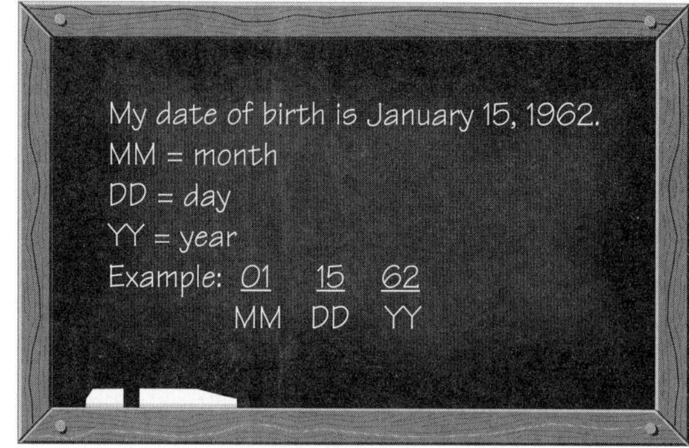

Fill in the application with your own or fictitious information as you read the contents aloud. Then have the students complete the application with their information. Go around and check their work.

Have the students compare their work with a partner.

Finally, call on different students to write their information on the board.

7 Road signs

LEARNING POINT
Understanding and reading road signs

NEW LANGUAGE

bus stop	road sign
hospital	speed limit
No Parking Any Time	stop
one way	

Listen.

Have the students open their books and examine the illustrations.

Have the students listen with their books closed.

1. Bus Stop

2. Speed Limit thirty-five

3. Stop

4. One Way

5. Hospital

6. No Parking Any Time

Then have them open their books, look at the illustrations, and listen again as they follow along.

Listen and say.

Have the students listen to and repeat each line separately. Stop the tape or CD after each line or read aloud the separate lines with pauses.

Then call on individual students to listen and repeat after you.

Write. Complete the road signs.

Point out the first sign and copy it on the board. Then write the sample answer as you explain to the students that they must complete the other signs by writing in the missing words.

Go around the room and check their work.

When the students finish, have them check their work with a partner. Then have different pairs come to the board to draw the signs and fill in the missing words.

ANSWERS:

1. H

2. One Way

Circle the problem.

Point out the two situations in the first item. Point to and read the No Parking sign. Then you shake your head and point to the parked car.

Have the students examine the sets of illustrations and complete the activity. Go around the room and check their work.

Have the students compare their answers with a partner.

Finally, have a student point to the choices he or she circled.

ANSWERS:

1. illustration on the right

2. illustration on the right

8 How often does the train leave?

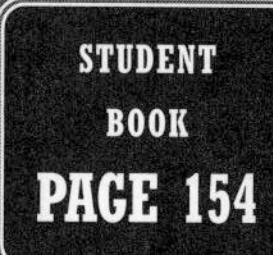
STUDENT BOOK PAGE 154

LEARNING POINT
Understanding and asking about departure schedules

NEW LANGUAGE
every15 minutes/half hour/hour
How often does the ______ leave?
It leaves every _______.
Oh good. At ____, ____, and ____.

Listen.

Have the students listen with their books closed.

Carlos: How often does the B Train leave?

Isabel: It leaves every hour.

Carlos: Oh good. At 4:00, 5:00, and 6:00.

Have the students listen again as they follow along with their books open.

Point out the times in the conversation to show that the train leaves every hour, at 4:00, 5:00, 6:00, etc.

Listen and say.

Have the students listen to and repeat each line separately. Stop the tape or CD after each line or read aloud the separate lines with pauses.

Then call on individual students to listen and repeat after you.

Listen.

Repeat the procedure from the previous **Listen.**

Grace: How often does the 5 Bus leave?

Paul: It leaves every half hour.

Grace: Oh good. At 12:00, 12:30, and 1:00.

Listen and say.

Repeat the procedure from the previous **Listen and say.**

Listen.

Repeat the procedure from the previous **Listen.**

Tien: How often does the subway leave?

Leo: It leaves every 15 minutes.

Tien: Oh good. At 10:15, 10:30, and 10:45.

Listen and say.

Repeat the procedure from the previous **Listen and say.**

 WORKBOOK PAGE 112

8 How often does the train leave?

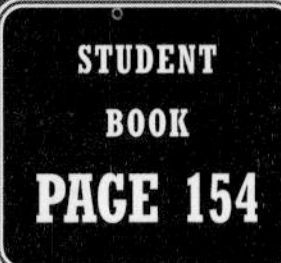

Match.

Point out the first item and go over it with the students. Then have them match the remaining items.

Have them compare answers with a partner.

Finally, call on a student to read the answers aloud as you write them on the board.

ANSWERS:

1. c

2. b

3. a

Listen and circle.

Have the students listen with their books closed.

1. Miami

Man: When does the bus to Miami leave?

Woman: It leaves every half hour.

2. Chicago

Man: When does the train to Chicago leave?

Woman: It leaves every 15 minutes

3. Dallas

Man: When does the train to Dallas leave?

Woman: It leaves every hour.

Copy the first line on the board. Play or say the first item. Tell the students to listen for time words. Circle "every half hour."

Then have the students listen again and complete the activity. Stop the tape or CD, or pause after each conversation, so students have time to circle the appropriate choice.

Have the students compare their answers with a partner. Then have them listen again as they check their work.

Finally, call on individual students to read aloud the items they circled.

ANSWERS:

Miami: every half hour

Chicago: every 15 minutes

Dallas: every hour

9 Reading a schedule

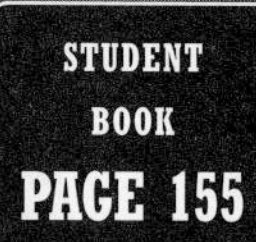

LEARNING POINT
Reading a bus schedule

NEW LANGUAGE
schedule

When does the bus leave _____?
When does the next bus leave?

Listen and read.

Have the students open their books and read the paragraph.

Have the students listen with their books closed.

This is a bus schedule for the K-52 bus. It leaves Pond Street every 15 minutes. The bus goes to Westside Park, City Library, Weston School, and Northway Airport. It's 4:35. The next bus leaves at 4:45.

Then have them open their books, look at the paragraph, and listen again as they read along.

Look at the bus schedule. Answer the questions.

Have the students examine the bus schedule. Point out the first item and the sample answer. Then point to the relevant information on the schedule.

Have the students complete the activity. Go around and check their work.

Have the students compare their work with a partner.

Finally, call on students to read the answers.

ANSWERS:

1. 4:30, 4:45, 5:00, 5:15, and 5:30

2. 5:15, 5:30, 5:45, 6:00, and 6:15

3. 5:15

4. 5:30

5. 6:45

EXPANSION ACTIVITY: Talk about the bus schedule.

Have the students look at the bus schedule on page 155 of the Student Book. Refer them to Activity B, item 3, and read the item aloud. Prompt the class to respond to the question. Then pick another time and ask about a different location. For example, say, "It's 4:30. When does the next bus leave Westside Park?" Prompt the class to answer, "4:45." Perform the exchange with a few individual students to be sure that the class understands how to do the activity.

Write a list of times on the board (5:00, 5:15, 5:30, 5:45). Have the students work in pairs to ask each other about the bus schedule. Tell them to use the times you wrote on the board.

10 Review

STUDENT BOOK PAGES 156-157

A Listen and write.

Have the students listen with their books closed.

A: Excuse me. Where is the drugstore?

B: It's on the left. Next to the movie theater.

Have the students open their books. Play or say the first item and point out the example.

Have the students listen again and fill in the blanks with the words they hear. Stop the tape or CD, or pause after each sentence, so students have time to write. Go around the room and check their answers.

Have students compare their answers with a partner. Then have them listen again as they check their work.

Finally, call on different students to read aloud the completed sentences as you write the answers on the board.

ANSWERS:

A: Where is

B: left

B Listen and √ check.

Have the students listen with their books closed.

1. How do you get to work?

2. How do you get to school?

3. Excuse me. Where is the police station?

4. When does the next bus to Portland leave?

5. Excuse me. How do I get to Central Park?

6. How often does the train leave?

Copy the first item on the board. Play or say the first question. Write a check mark next to "I take a subway."

Then have the students listen again and complete the exercise. Stop the tape or CD, or pause after each question, so students have time to check the appropriate response.

Have the students compare their answers with a partner. Have them listen again to check their work.

Finally, ask a student to write the answers on the board.

ANSWERS:

1. I take a subway.

2. I take a bus.

3. Straight ahead.

4. It leaves at 2:00.

5. Take the Blue Line.

6. It leaves every 15 minutes.

C Complete the road signs.

Have the students examine the road signs.

Tell the students to write the words in the signs.

Have the students complete the activity. Go around the room and check their work.

Have the students compare their answers with a partner.

Finally, call on different students to draw the signs on the board.

10 Review

STUDENT BOOK PAGES 156-157

ANSWERS:

1. ONE WAY

2. STOP

3. NO PARKING ANY TIME

4. H

D Write the letters in your name. Write words.

Read the directions aloud and go over the sample with the students. Talk about the entries.

Teacher:
The first letter in Carlos's name is C.
"Car" starts with C.

Have the students complete the activity. Go around the room and check the students' work. For letters where they've left blank spaces, help them find words from earlier units.

Finally, call on different students to copy their charts on the board.

E Learning Log

Write five words or phrases you remember.

Review the purpose of a learning log.

Tell the students to try to fill in the log without looking back in their books for words. Then have them compare answers with a partner.

Finally, copy the Learning Log on the board. Call several students to the board and have them write one word in each column of the log. Check their work.

SAMPLE ANSWERS:

Directions	Transportation	Road signs
straight ahead	bus	No Parking
on the left	bike	H
on the right	car	Stop
	subway	One Way
	train	Bus Stop

√ Check what you can do.

Tell the students to complete the checklist. Go around the room and check their work.

Finally, call on different students to read aloud the items they checked and what they filled in for item No. 5.

1. I can understand directions. ____

2. I can give directions. ____

3. I can understand road signs. ____

4. I can read a bus schedule. ____

5. I can ________________. ____

Looking Back

Look at page 146. What new words do you know? Now write three more words in your Learning Log.

Have the students look at the illustration on page 146 and add three words to their Learning Logs. Then have them compare their additions with a partner.

Finally, call on different students to read aloud the headings and the words they added.

10-12 Grammar Spotlight for Units 10-12

STUDENT BOOK
PAGES 158-159

A Can/Can't

Point out and read aloud the possible sentences from the chart.

> **Teacher: I can drive. I can't speak Spanish.**

Have the students repeat after you.

I	can/can't	drive.
You		cook.
He		use a computer.
She		fix things.
It		walk.
We		speak Spanish.
They		ride bicycles.

Explain that we use "can" to talk about ability.

Write *can* or *can't.*

Point out the sample item, read it aloud, and go over the answer with the students. Explain that *can* is the correct answer because Don can learn to drive with a learner's permit. Next have the students complete the exercise. Then have them compare answers with a partner. Go around and check their work.

Finally, call on different students to write the answers on the board.

ANSWERS:

1. can

2. can't

3. can

4. can

5. can't

6. can't

7. can

8. can

B Complete with *next to* or *between.*

Point out the illustration and talk about it.

Next have the students complete the sentences with *next to* or *between.* Remind them to use the illustration. Go around the room and check their work.

Have the students compare answers with a partner.

Finally, call on a student to write the complete sentences on the board.

ANSWERS:

1. next to

2. between

3. next to

10-12 Grammar Spotlight for Units 10-12

STUDENT BOOK PAGES 158-159

Complete the sentences with *in* or *on*.

Point out the illustration and talk about it.

Next have the students complete the sentences with *in* or *on*. Remind them to use the illustrations. Go around the room and check their work.

Have the students compare answers with a partner.

Finally, call on a student to write the complete sentences on the board.

ANSWERS:

1. in

2. on

3. on

4. in

5. on

10-12 Review for Units 10-12

STUDENT BOOK PAGES 160-161

Match.

Point out the sample question and corresponding answer and read them aloud as the students follow along in their books.

Teacher:
What's the matter?
C. I have a headache.

Then have the students match the remaining items. Go around the room and check their work.

Have the students compare their answers with a partner.

Finally, read the questions aloud and ask for volunteers to read the matching answers.

ANSWERS:

1. c

2. d

3. b

4. a

5. f

6. g

7. e

B Listen. Complete.

Have the students listen with their books closed.

1. Grace

Grace: Hello. This is Grace Lee. I have a cold. Can Dr. Brown see me today?

Woman: Dr. Brown can see you at eleven o'clock.

Grace: At eleven o'clock? That's fine. Thank you.

2. Paul

Paul: This is Paul Lemat. I have a headache. Can the doctor see me today?

Woman: Yes. Dr. Brown can see you at three-thirty this afternoon.

Paul: At three-thirty? Thank you.

3. Tien

Tien: Hello. This is Tien Lam. I have a toothache. Can I see Dr. Green today?

Woman: Dr. Green can see you at twelve-thirty.

Tien: At twelve-thirty? Fine.

4. Carlos

Carlos: This is Carlos Avila. I have an infection.

Woman: Can you come at four-fifteen?

Carlos: Four-fifteen? Yes, I can be there at four-fifteen.

Review for Units 10-12

STUDENT BOOK PAGES 160-161

5. Maria

Maria: Hello. This is Maria Cruz. I have a backache. Can I see Dr. Brown today?

Woman: Dr. Brown can see you at one forty-five.

Maria: At one forty-five? That's fine. Thank you.

Have the students open their books. Play or say the first item and point out the example.

Have the students listen again and complete the activity. Stop the tape or CD, or pause after each conversation, so students have time to write responses.

Have the students compare their answers with a partner. Then have them listen again as they check their work.

Finally, call on different students to read aloud the answers as you write them on the board.

ANSWERS:

1. a cold; 11:00

2. a headache; 3:30

3. a toothache; 12:30

4. an infection; 4:15

5. a backache; 1:45

C What's the job?

Go over the sample answer with the students. Then have them complete the activity. Tell them to use the words in the Word List. Go around and check their work.

Have them compare their answers with a partner.

Finally, call on a pair of students to write the complete words on the board.

ANSWERS:

1. waiter

2. cashier

3. receptionist

4. cook

5. delivery person

6. custodian

7. taxi driver

D Community Challenge: Bus schedule

Have the students study the schedule. Then point out the sample items and go over the answers with them. Next have the students complete the remaining sentences. Go around the room and check their work.

Then have them compare their answers with a partner or in a small group.

Finally, call on two students to write the complete sentences on the board.

ANSWERS:

1. 84; 7:15 a.m.; 5:00 p.m.

2. 343; 11:45 p.m.; Sacramento; 9:45 a.m.

3. 113; 9:00 a.m.; Oakland; 7:25 p.m.

4. 76; 6:00 a.m; San Diego; 10:00 a.m.

5. 202; 11:00 a.m.; Las Vegas; 4:45 p.m.

Workbook Answer Key

Page 2

A. Complete.

Jane: Hello, I'm Jane.

Soo Jin: Hi, Jane. I'm Soo Jin. Nice to meet you.

Jane: Nice to meet you too, Soo Jin.

B. Complete.

Alex: Hi. I'm Alex. I'm from Mexico.

Mei: Hello. My name is Mei. I'm from China.

C. Write your name.

(student's name)

Page 3

A. Complete.

A B C D E F G H I J K L M

a b c d e f g h i j k l m

B. Complete.

N O P Q R S T U V W X Y Z

n o p q r s t u v w x y z

C. Complete.

Eva: Hello. I'm Eva Martinez. What's your name?

Ivan: My name is Ivan Stoli.

Eva: How do you spell that?

Ivan: My first name is I-V-A-N. My last name is S-T-O-L-I.

D. Complete the sentences about you.

(student's first name)

(student's last name)

Page 4

A. Complete.

1. backpack
2. desk
3. door
4. student
5. board
6. pen
7. book
8. teacher
9. chair

Page 5

A. Circle.

d

B. Check.

d

C. Complete.

(student's name)

D. Match.

1. b
2. c
3. a
4. d

Page 6

A. Circle.

1. illustration on the right
2. illustration on the left
3. illustration on the left
4. illustration on the left

B. Check

1. a
2. c
3. a

Page 7

A. Write.

one; two; three; four; five; six; seven; eight; nine; ten

B. Write the numbers.

1. 1
2. 9
3. 7
4. 4
5. 2
6. 5

C. Complete.

1. phone number
2. address
3. e-mail address

Page 8

A. Complete the form about you.

(student's first and last names)

(student's emergency contact)

(emergency contact's phone number)

B. Write the names of three students in your class.

1. (a classmate's name)
2. (a classmate's name)
3. (a classmate's name)

Page 9

A. Unscramble the letters. Write the words.

1. name
2. hello
3. my
4. hi
5. spell
6. board
7. nice
8. paper

B. Find the words.

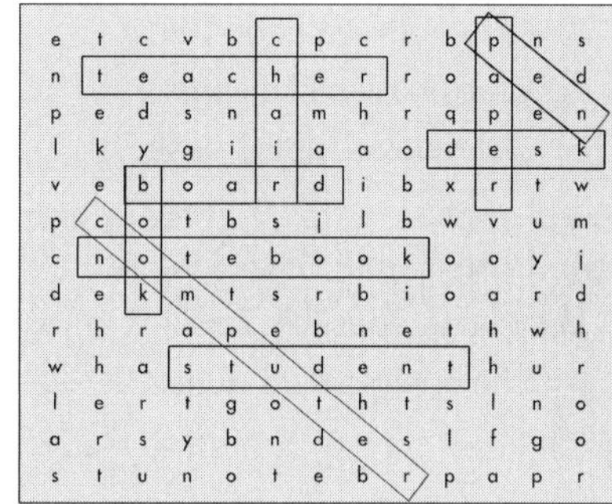

Page 11

A. Complete.

Alex: I'm from Mexico. Where are you from?

Mei: I'm from China.

B. Complete.

A: Where is Alex from?

B: He's from Mexico.

A: Where is Mei from?

B: She's from China.

C. Complete about you.

I'm from (student's country).

Page 12

A. Complete.

Ivan: I speak Russian. What language do you speak?

Soo Jin: I speak Korean.

B. Complete.

Mei: I speak Chinese. What language do you speak?

Marco: I speak Spanish.

C. Complete about you.

My name is (student's name). I'm from (student's country)

I speak (student's language).

Page 13

A. Read. Complete.

1.

A: Marco is from Colombia. What language does he speak?

B: He speaks Spanish.

2.

A: Ly is from Vietnam. What language does she speak?

B: She speaks Vietnamese.

3.

A: Luna is from Brazil. What language does she speak?

B: She speaks Portuguese.

4.

A: Alex is from Mexico. What language does he speak?

B: He speaks Spanish.

5.

A: Mei is from China. What language does she speak?

B: She speaks Chinese.

Page 14

A. Circle.

1. a. married
2. c. divorced
3. d. widowed

B. Complete.

1. Eva is widowed.
2. Mary and Kim are single.
3. Alex is married.
4. Marco is divorced.

Page 15

A. Complete.

1. Lin is tall.
2. Soo Jin is average height.
3. Alex is tall.
4. Mei is short.

B. Write about the people.

1. Soo Jin wears glasses.
2. Alex and Mei don't wear glasses.

Page 16

A. Complete.

eleven; twelve; thirteen; fourteen; fifteen

sixteen; seventeen; eighteen; nineteen

B. Write the numbers.

1. 11
2. 19
3. 14
4. 16
5. 15
6. 12

C. Complete.

A: What's your address?

B: My address is 324 Short Street.

A: What's your zip code?

B: My zip code is 92924.

D. Complete.

(student's address)

(student's zip code)

Page 17

A: Complete the form for Luna.

Gilbert; Luna; J.

324 Lake Street; Troy; NY; 12183

widowed

brown

black

Page 18

A. Complete.

1. English
2. Spanish
3. Portuguese
4. Vietnamese
5. Korean
6. Russian
7. Chinese

B. What are the words?

Across

3. address
6. hello

Down

1. name
2. meet
4. spell
5. your

Page 20

A. Complete.

1. Van
2. Tam
3. Loc

B. Complete. Look at the pictures in Activity A.

1. brother
2. niece
3. daughter
4. sister-in-law

Page 21

A. Complete. Look at the pictures on page 20.

1.
A: Who is Loc?
B: Loc is Ly's father.

2.
A: Who is Tam?
B: Tam is Ly's mother.

3.
A: Who is Doug?
B: Doug is Ly's son.

B. Read and check. Look at the pictures on page 20.

1. Ly's father.
2. Ly's niece.
3. Ly's mother.
4. Ly's son.
5. Ly's sister-in-law.
6. Ly's husband.

Page 22

A. Complete.

Soo Jin: Do you have children, Ly?
Ly: Yes, I have a son and a daughter.
Soo Jin: No, I don't.

Alex: Do you have children?
Jane: No, I don't.
Alex: Yes, I have a son.

B. Write about you.

(No, I don't. / Yes, I have a...)

Page 23

A. Write *Mr., Mrs.*, or *Ms*. Look at the picture on page 20.

1. Mr. Van Tran
2. Mr. and Mrs. Cao
3. Ms. Jade Tran
4. Ms. or Mrs. Nu Cao
5. Mr. Doug Tran

Page 24

A. Complete Ivan's family tree.

Igor = grandfather
Olga = grandmother
Elena = mother
Sasha = father
Anton = brother
Mila = sister-in-law
Lara = niece

B. Write *middle-aged, old,* or *young*.

1. young
2. old
3. middle-aged

Page 25

A. Write the numbers.

1. 90
2. 50
3. 30
4. 100
5. 60
6. 22
7. 70
8. 40
9. 50
10. 80

B. Write the numbers.

20 30 40 50 60 70 80 90 100

C. Complete.

Soo Jin: How old are you, Luna?
Luna: I'm 52 years old.
Luna: How old are you, Eva?
Eva: I'm 68 years old.

D. Write about you.

(student's age)

Page 26

B. Complete Alex's census form.

178 Old Street
Albany; NY; 12203

1. Mr. Alex; P.; Reyes; 48
2. Mr. Juan; R.; Reyes; 70
3. Mrs. Anita; L.; Reyes; 70
4. Mrs. Linda; T.; Reyes; 46
5. Mr. Ben; S.; Reyes; 15
6. Ms. Lola; J.; Reyes; 17

Page 27

A. Complete.

1. f a t h e r
2. d a u g h t e r
3. s o n
4. b r o t h e r
5. m o t h e r
6. h u s b a n d

B. Write the letters from Activity A.

Y o u a r e s m a r t !

Pages 28–29

A. Pronouns.

Circle the pronouns.

(I) am Ly. (I) am from Hue, Vietnam. (I) speak Vietnamese and English. (I) am married. (I) have a brother and a sister-in-law. (They) speak Vietnamese and English, too. (We) live in the United States. (I) have a husband. (He) is from Vietnam, too. (We) have two children.

B. Present Tense of *BE*.

Write *am, is,* or *are*.

1. is
2. are
3. am
4. are
5. are
6. are

Write *'m, 's,* or *'re.*

1. He's
2. We're
3. They're
4. I'm
5. She's
6. I'm
7. You're
8. She's

C. *BE* with Negatives.

Write negative sentences.

1. He's not
2. She's not
3. He's not
4. They're not
5. I'm not
6. She's not
7. They're not
8. We're not
9. I'm not

D. Present tense of *HAVE*.

Write *have* or *has*.

1. has
2. has
3. have
4. has
5. have
6. have

Page 31

A. Complete.

1. kitchen
2. bathroom
3. bedroom
4. living room
5. yard
6. dining room

B. Look at the pictures in Activity A. Complete.

1. Nu and Ly are in the kitchen.
2. Loc is in the living room.
3. Jade is in the bedroom.

Page 32

A. Complete.

Luna: Is there a chair in the living room?

Erik: Yes, there is.

Luna: Is there a lamp in the kitchen?

Erik: No, there isn't.

B. Circle the answers.

1. Yes, there is.
2. No, there isn't.
3. Yes, there is.

Page 33

A. Circle.

1. bathroom
2. hall
3. yard
4. kitchen
5. bathroom
6. bedroom
7. bathroom

B. Complete.

1. apartment
2. house
3. rented room

C. Complete.

1. rented room
2. apartment
3. house

Page 34

B. Complete.

Kim has a: lamp, chair, desk, sofa

Kim needs a: dresser, table

C. Complete.

Eva: What do you need?

Kim: I need a bed.

Eva: Do you need a lamp?

Kim: No, I don't. Thanks.

Page 35

A. Complete.

1.

A: Where do you shower?

B: I shower in the bathroom.

2.

A: Where do you cook?

B: I cook in the kitchen.

3.

A: Where do you study?

B: I study in the living room.

4.

A: Where do you sleep?

B: I sleep in the bedroom.

B. Complete.

1. in the city
2. at the beach
3. in the country

Page 36

A. Write the numbers.

1. 30
2. 13
3. 18
4. 80
5. 12
6. 20
7. 90
8. 19

B. Write the numbers.

1. seventy
2. seventeen
3. sixteen
4. sixty
5. fifty
6. fifteen

C. Write the numbers.

1. 20
2. 60
3. 18
4. 14
5. 12

Page 37

A. Match.

1. e
2. b
3. d
4. c
5. a

Page 38

A. Find the words.

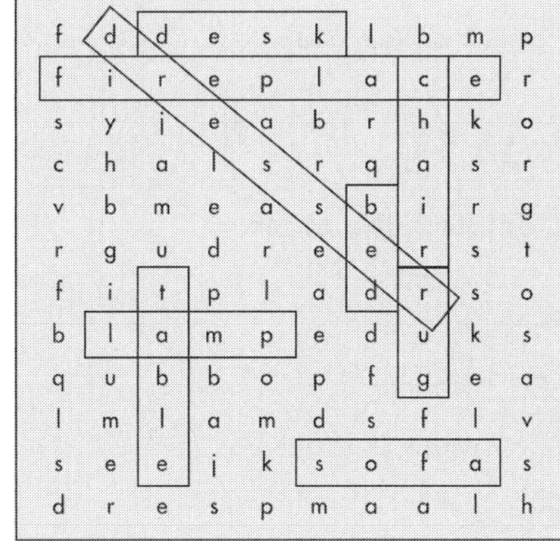

B. Write the words.

1. A: Is there a shower in the bathroom?
2. A: Where are your parents?

Page 40

A. Match.

1. c
2. e
3. a
4. f
5. d
6. b

B. Complete.

Soo Jin: What do you do every day?

Eva: I brush my teeth.

Page 41

A. Complete the calendar.

Calendar: Sunday; Monday; Tuesday; Wednesday; Thursday; Friday; Saturday

B. Complete. Look at the calendar in Activity A.

1. Sunday
2. Friday
3. Sunday and Tuesday
4. Monday and Wednesday

C. Complete.

1. August
2. March
3. January
4. February
5. December
6. October

Page 42

A. Match.

1. b
2. c
3. a
4. d

B. Complete the sentences about Kim's day.

1. 6:30
2. 6:45
3. 7:15
4. 9:00

Page 43

A. Complete.

Alex: I'd like to make an appointment for a tune-up.

Man: Can you come on Monday at 7:00?

Alex: Monday at 7:00? That's fine.

B. Complete.

Eva: I'd like to make an appointment for a haircut.

Woman: Can you come on Friday at 3:45?

Eva: Friday at 3:45? That's fine.

Eva: I'd like to make an appointment for a cleaning.

Woman: Can you come on Wednesday at 10:30?

Eva: Wednesday at 10:30? That's fine.

Page 44

A. Complete.

Luna: How often do you cook dinner?

Erik: Once a week.

Kim: Once a month.

B. Circle.

1. once a week
2. once a month
3. every day

Page 45

A. Match.

1. f
2. g
3. a
4. h
5. b
6. d
7. e
8. c

B. Write the numbers.

1. 9th
2. 11th
3. 14th
4. 1st
5. 13th
6. 5th
7. 3rd
8. 7th
9. 8th
10. 6th
11. 9th
12. 12th

Page 46

A. Complete the chart for Eva.

Martinez; Eva; S.; September 6, 1959

B. Complete Eva's calendar for this week.

Days: Sunday; Tuesday; Wednesday; Thursday; Saturday

Sunday: garage sales

Monday: cleaning

Tuesday: English class

Wednesday: tune-up

Thursday: English class

Friday: (nothing)

Saturday: basketball

Page 47

A. Complete.

1. A p r i l
2. A u g u s t
3. J a n u a r y
4. J u n e
5. D e c e m b e r
6. O c t o b e r
7. F e b r u a r y
8. M a r c h

B. Write the letters from Activity A. Answer the question.

W h e n i s y o u r b i r t h d a y ?

It's in (month).

Page 49

A. Complete.

1. shoes
2. coat
3. suit
4. watch
5. pants
6. sweater
7. dress
8. skirt

B. Complete.

Luna: Excuse me, I'm looking for a watch.

Clerk: Follow me, please.

Luna: Thank you.

C. Complete.

Clerk: May I help you?

Alex: Yes, I'm looking for a jacket.

Page 50

A. Complete.

Kim: What are you wearing to the party?

Soo Jin: I'm wearing black pants and a blue shirt. What are you wearing?

Kim: I'm wearing a purple dress.

B. Circle.

1. pants and a shirt
2. a skirt and a sweater
3. a skirt
4. a blouse
5. a shirt
6. a suit

Page 51

A. Complete the sentences.

A: What is your favorite color?

B: My favorite color is blue.

B. Complete the sentences.

A: What color is your dress.

B: Red.

A: What color are your shoes?

B: Brown.

C. Write about your clothes.

I'm wearing (clothing items).

My shoes are (color).

My shirt is (color).

Page 52

A. Match.

1. b
2. a
3. c

B. Write *small, medium,* or *large.*

1. medium
2. small
3. large

C. Complete about you.

(student's size)

Page 53

A. Complete.

1. too long
2. too small
3. too small
4. too big
5. too short

B. Write three sentences about Nick's clothes.

1. too long
2. too small/short
3. too small/short

Page 54

A. Complete the chart.

1. 1 cent
2. a nickel
3. 10 cents
4. a quarter; 25¢

B. Circle.

1. $25.25
2. $16.11
3. $5.40
4. $1.40

Page 55

C. Complete.

December 20, 2005

Stanford's Department Store; $26.05

twenty-six and 05/100 ———

sweater; (signature)

Page 56

A. What are the words?

Across

2. penny
5. dollar

Down

1. dime
3. nickel
4. quarter

B. Find the words.

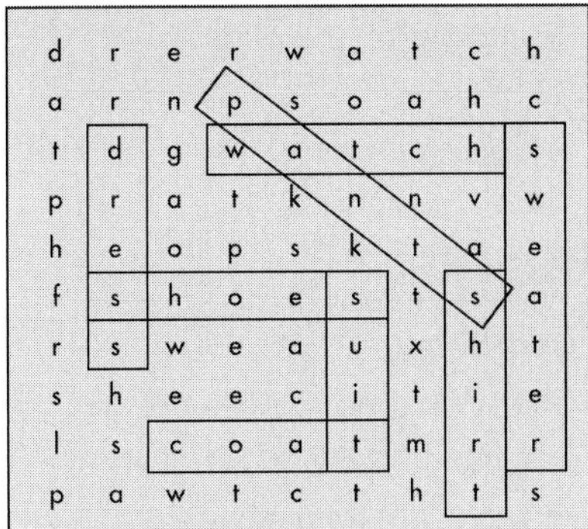

Pages 57–58

A. Singular and Plural Nouns

Write the plural nouns.

1. coats
2. dresses
3. dollars

Circle the plural nouns.

Soo Jin, Eva, Kim, and Luna are at a garage sale. Soo Jin needs a bike. He also needs a desk. Eva needs chairs and a bed. Kim needs CDs. She needs two fans and a backpack, too. Luna needs a dresser, a coat, and tables.

Mei and Marco are at the garage sale. Mei needs a table and chairs. She needs a dress. Marco needs shirts and pants. He needs a sofa and two lamps.

B. A/an

Write *a* or *an*.

I'm looking for a house. I live in an apartment. My apartment building has an elevator. It has a bedroom, a kitchen, and a bathroom.

I'm looking for an apartment with two bedrooms, a kitchen, a yard, a bathroom, and a living room.

C. Simple Present Tense.

Complete.

1. eat
2. cooks
3. plays
4. work
5. needs
6. shops
7. gets
8. study
9. sleep
10. talks

Page 60

A. Complete.

1. carrots
2. eggs
3. potatoes
4. milk
5. apples
6. ice cream

B. Complete.

A: We need apples.

B: That's right. We need milk, too.

Page 61

A. Match.

1. e
2. g
3. d
4. a
5. b
6. c
7. f

B. Complete.

A: Excuse me. I'm looking for milk.

B: It's in Aisle 3.

A: Excuse me. I'm looking for bread.

B: It's in Aisle 4.

Page 62

A. Complete.

Kim: What do you have for breakfast?

Eva: I usually have eggs. Sometimes I have cereal.

Kim: What do you have for lunch?

Eva: I usually have a sandwich. Sometimes I have a hot dog.

Kim: What do you have for dinner?

Eva: I usually have fish. Sometimes I have chicken.

B. Match.

1. b
2. a
3. c

Page 63

A. Complete.

1. pizza
2. hamburger
3. tuna sandwich
4. coffee
5. soda
6. cherry pie

B. Complete.

Server: May I help you?

Soo Jin: Yes, I'll have a hamburger, please.

Server: Anything else?

Soo Jin: Yes. I'll have a soda, too.

Page 64

A. Complete.

Ivan: Do you have hamburgers for dinner?

Thomas: No, I don't.

Ivan: Do you have pizza for dinner?

Thomas: Yes, I do.

B. Complete.

Thomas: Do you have eggs for breakfast?

Ivan: Yes, I do. Do you have chicken for lunch?

Page 65

A. Match.

1. b
2. a
3. c
4. f
5. e
6. d

B. Look at the containers in Activity A. Complete.

1. bottle
2. bunch
3. bag
4. package
5. can
6. box

Page 66

B. Check *True* or *False*.

1. True
2. True
3. False
4. True
5. False

C. Complete about you.

(student's favorite food)

Page 67

A. Find the words.

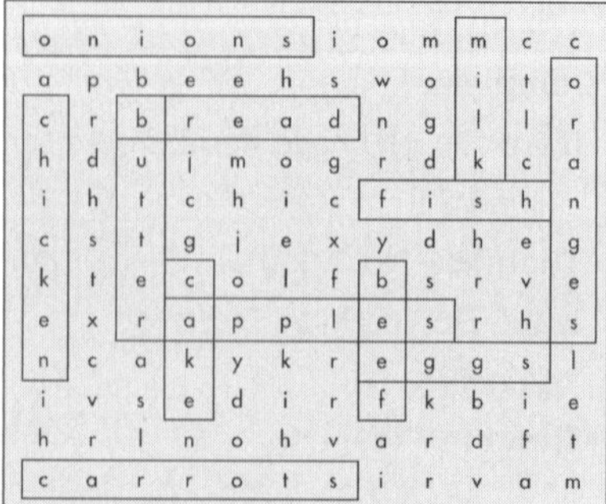

B. Write the words.

1. bottle
2. bunch
3. box
4. can

Page 69

A. Complete.

1. sunny
2. rainy
3. windy
4. hot
5. cold
6. snowy

B. Complete.

Lola: How's the weather in New York?

Alex: It's cold. How's the weather in Los Angeles?

Lola: It's hot.

Page 70

A. Write the seasons.

1. summer
2. winter
3. fall
4. spring

B. Complete.

Eva: What's your favorite season?

Ly: Summer. What's your favorite season?

Eva: Spring.

C. Write about you.

(student's favorite season)

Page 71

A. Match.

1. d
2. b
3. a
4. f
5. c

b. e

B. Write.

1. dancing.
2. talking on the phone.
3. reading.
4. playing soccer.

Page 72

A. Complete.

Mei: What do you like doing in the summer?

Ivan: I like swimming.

B. Complete.

1.

Ly: What do you like doing in the spring?

Kim: I like walking.

2.

Ly: What do you like doing in the winter?

Thomas: I like reading.

3.

Ly: What do you like doing in the summer?

Eva: I like swimming.

4.

Ly: What do you like doing in the fall?

Erik: I like cooking.

Page 73

A. Write about the weather.

1.

It's cold and snowy.

2.

It's hot and sunny, too.

3.

It's cold and cloudy.

4.

It's rainy and windy.

Page 74

A. Complete.

1. 30°
2. 95°
3. 70°
4. 50°

Page 75

A. Complete the chart.

Seattle: 55° F; Rainy
Los Angeles:75° F; Cloudy
Dallas: 80° F; Sunny
Chicago: 30° F; Snowy
Miami: 70° F; Sunny

B. Write a weather report for Dallas.

Sample response: This is a weather report for Dallas. The temperature is 80° F. The weather is sunny.

Page 76

A. What are the words?

Across

1. weather
3. sunny
4. rainy

Down

1. windy
2. hot
3. snowy

Page 78

A. Write the places.

1. library
2. gas station
3. fire station
4. hospital
5. bank
6. police station

B. Complete.

Thomas: Where are you going?
Erik: I'm going to the bank.

Page 79

A. Write.

1. Cherry Street
2. Paper Street
3. Cherry Street

Page 80

A. Write the places.

1. restaurant
2. park
3. movie theater
4. bus stop
5. laundromat
6. supermarket

B. Complete.

Ly: Is there a restaurant in your neighborhood?
Nick: Yes, there is.
Ly: Is there a library in your neighborhood?
Nick: No, there isn't.

Page 81

A. Complete.

Pedro: Where's the drugstore?
Ly: It's between the post office and the restaurant.
Pedro: Where's the laundromat?
Ly: It's next to the bank.

B. Look at the picture in Activity A. Complete.

1. The bank is between the laundromat and the movie theater.
2. The movie theater is next to the restaurant.
3. The laundromat is on 1st Street.

Page 82

A. Complete.

Eva: Do you live near a post office?
Kim: Yes, I do.
Eva: Do you live near a bank?
Kim: No, I don't.

B. Match.

1. b
2. d
3. a
4. c

C. Write about you.

1. Yes, I do./No, I don't.
2. Yes, I do./No, I don't.
3. At a post office.

Page 83

B. Complete.

1. October 25, 2005
2. 123-6545
3. $695.75
4. savings
5. three

Page 84

B. Circle.

1. 1256
2. withdrawal
3. checking
4. $100.00

Page 85

A. Where do you...?

1. m o v i e t h e a t e r
2. l a u n d r o m a t
3. b a n k
4. p a r k
5. d r u g s t o r e
6. s u p e r m a r k e t
7. r e s t a u r a n t

B. Write the letters from Activity A. Answer the question.

W h a t ' s y o u r f a v o r i t e m o v i e ?
It's (student's favorite movie).

Pages 86–87

A. Present Continuous

Write the present continuous.

1. She's studying
2. They're playing
3. She's buying
4. He's cooking
5. She's talking
6. It's playing
7. They're eating

8. You're watching
9. We're buying
10. He's reading

B. Question Words

Match.

1. b
2. h
3. e
4. a
5. f
6. g
7. d
8. c

Write *How, Where,* or *What*.

1. Where
2. How
3. Where
4. What
5. How
6. Where
7. What
8. Where
9. How
10. What

Page 89

A. Write.

1. a sore throat
2. a stomachache
3. a cold

B. Write.

1. hand
2. leg
3. finger
4. foot

C. Complete.

Mei: What's the matter?
Eva: I have a headache.
Mei: What's the matter with Marco?
Eva: His arm hurts.

Page 90

A. Complete.

Ben: I feel bad. My stomach hurts.
Alex: You need to see a doctor.

B. Complete.

Alex: Hello. This is Alex Reyes. My son is sick. Can Dr. Black see him today?
Woman: Yes. Dr. Black can see him at 8:30.
Alex: Today at 8:30? That's fine. Thank you.

C. Write.

Ben's stomach hurts. He has an appointment to see Dr. Black today at 8:30.

Page 91

A. Write.

1. a fever
2. a cough
3. an infection
4. a cut

B. Complete.

1. aspirin
2. an antibiotic
3. cough syrup
4. a bandage

C. Complete.

Soo Jin: Luna has a cut on her leg.
Eva: That's too bad. She needs a bandage.

Page 92

A. Match.

1. c
2. a
3. d
4. b

B. Complete.

1. Stretch.
2. Touch your toes.
3. Raise your arms.
4. Jump.

Page 93

B. Complete the diagram.

Lin: 44, plays soccer, likes carrots
May: 74, dances, likes apples
Both: healthy, exercises every day, walks in the park, eats healthy food

C. Write about you.

(something student does everyday to stay healthy)
(something student does once a week to stay healthy)

Page 94

B. Circle.

Luna: pill; 2x
Lola: capsule; 3x

Page 95

B. Fill in the form for Lin.

Lin Kwok; (today's date)
3/19/60
Hong Kwok
family
4769ALR
YES; $5.00

Page 96

A. Find the words.

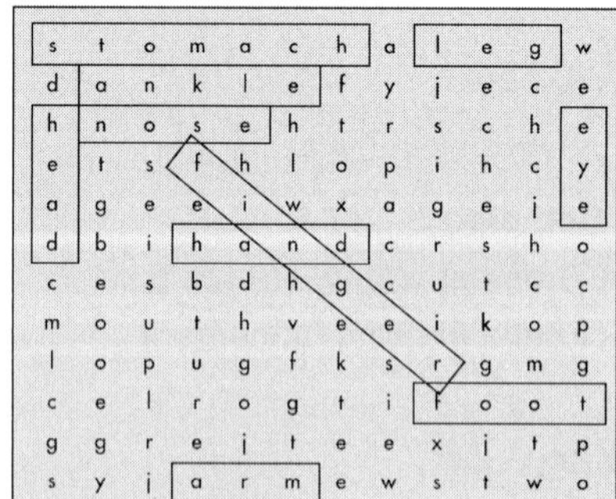

B. Write the words.

1. Stretch
2. Jump
3. Raise
4. Touch

Page 98

A. Write the jobs.

1. cashier
2. delivery person
3. waiter
4. custodian
5. gardener

B. Complete.

Erik: What do you do?
Mei: I'm a delivery person. And you?
Erik: I'm a cook.

Page 99

A. Check who uses it.

receptionist: A telephone
cook: Pots and pans
cashier: A cash register
custodian: A broom

B. Complete.

1. receptionist
2. cook
3. custodian

C. Complete the chart.

waiter: Indoors; With People
gardener: Outdoors; With Machines
receptionist: Indoors; With People; With Machines
delivery person: Indoors; Outdoors; With People
taxi Driver: Outdoors; With People

Page 100

A. Write.

1. sell
2. drive
3. fix
4. use

B. Complete.

Luna: What can you do?
Ly: I can fix things. And you?
Luna: I can use a computer.

C. Complete.

Marco: Can you drive a car?
Alex: Yes, I can. Can you use a computer?
Marco: No, I can't.

Page 101

A. Read and circle the job.

1. taxi driver
2. gardener
3. custodian
4. receptionist

B. Match.

1. b
2. e
3. d
4. c
5. a

C. Read. Write the ad number from Activity A.

1. #3
2. #2
3. #4
4. #1

Page 102

A. Write.

Lin: I was a salesclerk in Hong Kong. What was your job before?
Marco: I was a waiter in Colombia.
Luna: I was a receptionist in Brazil. What was your job before?
Thomas: I was a taxi driver in Haiti.

C. Complete the form for Lin Kwok.

Lin Kwok
474 Jones Street, Troy, NY, 12183
518-555-6263
salesclerk; Kane's Department Store; 1990-1997

Page 103

B. Circle.

1. Ivan Stoli
2. Jake's Restaurant
3. 25 hours
4. $187.48
5. $44.48
6. $10.95

C. Write.

$187.48

Page 104

B. Complete the form for Luna.

Gilbert; Luna; J
324 Lake Street; Troy; NY; 12183
518-555-1572
cook
Lucky Restaurant
14 (years)

Page 105

A. What are the words?

Across

1. cook
5. receptionist
6. gardener

Down

1. cashier
2. taxi driver
3. custodian
4. waiter

Page 107

A. Write.

1. drive a car
2. take a bus
3. ride a bike
4. take a subway

B. Complete.

Marco: How do you get to school?

Ivan: I ride a bike.

Thomas: I drive a car.

Lin: I walk.

Alex: I take a bus.

Page 108

A. Complete.

Man: Excuse me. Where is the post office?

Eva: It's straight ahead.

Woman: Excuse me. Where is the restaurant?

Eva: It's between the drug store and the library.

B. Circle the answers.

1. It's across from the bank.
2. It's across from the restaurant.
3. It's next to the hospital.

Page 109

A. Match.

1. d
2. c
3. a
4. b

B. Write.

Kim: How do I get to the East Beach?

Thomas: Take the 12 Bus.

Kim: How do I get to Riverton Airport?

Thomas: Take the J Train.

C. Complete.

Marco: When does the next train to Dallas leave?

Woman: It leaves at 7:30.

Marco: At 7:30? Thanks.

Page 110

B. Circle the answers.

1. a learner's permit
2. Tuesday
3. 10:00
4. $34

C. Read. Complete the form.

1. Stoli; Ivan; P.
2. 09/15/82
3. blue
4. yes
5. male
6. blond; (signature)

Page 111

A. Write.

1. Hospital
2. Bus Stop
3. Stop
4. One Way
5. No Parking
6. Speed Limit

B. Circle the problem.

1. b
2. a

Page 112

A. Complete.

Marco: How often does the D Train leave?

Woman: It leaves every half hour.

Marco: Oh, good. At 2:00, 2:30, and 3:00.

Eva: How often does the subway leave?

Woman: It leaves every 15 minutes.

Eva: Oh, good. At 12:00, 12:15, and 12:30.

Kim: How often does the bus leave?

Woman: It leaves every hour.

Kim: Oh, good. At 6:00, 7:00, and 8:00.

B. Circle.

1. every half hour
2. every hour
3. every half hour
4. every 15 minutes
5. every hour

Page 113

B. Write.

1. 3:25
2. 6:10
3. 3:25
4. 4:10
5. 3:40

Page 114

A. Write the words.

1. Take
2. Ride
3. Drive
4. Take
5. Take
6. Walk

B. The signs are wrong. Correct the signs.

No Parking; Bus Stop; Stop

Pages 115–116

A. Can/Can't

Write *can* or *can't*.

1. can't
2. can't
3. can
4. can't
5. can
6. can
7. can't
8. can
9. can't
10. can't

B. Complete with *in, next to, between.*

Complete the sentences.

1. in
2. next to
3. between

C. Prepositions of Time: *on, at*

Complete the sentences.

1. on
2. at
3. on
4. at
5. at; on

Tests

Introduction to the *Taking Off* Tests

The Teacher's Edition contains a reproducible unit test for each of the twelve units of *Taking Off*. Each two-page test assesses students' knowledge of the vocabulary and language structures taught within the unit. Given the low level of *Taking Off*, the tests do not assess students' understanding of specific grammatical structures. Each test is worth 20 points.

The first page of each test consists of two listening activities. The first activity asks students to listen to a question or statement and choose one of two possible responses. The second asks students either to listen to a sentence and determine which of the two sentences shown is the one they heard, or to listen and choose the vocabulary item they heard. The audio portion of each test is provided on the *Taking Off* CDs or cassettes.

The second page of the tests consists of two written activities which might ask students to label illustrations, match words to illustrations, or complete items in a series.

Name ______________________ Date __________ Score ________

Listen and check the answer.

1. ____ Hello, Maria. I'm Carlos.
   ____ Hello, Carlos. I'm Maria.

2. ____ Hi, Carlos. I'm Don. Nice to meet you.
   ____ Hi. My name is Carlos. I'm from Brazil.

3. ____ I'm from Brazil.
   ____ My name is Maria Cruz.

4. ____ My first name is M-A-R-I-A.
   ____ My first name is Maria.

5. ____ I'm Isabel.
   ____ A desk.

6. ____ My first name is S-A-N-D-Y.
   ____ My name is Sandy Johnson.

7. ____ It's a computer.
   ____ Point to the door.

Listen and circle.

1.  

2.  

3.  

C Write.

backpack	book	chair	notebook	paper

1. ____________ **2.** ____________ **3.** ____________

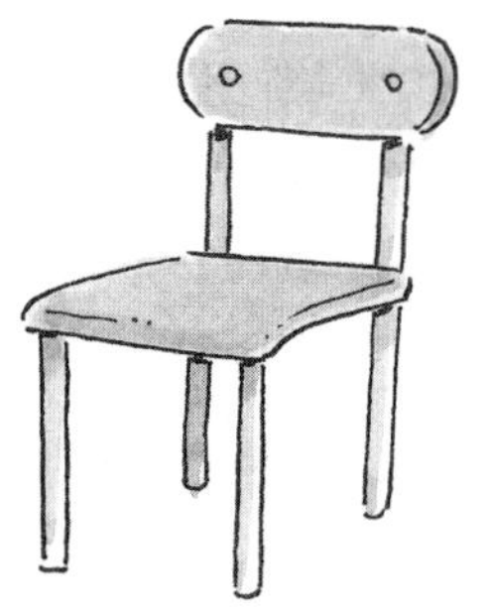

4. ____________ **5.** ____________

D Write the number.

1	4	7	8	10

1. ____ four

2. ____ seven

3. ____ one

4. ____ eight

5. ____ ten

Name ______________________ **Date** __________ **Score** ______

A Listen and check the answer.

1. ____ I speak Chinese.
   ____ I'm from China.

2. ____ He speaks Russia.
   ____ He speaks Russian.

3. ____ I speak Spanish.
   ____ I'm from Korea.

4. ____ I'm from Brazil.
   ____ My address is 142 Book Street.

5. ____ My zip code is 95945.
   ____ My address is 95 Pen Street.

B Listen and circle.

1.  

4.  

2.  

5.  

3.  

REPRODUCIBLE

C Write.

average height	average height	short	tall	tall

1. Leo is ______________________.
2. Paul is ______________________.
3. Carlos is ______________________.
4. Don is ______________________.
5. Tien is ______________________.

D Match.

1. ____ fifteen — a. 12
2. ____ fourteen — b. 17
3. ____ twelve — c. 15
4. ____ seventeen — d. 11
5. ____ eleven — e. 14

Name ______________________ Date __________ Score ________

A Listen and check the answer.

1. ____ I'm twenty-two years old.
   ____ My grandfather is old.

2. ____ Her name is Ann.
   ____ His name is John.

3. ____ Yes, I do.
   ____ No, I do.

4. ____ Yes, I have two sons.
   ____ She's twenty-seven years old.

5. ____ Tom is thirty-five years old.
   ____ Tom is Andy's brother.

B Listen and circle.

1. Mary is my __________.	sister	mother
2. John is my __________.	father	brother
3. Andy is my __________.	father	brother
4. Cathy is my __________.	sister	mother
5. Tina is my __________.	daughter	mother

C Write.

Mrs.	Mr.	middle-aged	old	young

1. Don's sister is ________________.

2. Leo's mother is ________________.

3. Don's parents are ________________.

4. ________________ Paul Lemat

5. ________________ Sandy Johnson

D Match.

1. ____ fifty **a.** 30

2. ____ twenty-four **b.** 100

3. ____ twenty **c.** 24

4. ____ thirty **d.** 50

5. ____ one hundred **e.** 20

Name ______________________ Date __________ Score ________

A Listen and check the answer.

1. _____ He's in the yard.
   _____ I live in a house.

2. _____ She's in the kitchen.
   _____ There's a stove in the kitchen.

3. _____ Yes, there is.
   _____ In the living room.

4. _____ I'm in the living room.
   _____ I live in a rented room.

5. _____ I need a sofa.
   _____ I have a sofa.

B Listen and circle.

1. 14 40
2. 18 80
3. 17 70
4. 16 60
5. 15 50

C Circle.

1. There's a tub in the ________. bathroom bedroom

2. There's a stove in the ________. backyard kitchen

3. There's a ________ in the bedroom. refrigerator bed

4. There's a sink in the ________. kitchen hall

5. There are ________ in the dining room. tubs windows

D Circle.

1. shower 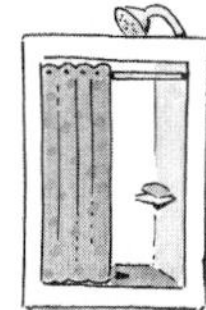 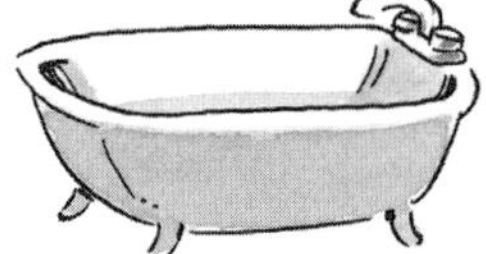

2. hall  

3. sink 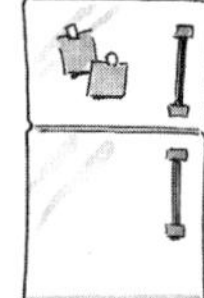 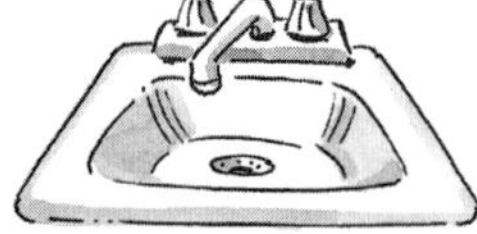

4. microwave oven  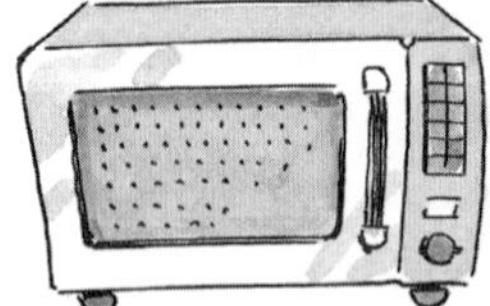

5. rug 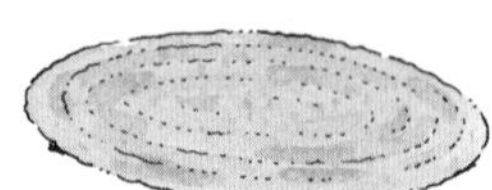 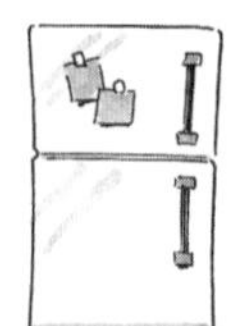

Name ________________ Date ________ Score ______

A Listen and circle.

1. 8th 7th
2. 10th 11th
3. 3rd 13th
4. 2nd 5th
5. 4th 14th

B Listen and check the answer.

1. ____ January 12, 1971. ____ Friday at 10:30.
2. ____ Tuesday at 3:15. ____ It's in December.
3. ____ Wednesday at 8:15. ____ 8:15.
4. ____ Once a week. ____ In March.
5. ____ Saturday at 9:45? That's fine. ____ Saturday at 9:15? That's fine.

REPRODUCIBLE

C Check the time.

1. 

____ 2:30

____ 2:00

2. 

____ 7:00

____ 7:15

3. 

____ 4:45

____ 4:15

4. 

____ 8:45

____ 8:15

5. 

____ 12:30

____ 12:00

D Match.

1. ____ I work on my computer. a. 

2. ____ I talk on the phone. b. 

3. ____ I play basketball. c. 

4. ____ I brush my teeth. d.

5. ____ I read the newspaper. e. 

Name ________________ Date ________ Score ______

A Listen and check the answer.

1. ____ Yes, I'm looking for a sweater.
   ____ Sweaters are over there.

2. ____ A blue coat.
   ____ Blue.

3. ____ I'm wearing a brown suit.
   ____ It's purple.

4. ____ I'm looking for pants.
   ____ Black.

5. ____ I'm wearing sneakers.
   ____ I'm a medium.

B Listen and circle.

1.  

4.  

2.  

5.  

3.  

Complete.

a blouse	a dress	sneakers	a suit	a watch

1. Maria is looking for ________________. 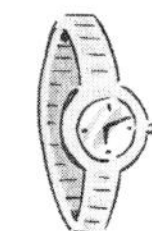

2. Grace is looking for ________________. 

3. Sandy is looking for ________________. 

4. Don is looking for ________________. 

5. Paul is looking for ________________. 

D Match.

1. ____ five dollars and fifty cents — **a.** 

2. ____ three dollars — **b.** 

3. ____ seventy-five cents — **c.** 

4. ____ two dollars and fifty-three cents — **d.**  

5. ____ seven dollars and five cents — **e.** 

Name ______________________ Date __________ Score ________

A Listen and check the answer.

1. ____ We need milk.
   ____ Yes, we do.
2. ____ Me, too. Let's have breakfast.
   ____ I usually have orange juice and eggs.
3. ____ Me, too. Let's have dinner.
   ____ Me, too. Let's have lunch.
4. ____ Yes. I'll have a hamburger, please.
   ____ No, we don't.
5. ____ Yes. I'll have a soda, too.
   ____ I usually have a soda.

B Listen and circle.

1. We need __________.	beef	bread
2. We need __________.	chicken	cheese
3. We need __________.	beef	bread
4. We need __________.	apples	oranges
5. We need __________.	cake	ice cream

C Write.

bread	butter	cheese	eggs	oranges

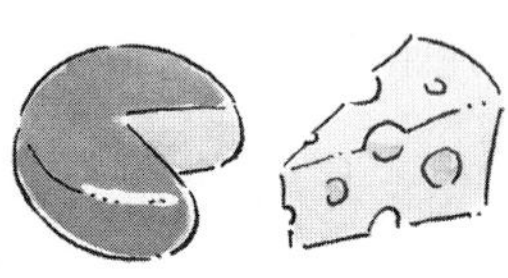

1. ______________ 2. ______________ 3. ______________

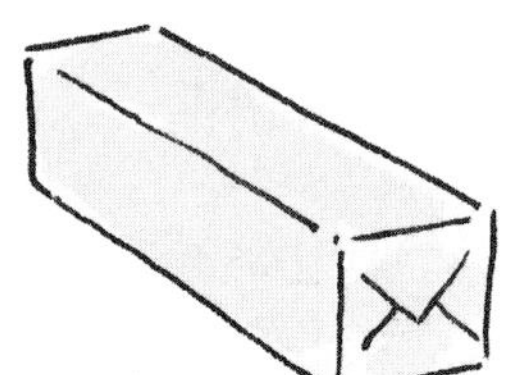

4. ______________ 5. ______________

D Complete.

bag	bottle	box	bunch	can

1. 

a ______________ of tomato soup

2. 
a ______________ of grapes

3. 

a ______________ of rice

4. 

a ______________ of oil

5. 

a ______________ of cereal

Name ______________________ Date __________ Score ________

A Listen and check the answer.

1. _____ It's winter.
   _____ It's sunny.

2. _____ Fall.
   _____ It's rainy.

3. _____ I'm reading.
   _____ I like dancing.

4. _____ I like swimming.
   _____ I like soda.

5. _____ I'm listening to music.
   _____ She's listening to music.

B Listen and circle.

1.  

2.  

3.  

4.  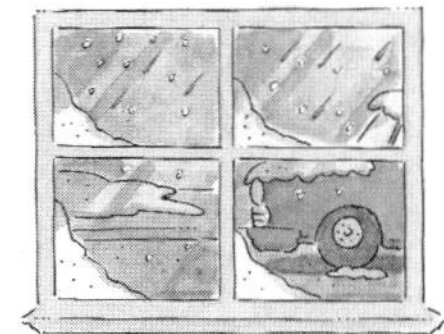

5.  

REPRODUCIBLE

 **Write.**

cooking	dancing	listening to music	reading	watching TV

1. ______________ 2. ______________ 3. ______________

4. ______________ 5. ______________

 **Write.**

playing soccer	playing basketball	swimming	talking	walking

1. ______________ 2. ______________ 3. ______________

4. ______________ 5. ______________

Name ______________________ Date __________ Score ________

A Listen and check the answer.

1. _____ She's going to the drugstore.
   _____ I'm going to the drugstore.

2. _____ He's next to the library.
   _____ It's on Main Street.

3. _____ Yes, there is.
   _____ In the bank.

4. _____ It's on First Street.
   _____ No, I don't.

5. _____ At the bank.
   _____ At a laundromat.

B Listen and circle.

1. bank	post office
2. library	supermarket
3. fire department	drugstore
4. post office	bank
5. laundromat	restaurant

Name ______________________ Date __________ Score ______

C Write.

bus stop	laundromat	supermarket	movie theater	restaurant

1. ______________ 2. ______________ 3. ______________

4. ______________ 5. ______________

D Complete.

between	between	in	next to	on

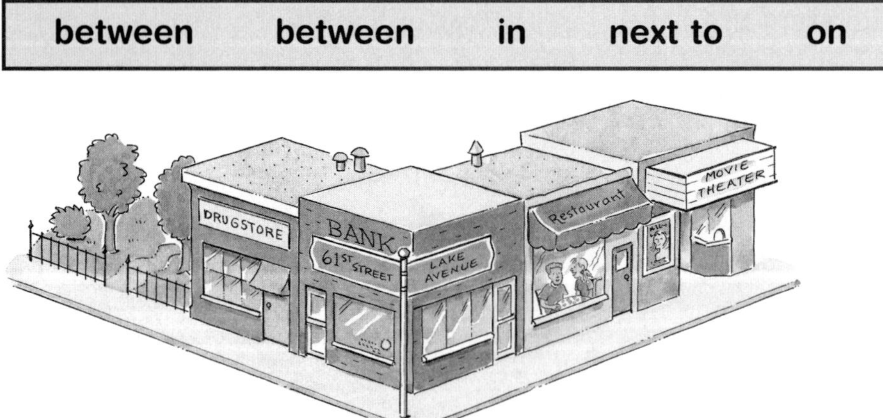

1. The movie theater is ______________ the restaurant.
2. The drugstore is ______________ the bank and the park.
3. Paul is ______________ the restaurant.
4. The restaurant is ______________ Lake Avenue.
5. The restaurant is ______________ the bank and the movie theater.

Name ______________________ Date __________ Score ________

A Listen and check the answer.

1. ____ I have a cold.
   ____ He needs an antibiotic.

2. ____ His foot hurts.
   ____ Her leg hurts.

3. ____ He needs a bandage.
   ____ Dr. Smith can see him at 9:30.

4. ____ That's too bad. Yes, he needs some aspirin.
   ____ That's too bad. Yes, he needs a stomachache.

5. ____ That's too bad. She needs a bandage.
   ____ That's too bad. She needs an antibiotic.

B Listen and circle.

1.  

4. 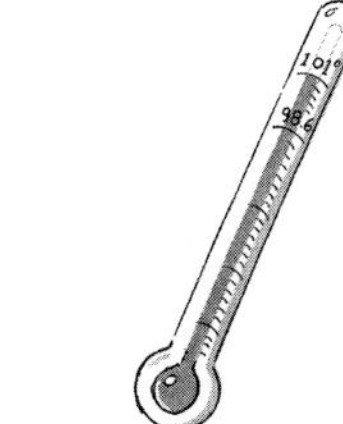 

2.   

5.   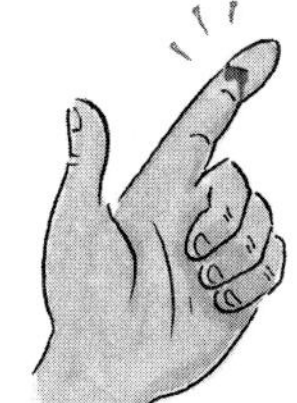

3.   

C Match.

1. ____ foot
2. ____ hand
3. ____ head
4. ____ chest
5. ____ arm

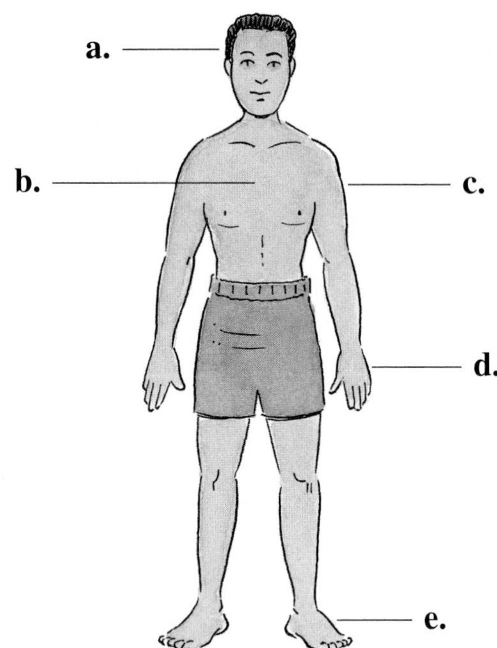

D Match.

1. ____ finger
2. ____ leg
3. ____ stomach
4. ____ eye
5. ____ nose

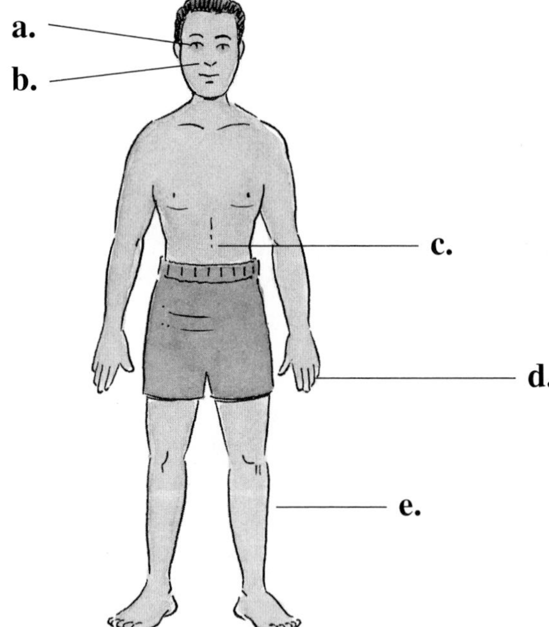

Name ______________________ **Date** __________ **Score** ________

Listen and check the answer.

1. ____ I'm a gardener.
   ____ I can fix things.

2. ____ No, I don't.
   ____ I'm a waiter.

3. ____ I'm a custodian.
   ____ I can use a computer.

4. ____ I can sell clothes.
   ____ Yes, I can.

5. ____ I was a cook.
   ____ I'm a taxi driver.

Listen and circle.

1.  

4.  

2.  

5. 

3.  

C Write.

a cashier	a delivery person	a gardener	a receptionist	a waiter

1. ______________ 2. ______________ 3. ______________

4. ______________ 5. ______________

D Check.

Jobs	Indoors	Outdoors	With People	With Machines
1. taxi driver				
2. custodian				
3. cook				
4. receptionist				
5. gardener				

Name ______________________ Date __________ Score ________

A Listen and check the answer.

1. ____ I take a bus.
   ____ It's on the left.

2. ____ Take the Blue Line.
   ____ It's straight ahead.

3. ____ It leaves at 4:30.
   ____ It leaves every fifteen minutes.

4. ____ Take the M train.
   ____ It's on the left.

5. ____ It leaves at 2:00.
   ____ I take a taxi.

B Listen and circle.

1. 1:30; 1:45; 2:00	3:00; 4:00; 5:00
2. 2:00; 2:30; 3:00	2:30; 3:30; 4:30
3. 4:15; 5:15; 6:15	4:15; 4:30; 4:45
4. 7:30; 7:45; 8:00	7:30; 8:00; 8:30
5. 3:15; 3:45; 4:15	3:15; 3:30; 3:45

Circle.

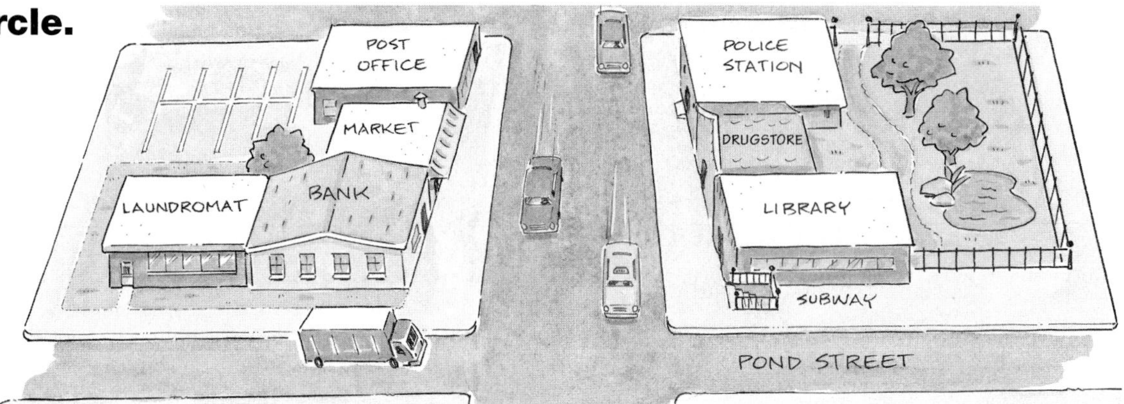

1. The bank is ____.	on the corner	next to the post office
2. The park is ____.	on the left	next to the police station
3. The laundromat is ____.	next to the bank	between
4. The library is ____.	straight ahead	on the corner
5. The market is ____.	next to the laundromat	between the bank and the post office

D Write.

Bus Stop	No Parking	One Way	Speed Limit	Stop

ANY TIME

35

1. __________ **2.** __________ **3.** __________

4. __________ **5.** __________

Tests Listening Script

UNIT 1

A. Listen and check the answer.

1. Hello. I'm Maria.
2. Hello. I'm Don. I'm from Korea.
3. I'm Tien Lam. What's your name?
4. How do you spell that?
5. What's this?
6. What's your name?
7. What's this?

B. Listen and circle.

1. Take out the pen.
2. Point to the computer.
3. Close the book.

UNIT 2

A. Listen and check the answer.

1. What language do you speak?
2. Leo is from Russia. What language does he speak?
3. I'm from Mexico. Where are you from?
4. What's your address?
5. What's your zip code?

B. Listen and circle.

1. Maria is widowed. She's not married now.
2. I am single. I'm not married.
3. They're married.
4. I'm divorced. I'm not married now.
5. She's married.

UNIT 3

A. Listen and check the answer.

1. How old are you?
2. What's your father's name?
3. Do you have two daughters?
4. Do you have children?
5. Who is Tom?

B. Listen and circle.

1. Mary is my sister.
2. John is my father.
3. Andy is my brother.
4. Cathy is my mother.
5. Tina is my daughter.

UNIT 4

A. Listen and check the answer.

1. Where is John?
2. Where is Sandy?
3. Is there a closet in the bedroom?
4. Where do you live?
5. What do you need?

B. Listen and circle.

1. I'm forty years old.
2. I have eighty dollars.
3. I need 17 pens.
4. My mother is sixty years old.
5. We have fifteen chairs.

UNIT 5

A. Listen and circle.

1. seventh
2. eleventh
3. third
4. second
5. fourth

B. Listen and check the answer.

1. What is your date of birth?
2. When is your birthday?
3. What time is it?
4. How often do you cook dinner?
5. Can you come on Saturday at nine forty-five?

UNIT 6

A. Listen and check the answer.

1. May I help you?
2. What's your favorite color?
3. What are you wearing to the party?
4. What color are your pants?
5. What size are you?

B. Listen and circle.

1. The shirt is too long.
2. The blouse is too big.
3. The pants are too short.
4. The jacket is too small.
5. The shirt is too small.

UNIT 7

A. Listen and check the answer.

1. Do we need milk?
2. What do you have for breakfast?
3. It's 6:00. I'm so hungry!
4. May I help you?
5. Anything else?

B. Listen and circle.

1. We need bread.
2. We need cheese.
3. We need beef.
4. We need apples.
5. We need ice cream.

UNIT 8

A. Listen and check the answer.

1. How's the weather?
2. What's your favorite season?
3. What are you doing?
4. What do you like doing in the summer?
5. What's Maria doing?

B. Listen and circle.

1. It's cold.
2. It's sunny.
3. It's windy.
4. It's snowy.
5. It's rainy.

UNIT 9

A. Listen and check the answer.

1. Where are you going?
2. Excuse me. Where's the bank?
3. Is there a post office in your neighborhood?
4. Do you live near a hospital?
5. Where do you wash clothes?

B. Listen and circle.

1. You buy stamps at the post office.
2. You read at the library.
3. You buy aspirin at the drugstore.
4. You deposit money at the bank.
5. You wash clothes at the laundromat.

UNIT 10

A. Listen and check the answer.

1. What's the matter?
2. What's the matter with Andy?
3. My son is sick. Can Doctor Smith see him today?
4. Paul has a fever.
5. Isabel has an infection.

B. Listen and circle.

1. I have a headache.
2. I have a stomachache.
3. I have a sore throat.
4. I have a fever.
5. I have a cut.

UNIT 11

A. Listen and check the answer.

1. What do you do?
2. Do you like to work with machines?
3. What can you do?
4. Can you drive a car?
5. What did you do before?

B. Listen and circle.

1. I can drive a car.
2. I can fix things.
3. I can sell clothes.
4. I can use a computer.
5. I can use a cash register.

UNIT 12

A. Listen and check the answer.

1. How do you get to school?
2. Excuse me. Where is the drugstore?
3. How often does the 5 bus leave?
4. How do I get to the beach?
5. When does the next plane to New York leave?

B. Listen and circle.

1. It leaves every hour.
2. It leaves every half hour.
3. It leaves every fifteen minutes.
4. It leaves every half hour.
5. It leaves every fifteen minutes.

Tests Answer Key

UNIT 1

A. Listen and check the answer.

1. Hello, Maria. I'm Carlos.
2. Hi, My name is Carlos. I'm from Brazil.
3. My name is Maria Cruz.
4. My first name is M-A-R-I-A.
5. A desk.
6. My name is Sandy Johnson.
7. It's a computer.

B. Listen and circle.

1. illustration on the left
2. illustration on the right
3. illustration on the left

C. Write.

1. book
2. notebook
3. paper
4. backpack
5. chair

D. Write the number.

1. 4
2. 7
3. 1
4. 8
5. 10

UNIT 2

A. Listen and check the answer.

1. I speak Chinese.
2. He speaks Russian.
3. I'm from Korea.
4. My address is 142 Book Street.
5. My zip code is 95945.

B. Listen and circle.

1. illustration on the left
2. illustration on the left
3. illustration on the left
4. illustration on the left
5. illustration on the right

C. Write.

1. tall
2. tall
3. average height
4. average height
5. short

D. Match.

1. c
2. e
3. a
4. b
5. d

UNIT 3

A. Listen and check the answer.

1. I'm twenty-two years old.
2. His name is John.
3. Yes, I do.
4. Yes, I have two sons.
5. Tom is Andy's brother.

B. Listen and circle.

1. sister
2. father
3. brother
4. mother
5. daughter

C. Write.

1. young
2. old
3. middle-aged
4. Mr.
5. Mrs.

D. Match.

1. d
2. c
3. e
4. a
5. b

UNIT 4

A. Listen and check the answer.

1. He's in the yard.
2. She's in the kitchen.
3. Yes, there is.
4. I live in a rented room.
5. I need a sofa.

B. Listen and circle.

1. 40
2. 80
3. 17
4. 60
5. 15

C. Check.

1. bathroom
2. kitchen
3. bed
4. kitchen
5. windows

D. Circle.

1. illustration on the left
2. illustration on the right
3. illustration on the right
4. illustration on the right
5. illustration on the left

UNIT 5

A. Listen and circle.

1. 7th
2. 19th
3. 3rd
4. 2nd
5. 4th

B. Listen and circle.

1. January 12, 1971.
2. It's in December.
3. 8:15.
4. Once a week.
5. Saturday at 9:45? That's fine.

C. Check the time.

1. 2:00
2. 12:30
3. 4:45
4. 8:15
5. 7:15

D. Match.

1. d
2. c
3. a
4. b
5. e

UNIT 6

A. Listen and check the answer.

1. Yes, I'm looking for a sweater.
2. Blue.
3. I'm wearing a red dress.
4. They're black.
5. I'm a medium.

B. Listen and circle.

1. illustration on the left
2. illustration on the left
3. illustration on the right
4. illustration on the left
5. illustration on the right

C. Complete.

1. a watch
2. a dress
3. a blouse
4. a suit
5. sneakers

D. Match.

1. b
2. d
3. e
4. c
5. a

UNIT 7

A. Listen and check the answer.

1. Yes, we do.
2. I usually have orange juice and eggs.
3. Me, too. Let's have dinner.
4. Yes. I'll have a hamburger, please.
5. Yes. I'll have a soda, too.

B. Listen and circle.

1. bread
2. cheese
3. beef
4. apples
5. ice cream

C. Write.

1. oranges
2. cheese
3. eggs
4. bread
5. butter

D. Complete.

1. can
2. bunch
3. bag
4. bottle
5. box

UNIT 8

A. Listen and check the answer.

1. It's sunny.
2. Fall.
3. I'm reading.
4. I like swimming.
5. She's listening to music.

B. Listen and circle.

1. illustration on the right
2. illustration on the right
3. illustration on the left
4. illustration on the right
5. illustration on the right

C. Write.

1. listening to music
2. cooking
3. watching TV
4. reading
5. dancing

D. Write.

1. swimming
2. playing soccer
3. talking
4. walking
5. playing basketball

UNIT 9

A. Listen and check the answer.

1. I'm going to the drugstore.
2. It's on Main Street.
3. Yes, there is.
4. No, I don't.
5. At a laundromat.

B. Listen and circle.

1. post office
2. library
3. drugstore
4. bank
5. laundromat

C. Write.

1. bus stop
2. supermarket
3. laundromat
4. movie theater
5. restaurant

D. Complete.

1. next to
2. between
3. in
4. on
5. between

UNIT 10

A. Listen and check the answer.

1. I have a cold.
2. His foot hurts.
3. Dr. Smith can see him at 9:30.
4. That's too bad. Yes, he needs some aspirin.
5. That's too bad. She needs an antibiotic.

B. Listen and circle.

1. illustration on the left
2. illustration on the right
3. illustration on the left
4. illustration on the left
5. illustration on the right

C. Match.

1. e
2. d
3. a
4. b
5. c

D. Match.

1. d
2. e
3. c
4. a
5. b

UNIT 11

A. Listen and check the answer.

1. I'm a gardener.
2. No, I don't.
3. I can use a computer.
4. Yes, I can.
5. I was a cook.

B. Listen and circle.

1. illustration on the left
2. illustration on the right
3. illustration on the left
4. illustration on the left
5. illustration on the left

C. Write.

1. a delivery person
2. a gardener
3. a cashier
4. a receptionist
5. a waiter

D. Check.

1. taxi driver: Outdoors; With People
2. custodian: Indoors; With Machines
3. cook: Indoors; With People; With Machines
4. receptionist: Indoors; With People; With Machines
5. gardener: Outdoors; With Machines

UNIT 12

A. Listen and check the answer.

1. I take a bus.
2. It's straight ahead.
3. It leaves every fifteen minutes.
4. Take the M train.
5. It leaves at 2:00.

B. Listen and circle.

1. 3:00; 4:00; 5:00
2. 2:00; 2:30; 3:00
3. 4:15; 4:30; 4:45
4. 7:30; 8:00; 8:30
5. 3:15; 3:30; 3:45

C. Circle.

1. on the corner
2. next to the police station
3. next to the bank
4. on the corner
5. between the bank and the post office

D. Write.

1. No Parking
2. Stop
3. Speed Limit
4. One Way
5. Bus Stop